FISCAL POLICY AND INTEREST RATES IN THE EUROPEAN UNION

Fiscal Policy and Interest Rates in the European Union

Klaas Knot
Monetary and Economic Policy Department
De Nederlandsche Bank NV
Amsterdam, The Netherlands

Edward Elgar
Cheltenham, UK • Brookfield, US

Published by
Edward Elgar Publishing Limited
8 Lansdown Place
Cheltenham
Glos GL50 2HU
UK

Edward Elgar Publishing Company
Old Post Road
Brookfield
Vermont 05036
US

A catalogue record for this book
is available from the British Library

Library of Congress Cataloguing in Publication Data
Knot, Klaas, 1967–
    Fiscal policy and interest rates in the European Union / Klaas
Knot.
    Includes bibliographical references and index.
    1. Fiscal policy—European Union countries. 2. Budget deficits–
–European Union countries. 3. Interest rates—European Union
countries.
    HJ1000.K66   1996   96–23173
                                                                CIP

ISBN 1 85898 429 7

Printed and bound in Great Britain by
Hartnolls Limited, Bodmin, Cornwall

Contents

Tables

Figures

Acknowledgements

This study resulted from a research project carried out at the Department of Economics at the University of Groningen between 1991 and 1995. Although the individuals who have been helpful in conducting the research are too numerous to mention all, I would like to mention a few. First of all I would like to express my thanks to my direct supervisor Jakob de Haan, whose 'to-the-point' approach always kept me on track and stimulated me a great deal over the course of the project. Moreover, he is also the coauthor of the second chapter of this book and of several papers that resulted from our joint efforts. In addition to that, I am indebted to Flip de Kam and Theo Dijkstra who, both in their own way, also participated during several phases of the project.

Thanks are also due to Willem Buiter, Sylvester Eijffinger, and Simon Kuipers for their willingness to read the entire manuscript and to provide me with some very useful comments. In a similar vein, I would like to thank Harry Garretsen, Hans Groeneveld, Lex Hoogduin, Jan Jacobs, Kees Koedijk, Clemens Kool, Elmer Sterken, and the participants of the various congresses I visited for their valuable comments on preliminary versions of the papers this book is based on. Excellent research assistance was provided by Gert-Jan van't Hag, Bernd-Jan Sikken, and Jan-Egbert Sturm; excellent editorial assistance was provided by Lies Baars. Financial support is gratefully acknowledged from the graduate school SOM, NWO, Royal Dutch/Shell, and the Stichting Organisatie van Effectenhandelaren te Rotterdam. I would like to thank the editors of *Banca Nazionale del Lavoro Quarterly Review, Empirical Economics, European Journal of Political Economy,* and *Journal of Banking and Finance* for their permission to let me use articles that have been published in these journals. Finally, I would like to thank the designers of the Wordperfect word processor for letting me encounter all kinds of most illogical problems one could possibly imagine.

The pleasant working atmosphere in Groningen also contributed a great deal to the final result. In this respect, a special mention goes to Bas Bakker and Cees Sterks who created a sociable research environment by never failing to put research and its results into perspective. Finally, I wish to thank my relatives for their continuous support and, of course, Tiny for her continuous efforts in preventing me to become a (total) workaholic.

1 Introduction and outline

*It is encouraging that governments everywhere acknowledge
that the re-emergence or persistence of large budget deficits
needs to be addressed as a matter of considerable urgency. A
failure to reduce substantially these imbalances over the
medium term would likely renew upward pressure on long-term
interest rates, reduce capital formation and the scope for new
job creation in the private sector, lower the rate of growth of
potential output and income, and continue to impede the
flexibility of fiscal policy.*

International Monetary Fund (1993), p.3

I   Introduction

So far, the debate on the supposedly detrimental economic effects of high
government budget deficits rages on. The quote heading this chapter refers to
a controversial issue: the relation between the size of government budget
deficits and such important variables as the level of saving, interest rates, and
capital accumulation. The prevailing view is that higher government deficits
reduce the supply of national saving, push up interest rates and reduce the
demand for investment. However, some economists argue that private saving
will rise with the deficit as consumers fully discount future tax liabilities
implied by current deficits, thereby offsetting lower government saving.
Supporters of this so-called Ricardian equivalence theorem, as revitalised by
Barro (1974), thus deny any influence from budget deficits on either the level
of national saving, or interest rates.

Recently, many empirical studies have concentrated on the relationship
between government budget deficits and interest rates; most of these studies
refer to the United States.[1] Thus far, the evidence is far from conclusive. The
relationship between government budget deficits and the interest rate appears
to be not very stable over time. Such mixed results have led some authors to
argue that the linkages between fiscal policy and asset returns have to be
considered from a global instead of a national perspective. Tanzi and Lutz
(1993) and Barro and Sala-i-Martin (1990) stress that because of increasing
international capital mobility and the growing integration of financial markets
the consequences of government budget deficits should be analysed from a
global perspective. However, according to Bhandari and Mayer (1990) and

1

Lemmen and Eijffinger (1995), financial markets are not very well integrated, except for countries participating in the European Monetary System (EMS).

The aim of this book is to investigate the relationship between fiscal policy and interest rates in a European setting. In particular the focus is on the question whether increasing budget deficits after the first oil crisis (1973–1974) have pushed up interest rates.[2] To this end the book presents some alternative forms to model the relationship between deficits and interest rates, covering the complete term structure of interest rates as far as possible.

Basically, we follow two different but complementary approaches. First, the importance of increased international capital mobility will be stressed. Foreign savings may offset a decline in national saving due to government dissaving. In models with costless international arbitrage in goods and financial assets, real interest rates of comparable securities should be equal across countries. But also in a world with less than perfectly integrated capital markets, interest determination in various countries is dominated by a number of common elements, albeit to a lesser extent. It is our contention that this situation more or less applies for the various member countries of the European Monetary System. Therefore, we pursue this line of thought by investigating the link between budget deficits and interest rates, assuming a sufficiently integrated European capital market where agents are able and willing to move financial assets across national borders in response to expected differences in returns on comparable securities.[3]

Apart from common elements in the determination of interest rates in the countries under consideration, small but persistent interest differentials among these countries continue to exist. Such interest differentials mainly reflect expectations concerning future exchange rate movements and subsequent risk premia. Despite the fact that most countries have tried to stabilise exchange rates by joining the Exchange Rate Mechanism (ERM) of the EMS, the commitment to this arrangement has often been challenged. Therefore, our second line of research will focus on the underlying determinants of interest differentials vis-à-vis Germany, the anchor country of the EMS. After having examined the link between budget deficits and interest rates in Germany, we will investigate to what extent fiscal variables in the countries under consideration may have caused differentials in interest rates.

This introductory chapter is structured as follows. Section II sketches the development of budget deficits and interest rates in EMS countries since the early 1960s. Section III briefly discusses some methodological issues which arise when conducting this kind of empirical research. Finally, section IV outlines the rest of the book.

II   A first look at the data

Figures 1.1–1.9 trace trends in government budget deficits and interest rates since 1960 in nine European countries: Austria, Belgium, Denmark, France, Germany, Ireland, Italy, the Netherlands, and the United Kingdom. This

Figure 1.1: Public deficits and interest rates: Austria

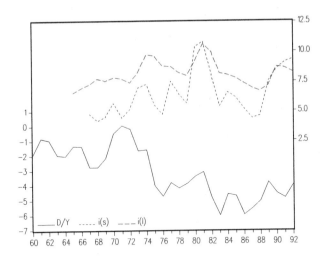

Figure 1.2: Public deficits and interest rates: Belgium

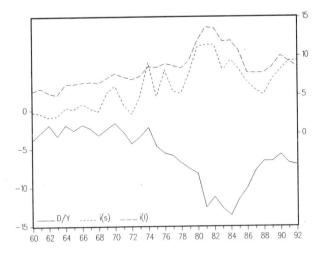

Figure 1.3: Public deficits and interest rates: Denmark

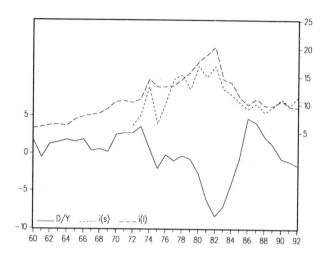

Figure 1.4: Public deficits and interest rates: France

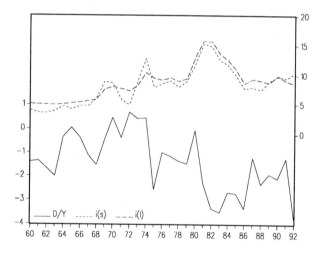

Figure 1.5: Public deficits and interest rates: Germany

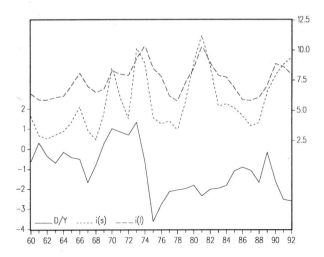

Figure 1.6: Public deficits and interest rates: Ireland

Figure 1.7: Public deficits and interest rates: Italy

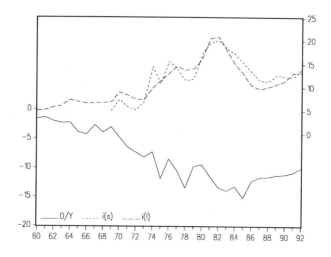

Figure 1.8: Public deficits and interest rates: The Netherlands

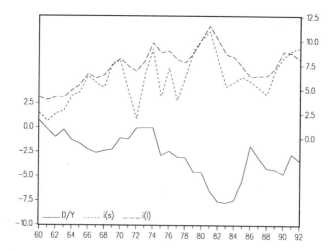

Figure 1.9: Public deficits and interest rates: United Kingdom

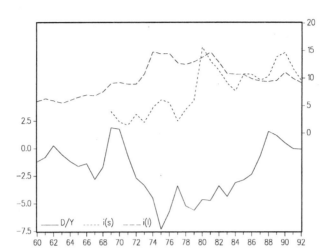

sample has been selected since the countries mentioned form a more or less homogeneous group which has aimed for economic integration ever since the foundation of the European Economic Community in the late 1950s.[4] Figures 1.1–1.9 present time-series plots of the development of consolidated central government budget deficits (D/Y, measured on the left-hand scale as the ratio between the budget balance and GNP) and interest rates (right-hand scale) in the countries under consideration. Data originate from the *International Financial Statistics* (IFS) from the International Monetary Fund (IMF). Long-term interest rates (i^l) are measured by government bond yields whereas short-term interest rates (i^s) are represented by three-month money market rates.[5] Table 1.1 presents summary statistics and partial correlation coefficients of the various time series.

From Figures 1.1–1.9 and the last column of Table 1.1 a strikingly strong correlation between budget deficits and interest rates emerges. In virtually all cases high budget deficits have been accompanied by high interest rates for a large part of our sample. The development of government budget deficits in most countries can be characterised by a 'double-dip' scenario. From the first oil crisis (1973) onwards, there is first a sharp and in most cases fairly prolonged deterioration in the fiscal position of the countries under investigation. For Italy and the United Kingdom the oil crisis and its aftermath merely represented an additional (adverse) shock which increased already large fiscal imbalances. A second dip can be located immediately after the second oil crisis (1979) when monetary policy contracted sharply in the

Table 1.1: Summary statistics

Variable	Mean	Standard deviation	Maximum	Minimum	Correlation with D/Y
Austria:					
i^s (1967–92)	6.47	1.94	10.82	4.14	−0.10
i^l (1965–92)	8.13	1.02	10.61	6.52	−0.13
D/Y	−3.12	1.75	0.06	−6.02	1.00
Belgium:					
i^s	6.10	2.90	11.47	2.11	−0.72
i^l	8.43	2.26	13.71	4.98	−0.84
D/Y	−5.82	3.56	−1.64	−13.63	1.00
Denmark:					
i^s (1972–92)	11.44	3.08	16.93	6.26	−0.62
i^l	11.10	3.73	20.39	5.76	−0.67
D/Y	−0.07	3.02	4.71	−8.40	1.00
France:					
i^s	8.21	3.19	15.30	3.61	−0.34
i^l	8.75	2.96	15.79	4.97	−0.40
D/Y	−1.42	1.23	0.69	−3.84	1.00
Germany:					
i^s	5.65	2.45	11.26	2.58	−0.07
i^l	7.47	1.29	10.40	5.80	−0.13
D/Y	−1.08	1.21	1.35	−3.62	1.00
Ireland:					
i^s (1971–92)	12.21	3.23	17.65	4.81	−0.61
i^l	10.68	3.69	17.26	5.45	−0.81
D/Y	−8.14	4.52	−0.95	−16.48	1.00
Italy:					
i^s (1969–92)	12.66	4.35	20.16	5.00	−0.67
i^l	10.75	4.30	20.90	5.01	−0.80
D/Y	−8.26	4.30	−1.38	−15.21	1.00
The Netherlands:					
i^s	6.07	2.42	11.01	1.72	−0.46
i^l	7.41	1.87	11.55	3.91	−0.59
D/Y	−2.90	2.30	0.70	−7.74	1.00
United Kingdom:					
i^s (1969–92)	7.90	4.38	15.62	1.42	0.09
i^l	9.93	2.85	14.77	5.43	−0.67
D/Y	−2.07	2.38	1.90	−7.30	1.00

Datasources are in the appendix. Sample: 1960–92 unless indicated otherwise.

Western world in order to combat persistently high levels of inflation, resulting in a severe recession accompanied by excessively (all-time) high budget deficits. The subsequent recovery in the second half of the 1980s enabled most governments to achieve a substantial degree of fiscal consolidation, although most deficits remained stuck at levels much higher than those before 1973. Furthermore, as economic conditions worsened towards the end of the 1980s, budget deficits again appeared to be highly sensitive to the business cycle. Despite the convergence criteria laid out in the Maastricht Treaty (1991), budget deficits deteriorated until deep into the 1990s.

On the other hand (and scale), in most countries interest rates rose after the first oil crisis, together with (expected) inflation. Despite the substantial decrease in inflation since the early 1980s, interest rates remained high during much of the decade. Apparently, either inflationary expectations or real interest rates proved to be persistent. Towards the end of the decade nominal interest rates in the Western world started to fall, but the relief appeared to be only temporary. During the beginning of the 1990s, the trend in interest rates in most of the countries under consideration was upward again.

The high correlation between deficits and interest rates reported in Table 1.1 does not necessarily mean causation. In the remainder of this book we will therefore investigate the potential channels through which deficits may swell interest rates. However, before proceeding, we will identify and describe a number of econometric techniques which may be of help in the intended investigation.

III Methodology: Reduced-form versus structural approach

This section discusses several methodological issues that are relevant to the elaboration of the purpose of this study. First, we summarise the debate concerning the pros and cons of reduced-form models as compared with structural models. Subsequently, we illustrate this issue by discussing the Dutch experience in modelling the relation between budget deficits and interest rates. Finally, we discuss the concept of Granger-causality within a vector autoregressive (VAR) setting, to be used in Chapter 6.

III.1 Comparison of both approaches

Van Loo (1984) has pointed out that empirical models of interest rate determination can roughly be divided into two distinct groups. The first category of studies includes the so-called class of structural models which seek to give an implicit explanation of the development of various interest rates by confronting behavioural equations of demand and supply of (various forms of) loanable funds. The other group of studies encompasses the so-called reduced-form models that explicitly try to relate the interest rate under consideration to a number of explanatory variables which should be exogenous to the interest rate itself. In comparing both approaches, the following advantages of using structural econometric models in the analysis of developments at financial markets can be distinguished:

i. Hypotheses concerning financial behaviour of individual sectors (for example banking sector, private sector) can be tested directly.
ii. Fluctuations in interest rates can be explained by behavioural equations describing demand and supply of the various sectors. This approach has the advantage of being derived from first principles, that is optimising behaviour of the different sectors, in such a way that all explanatory variables present in at least one of these behavioural equations implicitly affect all distinguishable interest rates. In contrast, in a reduced-form equation the number of potential determinants of any arbitrarily chosen interest rate is often limited by the presence of multicollinearity of the exogenous variables.
iii. Behavioural equations of the endogenous balance sheets of a certain sector can be estimated under the restriction that assets and liabilities of that sector must sum up to zero. Under these restrictions the financial structure can be modelled as a closed system, which simplifies the execution of dynamic simulations.

From these points it becomes clear that structural models are especially well-suited for analyses in which sectoral considerations play a role. Furthermore, these models are a prerequisite if one wants to perform a dynamic simulation of financial market behaviour. But these structural models also have several drawbacks, which seem to be less problematic in case of the reduced-form approach. In the context of financial market modelling these drawbacks may be summarised as follows:[6]

i. In structural models it is difficult to make a distinction between the impact of expected and unexpected events. Especially in explaining longer-term interest rates, expectations often play a significant role. The modelling of expectations in structural models usually remains restricted to adaptive expectations, which seems to be somewhat counterintuitive in the case of (often forward-looking) financial market behaviour.
ii. It is also difficult to distinguish between temporary and permanent events. In structural models uncertainty of this kind is sometimes being resolved by employing partial adjustment methods. Reduced-form analysis, on the other hand, facilitates the use of decomposition procedures for the identification of temporary versus permanent components in individual time-series, like Kalman filtering or the Beveridge–Nelson approach.[7]
iii. Lagged adjustment mechanisms that are often a part of structural models can be contradictory to the so-called Efficient Market Hypothesis, in which all available information is immediately incorporated in the process of

price formation. This type of problem is particularly relevant if term structure effects on interest rates are taken into account.

iv. Finally, construction and estimation of large structural models can be very expensive, in terms of time and money involved as well as in terms of computational efficiency. Often the number of degrees of freedom is limited for a considerable batch of equations, due to the large number of parameters to be estimated.[8] This drawback of large-scale macro-econometric models often applies over and above the fact that in earlier construction stages the model builders already have resorted to a-priori fixing of various other parameters.[9]

From this enumeration of advantages and disadvantages of both approaches it seems as if in general structural models embody a certain degree of overkill and may suggest would-be accuracy if one merely aims to perform a study of a partial nature, like the study of a single relationship between two variables.[10] The Dutch experience with modelling the relationship between budget deficits and interest rates underscores this point.

III.2   Deficits and interest rates in Dutch macro-econometric models

Large-scale structural models of OECD countries usually produce a rise in interest rates if the budget deficit increases (see Chan-Lee and Kato, 1984, p.116). Recent Dutch macro-econometric models, however, are less unanimous. The first thing to note in this respect is that the only Dutch models that employ a *purely* structural (implicit) approach to the determination of the various interest rates are the DUFIS model of Sterken (1990) and the IBS–CCSO model of Jacobs and Sterken (1995). Underlying this choice of modelling is a substantial degree of confidence in the market-clearing efficacy of interest rate adjustments, where no single market participant can effectively control or even set these rates. Behavioural equations have been specified for all categories of demand and supply of the various types of financial assets and have subsequently been estimated jointly and simultaneously. As a side effect, however, it becomes difficult to reveal the direct impact of one individual market participant, like, for example, public authorities, on equilibrium interest rates, for which purpose one has to resort to dynamic simulation exercises.

Such simulations with the DUFIS model exhibit a significant impact of budget deficits on interest rates. Here, an increase of the budget deficit by 1% of net national income leads to a rise of 1.79 percentage points in the (long-term) interest rate; a result that Sterken himself qualifies as 'extremely high' and 'by far the largest effect found in Dutch structural models' (Sterken, 1990, p.155). This large effect is ascribed to 'some of the special characteristics of our model' (ibid. p.155). The IBS–CCSO model, on the other hand, does not explicitly deal with any macroeconomic effects of budget deficits, since 'Traditional analysis of the effects of monetary and fiscal stimuli has become outdated. The Netherlands cannot pursue an independent money supply policy. The same holds for an expansionary fiscal stimulus. With the Maastricht Treaty in mind only balanced budget operations are allowed for' (Jacobs and Sterken, 1995, p.137).

Other large-scale Dutch macro-econometric models that were developed recently all have resorted to procedures different from implicit modelling of the various interest rate equations. In doing so, the HERMES model of Mot et al. (1989) as well as the MORKMON–II model of Fase et al. (1990) both build on a reduced-form specification in which, however, budget deficits play a minor role, if any. From Mot et al. (1989) we can infer that in the HERMES model 'The transmission of developments in the real sphere to the monetary sphere operates through a business cycle indicator, inflation and the current account of the balance of payments' (ibid. p.29) so that the potential effects of fiscal policy are excluded a priori.

In the MORKMON–II model the short-term (money market) interest rate is set by the central bank, based on a reaction function. This function is constructed along the lines of the uncovered interest parity relationship, where the deviation from central parity of the actual exchange rate vis-à-vis Germany and the current account of the balance of payments together proxy for market expectations of future exchange rate movements. In the equation for the long-term interest rate the latter expectations are being proxied by the inflation differential vis-à-vis Germany. Foreign (that is German) interest rates exert their influence directly as well as indirectly through short-term interest rates. Both transmission channels almost precisely sum up to one, so that, roughly spoken, in fact the long-term interest *differential* against Germany is modelled. Budget deficits only play a role in the determination of the long-term interest rate in MORKMON–II, albeit in a roundabout and at first sight somewhat far-fetched way. The long-term interest rate is modelled as a reduced-form equation, depending among others on a variable which aims to measure the tension on the capital market. This tension variable is related to the external capital market balance that is assumed to represent the net demand for loanable funds on the domestic capital market.[11] It consists of five components, one of them being the change in the supply of (Dutch) loanable funds from the part of the foreign sector. That foreign supply, in turn, is defined as the sum of a number of different variables, one of them being the change in the amount of (long-term) Dutch government debt outstanding (Fase et al., 1990, pp.56–7, 202–23). Despite all this, dynamic simulation analysis shows that a decrease in the budget deficit exerts no appreciable effect on long-term interest rates (ibid. p.182).

Finally, in the FKSEC model the financial sector is eliminated completely and replaced by a simple equation in which the change in the Dutch long-term interest rate is linked to the change in the corresponding German interest rate (Central Planning Bureau, 1992). The short-term interest rate has been made exogenous. This simplification is justified as the result of a combination of past experience and (adaptive) expectations: 'Because of the virtually fixed exchange rate regime that exists within most of the common market, Dutch interest rates very closely follow foreign interest rates, especially the German one. As the European financial integration continues under the terms of the European Monetary Union, it is to be expected that the deviations between the Dutch and other European (again, especially the German) interest rates will be even smaller in the future . . .' (ibid. p.67).[12] Although the authors emphasize that 'the elimination of the financial subsector does not imply that the influence of monetary factors within the model has been reduced' (ibid. p.67), it does imply that the impact of all potential domestic determinants on interest rates or differentials is excluded a priori.

In sum we can conclude that from the investigation of the relationship between budget deficits and interest rates in existing large-scale macro-econometric models of the Dutch economy a rather diverse picture emerges. In general, the evidence of a potential link is mixed, in some cases it is even excluded or neglected a priori. In this study we will therefore seek to employ a number of alternative forms to model the determination of interest rates, which allow for somewhat greater potential effect of fiscal policy.

III.3 VAR analysis and the concept of Granger-causality

One of these alternative forms to investigate the relationship between a pair of variables is the so-called vector autoregression (VAR) analysis. This modelling technique has been recommended by Sims (1980a, 1982) as a reliable alternative to the more conventional structural models as described in the previous section. Sims suggests to estimate unconstrained vector autoregressive models, treating all variables as endogenous in the first stage in order to avoid infecting the model by spurious or even false restrictions. In contrast, the VAR procedure imposes no restrictions based on supposed a priori knowledge of the dynamic linkages between the various variables in the model, which has led others to label the VAR approach as 'measurement without theory' (see for example Klein, 1988, p.8). However, after the model has been devised to summarise the data, hypotheses with economic content can be formulated and tested in the second stage. The general form of the VAR model is given by the following unrestricted reduced-form system:

$$Z_t = I + \Delta(L)Z_t + \eta_t, \qquad (1.1)$$

where Z_t is a column vector of endogenous variables, I a (column) vector of intercepts, and η_t a (column) vector of white-noise disturbances. $\Delta(L)$ is a matrix of lagged polynomial coefficients of which each element is defined in terms of the lag operator L such that:

$$\delta_{ij}^k(L) = \delta_{ij}^1 L^1 + \delta_{ij}^2 L^2 + ... + \delta_{ij}^k L^k. \qquad (1.2)$$

This procedure thus offers an opportunity to drop the standard restrictions based on a priori assumptions, while economically meaningful hypotheses can still be tested. However, some practical problems remain (Hsiao, 1981). If every variable is allowed to influence every other variable with a distributed lag of the same length without any restriction, the number of parameters to be estimated grows with the square of the number of variables and quickly exhausts the amount of degrees of freedom left in the data after fitting the model. This makes the interpretation of the tests based on asymptotic distribution theory difficult for a number of reasons. First, the tests are non-robust, as they become highly sensitive to non-normality. Second, different but seemingly reasonable and asymptotically equivalent formulas for the test statistic may result in very different significance levels for the same data. Finally, the distribution of the test-statistic is sensitive to the order of lags fitted to the first stage model.

Thornton and Batten (1985) have demonstrated that the specification of a lag structure in $\Delta(L)$ is crucial, if one aims to perform (Granger-) causality inferences. A comparison of several commonly used criteria for lag-length selection showed that *ad hoc* approaches, such as considering a few arbitrary lag structures or employing some 'rule of thumb', can produce misleading results. Furthermore, their analysis suggests that according to a standard, classical, hypothesis-testing norm Akaike's Final Prediction Error (*FPE*) criterion performed best relative to the others (Thornton and Batten, 1985). Overly generous lag lengths are then avoided, thus preserving degrees of freedom, while biased estimates of lag parameters are avoided by including lags of a sufficient length. This criterion prescribes the following procedure (compare among others Fackler, 1985, and Darrat, 1988):

i. After all variables z_i have been transformed into stationary series, each of them is regressed on a constant and its own lags to determine the appropriate lag order. A series of autoregressions are then estimated by varying the lag order m from 1 to the maximum number of lags considered. The lag m^* that minimises the following *FPE* value is considered appropriate:

$$FPE(m) = \frac{T+m+1}{T-m-1} \frac{SSR(m)}{T},$$ (1.3)

where T is the number of observations, and SSR is the sum of squared residuals. As Hsiao (1981) has pointed out, this criterion is appealing because it balances the risk due to the bias when a lower order is selected and the risk due to the increase of variance when a higher order is selected. When an additional lag is included, the first term in *FPE* increases, but simultaneously the second term decreases. When their product reaches a minimum, the two opposing factors are balanced.

ii. Once the appropriate number of own lags is determined, bivariate regressions are estimated comprising the appropriate own lag ($m*$) and lags of each of the remaining variables considered separately. For each additional variable the lag order is again varied from 1 to the maximum number of lags and the following modified *FPE* is calculated:

$$FPE(m^*,n) = \frac{T+m^*+n+1}{T-m^*-n-1} \frac{SSR(m^*,n)}{T} \qquad (1.4)$$

The appropriate lag length $n*$ for this bivariate system is that which minimises the *FPE* in equation (1.4).

iii. Given the bivariate results of equation (1.4), Caines et al. (1981) define the specific gravity of each variable j with respect to the variable i ($i \neq j$) as the reciprocal of the final prediction error in the bivariate z_i equation. Then one should begin with adding the variable z_j with the highest specific gravity in the equation for z_i, and proceed by adding the other variables in order of decreasing specific gravities, each with the (newly specified) lag length that yields the lowest *FPE* in the composite equation.

After performing the analysis of steps i to iii for each z_i that is caused by some other variable in the system, all the individual equations have to be estimated simultaneously by, for example, full information maximum likelihood (FIML).

Under fairly general conditions, Hsiao (1981) has shown that the inclusion of a variable based on the *FPE* criterion described above is evidence for a weak Granger-causal ordering. If it further exerts a statistically significant effect, then the Granger-causal impact can be identified as a strong form (Kawai, 1980). The concept of Granger-causality can perhaps best be illustrated by its definition as formulated by Granger himself (1969): '*X*2 "causes" *X*1 if and only if *X*1(*t*) is better predicted by using the past history of *X*2 than by not doing so with the past of *X*1 being used in either case'. This statistics-based definition of causality can be tested in several (closely related) ways. The test employed in the present study is similar to the interpretation of Sargent (1976), since Guilkey and Salemi (1982) have demonstrated that this test exhibits the best small sample properties.

IV   Outline of the rest of the book

This book consists of six chapters. After this introductory chapter, the next chapter will provide an overview of the existing literature on the theoretical aspects of fiscal policy. Central to Chapter 2 will be the questions why budget deficits do exist and what budget deficits do to the economy. Aside from the various theoretical insights in this field, Chapter 2 will present an empirical investigation into the determinants of budget deficits and a contemplation about the 'correct' way to measure the fiscal stance. After having discussed these prelims, we are able to subsequently focus on the main goal of this study: the impact of fiscal policy on interest rates. We proceed in Chapter 3 by looking at common elements in the determination of interest rates in the European Union. In doing so, we assume that capital markets within Europe are nearly perfectly integrated, which implies that it is appropriate to investigate the development of the average level of interest rates in (a number of countries of) the European Union. Consequently, we also address the question whether budget deficits in these countries have pushed up interest rates, for which we will consider short-term as well as long-term interest rates.

After having investigated these common elements in the determination of interest rates, we shift our attention towards the interest differentials among these countries, that have certainly not completely ceased to exist. For this purpose we chose Germany as the reference country, because of its anchor function in the EMS. In Chapter 4 we therefore first investigate the link between budget deficits and interest rates in Germany. To this end, we will employ the so-called 'announcement effect methodology'. The idea behind this approach is that in an efficient market, information about any determinant of interest rates will be immediately incorporated into observed interest rates. Observations for the period surrounding the German (re-)unification seem to form an excellent sample to test for this hypothesis, as deficit projections from various sources then succeeded each other swiftly.

Chapters 5 and 6 study the behaviour of the interest differentials vis-à-vis Germany in the other EMS countries, within the framework of the target zone model. The target zone model, in which exchange rates are determined by fundamentals and expectations, will be described in extenso in Chapter 5. Special attention will again be paid to the term structure of interest rates and differentials. In Chapter 6 the credibility of the various EMS target zones is examined through so-called 'interest corridor' analysis. Furthermore, we continue the analysis of interest differentials by extracting devaluation expectations from these differentials by means of the so-called 'drift-adjustment' method. Subsequently, we will investigate whether these devaluation expectations can accurately be explained by a collection of fundamental determinants, including the budget deficit.

Finally, Chapter 7 summarises our main results and offers a short contemplation concerning its policy implications.

Appendix: Definitions and sources of the variables used

i^s Money or commercial market rate (period averages) from *International Financial Statistics* (IMF) line 60b.

i^l Government bond yield (period averages) from *IFS* line 61.

D Government budget deficit(–) or surplus from *IFS* line 80.

Y Gross National Product from *IFS* line 99a.

Notes

1. See for example, Evans (1985), Hoelscher (1986), Tran and Sahwney (1988), Allen (1990), De Haan and Zelhorst (1990a), and Zelhorst and De Haan (1991).
2. Another channel through which fiscal policy may affect interest rates consists of the impact of government spending on interest rates. In an intertemporal setting, temporary government purchases may lead to an excess demand for goods, inducing a rise in interest rates (Aschauer, 1988). This view has been confirmed empirically by Barro (1987) for the UK and by Denslow and Rush (1989) for France, but is challenged by De Haan and Zelhorst (1992) for the Netherlands. Here we will mostly abstain from this line of research.
3. The degree of financial market integration in Europe can be measured in various ways. Lemmen and Eijffinger (1993) provide an overview of the various measures and their application to the European Union.
4. Despite the fact that Denmark and the UK (1973), and especially Austria (1995) joined the European Union (established in 1957) much later, economic policy in these countries has also been oriented to a certain extent to the development in (one of) the other countries in our sample.
5. Exact sources and definitions of the variables are in the appendix.
6. See Verbruggen (1992) for a more general treatment of the theoretical as well as econometric disadvantages of large-scale macro-econometric models.
7. For an extensive treatment of the Kalman filtering procedure see Schotman (1989). The Beveridge–Nelson approach was first described by Beveridge and Nelson (1981), and subsequently simplified by Cuddington and Winters (1987) and Miller (1988).
8. For a more thorough treatment of this issue see Basmann (1972a,b) and Fromm and Klein (1972).
9. See for example the discussion concerning the *FKSEC* model of the Central Planning Bureau (1992) in Bomhoff (1994a,b) and Okker (1994).
10. Of course, in such cases one has to take into consideration the big 'ceteris paribus' clause under which the various hypotheses are tested.
11. In MORKMON–I (De Nederlandsche Bank, 1984) this tension variable was directly related to the change in government debt outstanding. However, the impact of this tension variable on long-term interest rates turned out to be insignificant. Furthermore, its construction assumed a passive banking sector, which led to a number of implausible results concerning the effects of credit restrictions (Fase et al., 1990, p.56). With the modified definition of this new tension variable both (undesirable) properties were circumvented.
12. Note that this was written in the first half of 1992, right before the turbulence in the EMS took off.

2 Fiscal policy: Theory, determinants, and measurement

co-author: Jakob de Haan

> *When for the expenses of a years war 20 millions are raised by means of a loan, it is . . . twenty millions which are withdrawn from the productive capital of the nation. The million per annum which is raised by taxes to pay the interest of the loan, is merely transferred from the contributor of the tax to the national creditor . . . Governments might at once have required the twenty millions in the shape of taxes: in which case it would not have been necessary to raise annual taxes to the amount of a million. This however would not have changed the nature of the transaction. An individual instead of being called upon to pay 100 £ per annum, might have been obliged to pay 2000 £ once and for all.*
>
> Ricardo (1971), pp.252–3.

I Introduction

No issue in economic policy has generated more debate over the past decades than the effects of government budget deficits. However, paraphrasing a song by Bob Dylan, it appears that 'the times for fiscal policy are changing'. At the beginning of the 1960s the majority of academic and professional economists clearly regarded fiscal policy as the main instrument for stabilisation purposes. An instrument that was considered quite effective, especially if accommodated by monetary policy. This consensus has disappeared in thin air, due to two factors. First, as a consequence of the 'Monetarist/Neoclassical counter-revolution' and the New Classical 'rational expectations revolution', traditional Keynesian policy views came under severe attack. Second, according to many economists, the effectiveness of fiscal policy has been discredited by actual developments in most industrial countries during the 1970s, in particular the emergence of stagflation. Although the economics profession is still more or less divided over the issue, many economists share the view that deficits are harmful, and that excessive deficits may even be disastrous.

If economists and policymakers decry deficits, why then do they still exist? The answers provided thus far can roughly be subdivided into two groups containing normative and positive aspects of budget deficits and government debt. Until recently most economists studying the creation and existence of public deficits and debt only focussed on what governments ought to do. These so-called normative theories of government behaviour encompass a number of different arguments, arising from various schools of thought. In passing section II.1 will mention the potentially stabilising properties of fiscal policy, intertemporal considerations that emphasise the admissible financing of government investment by incurring public debt, and the so-called 'tax-smoothing' motive for government debt.[1] It is only recently that economists also started to formulate positive theories of government behaviour. Section II.2 summarises these positive arguments and presents an empirical investigation into the various determinants of budget deficits for the member countries of the European Union.

Despite the widespread concern over budget deficits, there is considerable controversy about what effects deficits have on the economy. The goal of section III is to clarify these effects. The central issue in this section is the question whether budget deficits do reduce national saving and raise interest rates accordingly. In section III we will disinguish between the Ricardian paradigm (III.1), the Neoclassical perspective (III.2), and a resurrection of the Keynesian view of *real* deficits as provided by Eisner and Pieper (III.3).

The debate concerning the effects of real deficits already touches upon the issue of an appropriate measurement of the fiscal policy itself. A government deficit is conventionally defined as the difference between government expenditures and revenues. Although this may seem rather obvious, various issues have to be discussed before one can proceed with the analysis of the consequences of budget deficits in the European Union. These issues are dealt with in section IV. Finally, section V presents our conclusions.

II   On the causes of budget deficits
II.1   Normative theories
II.1.1 Stabilisation

First and foremost, traditional Keynesian policy views stress the use of fiscal policy as a major instrument for stabilisation purposes, in order to keep the economy in balance. In the 1960s and early 1970s the instrument of fiscal policy was considered quite effective, especially if accommodated by monetary policy. We have to distinguish between active and passive stabilisation here. Passive stabilisation policies occur through the working of so-called 'automatic stabilisers' (Sterks, 1982, Wolswijk, 1991). In accordance with results of Roubini and Sachs (1989a,b) and De Haan and Sturm (1994), section II.2 will report evidence that among a set of political and institutional determinants, the business cycle indeed affects the stance of fiscal policy in most European countries.

The use of *active* stabilisation policies has been seriously challenged, however, due to two main lines of criticism. As a consequence of the 'Monetarist counterrevolution' and the 'rational expectations revolution', traditional Keynesian policy views came under severe attack (De Haan, 1989; see also section III.2). A first line of criticism questioned the *need* for stabilisation policies anyhow. Of particular relevance in this context is the Monetarist 'natural rate' hypothesis – as revived by Milton Friedman in his 1967 Presidential Address to the American Economic Association – that, 'there is always a temporary trade-off between inflation and unemployment; there is no permanent trade-off' (Friedman, 1969, p.104). This issue lies at the heart of the dispute about the need for stabilisation policies, and simply boils down to the question of whether the private economic sector is inherently stable or not. If it is, there is little need for an active stabilisation policy, neither through monetary nor fiscal policy instruments.

Additionally, the *effectiveness* of fiscal policy in this regard is also questioned.[2] On the one hand, the attention is directed towards the difficulties surrounding the (anti-cyclical) fine-tuning of fiscal policy, and towards the negative crowding-out effects of budget deficits on the productive potential of an economy in the longer run. The Keynesian view that 'a private enterprise economy using an intangible money needs to be stabilized, can be stabilized, and therefore should be stabilized by appropriate monetary and fiscal policies' (Modigliani, 1977, p.1) was further (and perhaps even more seriously) undermined by the incorporation of rational expectations in Friedman's natural rate model. As a consequence of the assumed market-clearing process combined with rational expectations, there is no trade-off between inflation and unemployment even in the short-run (see for example Lucas, 1972). Systematic government policies will have no stabilising impact, unless the authorities have access to superior information (Sargent and Wallace, 1976, 1981). On the other hand, an important offshoot of the rational expectations revolution has been provided by the revival of the Ricardian equivalence or debt neutrality proposition by Barro (1974). In section III.1 we will see that supporters of this theorem in its strictest version maintain that budget deficits simply do not exert any influence on the real economy whatsoever. As a consequence of its disputed need and its alleged ineffectiveness, by now most governments do not use fiscal policy to fine-tune the economy any longer and rely solely on automatic stabilisers (De Haan, Sterks, and De Kam, 1992).

II.1.2 Public consumption versus public investment
A second argument that has been brought forward to defend budget deficits originates from a Neoclassical perspective. Proponents of this school of thought emphasise the distinction between public consumption and public investment. In their view, the first category of government spending should be financed by current tax revenues only. Public investment, on the other hand, may also be financed by issuing government debt, so that the burden of taxation can be shifted onto the recipients of the future benefits of current investments.[3] Most important drawback of this intertemporal point of view is, however, a logical consequence of difficulties involved in the classification of

various forms of government spending, like for example spending on public education. 'Public choice'-like arguments point to the political process, that provides governments with a strong incentive to stress the investment character of most spending categories, thereby inducing a bias towards accepting budget deficits. Probably due to similar arguments, this intertemporal principle also seems to be at odds with the actual experience of fiscal retrenchment in most industrialised countries in the 1980s. In the beginning of the decade public investment shrank, while budget deficits rose dramatically. Subsequently, in order to reduce these (structural) deficits, governments appeared to be more inclined to cut public investment even further, rather than curtailing the ever expanding welfare state (De Haan, Sturm, and Sikken, 1996).

II.1.3 Tax-smoothing

A final argument in favour of budget deficits is the so called 'tax-smoothing' argument brought forward by Barro (1979), that has its roots in the 'equilibrium approach' to fiscal policy[4] as well as the Ricardian equivalence theorem (section III.1). Tax and deficit policies are viewed as the result of an intertemporal optimisation process by the budgetary authorities. The tax-smoothing theory assumes that the discounted value of current and future taxes is equal to the initial stock of government debt plus the discounted value of current and future government spending, its time-path given. Moreover, this theory assumes that the collection costs of taxation are homogeneous in taxes and the tax base and that the *marginal* collection costs are an increasing function of the tax rate. If a government chooses to minimise the excess burden of taxation under these circumstances, Barro (1979) has shown that the resulting first-order conditions require the marginal collection costs of raising taxes to be equalised over all periods.

The stabilisation of (anticipated) tax rates over time has some important implications for public debt behaviour. First, temporarily large government outlays should be financed by issuing debt, while a permanently higher level of public spending ought to be financed by taxes. Second, if real government expenditures exhibit little cyclical variation, a tax-smoothing policy entails deficits during recessions and surpluses during economic booms. Third, anticipated inflation is reflected in the growth rate of nominal debt. Finally, the policy of maintaining stable tax rates itself is independent of the initial stock of government debt. Barro (1979) concludes that government debt growth in the US can be explained by this theory. His results indicate that the magnitude of typical countercyclical debt has exceeded the amount as implied by the tax-smoothing theory, but his other findings corroborate the theory. Nevertheless, empirical evidence with respect to other countries have not unambiguously shown that governments behave accordingly (Roubini and Sachs, 1989a, De Haan and Zelhorst, 1993).[5]

II.2   Positive theories

II.2.1   *Theory*

In recent theoretical and empirical research the variation in political and institutional arrangements which may affect the process of national policy formation is called upon to explain cross-country differences with respect to fiscal policies pursued. A first class of models investigates how the *political system* affects the behaviour of policymakers (Grilli et al., 1991). According to these models two features of the political system are especially relevant: instability (that is the chance that policymakers will be thrown out of office) and polarisation (how strong is the disagreement between alternating governments). For instance, Persson and Svensson (1989) have shown that a conservative government, which favours a low level of government spending but knows that it will probably be replaced by a government in favour of higher spending levels, will borrow more than if it was certain to stay in office. For a two party system, Alesina and Tabellini (1990) show that public debt is positively correlated with the degree of polarisation between alternating governments, with the time between government changes and with the chance that a government will not be re-elected. Basically, these models imply that highly unstable and polarised political systems behave more myopically and therefore exhibit higher public debt-to-GDP ratios. Indeed, Grilli et al. (1991) found a strong negative correlation between debt accumulation and the frequency of government changes in their sample of eighteen OECD countries. Saunders and Klau (1985) report that the number of elections, reflecting opportunities for competitive fiscal bidding by political parties, is significantly positive in their cross-country regression which tries to explain the growth of the public sector.

A second class of models focusses on *disagreement* between *various decision makers* (see, for example, Alesina and Drazen, 1991). The greater the conflict, the more difficult it will be to enact deficit reduction measures. It is likely, that such policy conflicts are more important in countries with coalition governments. Game theory suggests that cooperation is harder when the number of players is large. In this view, coalition governments will have a hard time closing budget deficits after adverse shocks, since individual parties in the coalition will each veto spending cuts or tax increases that would impinge on their constituencies (see also Corsetti and Roubini, 1991). Roubini and Sachs (1989a) and Corsetti and Roubini (1991) found that their index of political power dispersion, which measures the type of government in power, helps explain government debt growth in their sample of fifteen OECD countries: large coalition governments have higher deficits, other things being equal, than do one-party, majoritarian governments. Edin and Ohlsson (1991) argue, however, that the political cohesion variable used by Roubini and Sachs captures the effects of minority governments rather than majority coalition governments. Roubini and Sachs (1989b) also argue that coalition governments will have a bias towards higher levels of government spending relative to majority party governments, as various parties in government make logrolling agreements so as to ensure higher outlays benefitting their individual constituencies. They report evidence in support of this view.

A third class of models, which predates the models outlined above, focuses on *ideological differences* (see for instance Hibbs, 1977, and Frey and Schneider, 1978). It is often maintained that left-wing governments aim for a higher share of government spending in total output, and are perhaps even more willing to accept rising government budget deficits than do right-wing governments. Cameron (1985) and Roubini and Sachs (1989b) found some support for this hypothesis, but De Haan and Zelhorst (1992) conclude that government debt growth in Germany is not influenced by the 'political colour' of government.

Finally, some authors have argued that *budgeting procedures*, that is the rules according to which budgets are drafted by the government, amended and passed by the parliament, and implemented by the government may have important consequences for the sustainability of fiscal policy (see for example Von Hagen, 1991, 1992). According to Von Hagen a budgeting procedure enabling a government to commit itself to fiscal discipline is an essential condition for fiscal stability. Indeed, Von Hagen (1992) using data from the European Union countries during the 1980s and characterisations obtained from an assesment of national budget procedures has found strong empirical support for the view that a budgetary process that gives the prime minister or the finance minister a dominant position over spending ministers, that limits the amendment power of parliament, and that leaves little room for changes in the budget during the execution process, is conducive to fiscal discipline.

II.2.2 Data
In the next section[6] we will build upon the literature outlined above and examine whether cross-country differences in debt accumulation and public sector size of member countries of the European Union during the 1980s can be explained using, inter alia, the following variables:

- the number of government changes;
- the share of cabinet portfolios or seats in parliament held by social democratic and other leftist parties;
- the Roubini and Sachs political power dispersion index;
- a variant of the Von Hagen budgetary process variable.

This section first presents these data. It appears that fiscal policy of EU member countries during the 1980s varies remarkably both across countries and over the years within the same country. So our sample provides ample opportunity to test various theories, which will be taken up in the next section.

The member countries of the European Union strive for the convergence of their fiscal policies. Although in this respect some progress has been

Table 2.1: Government debt-to-GDP ratio in EU member countries, 1981–89

	1981	1985	1989
Belgium	89.7	119.8	128.4
Denmark	53.3	76.8	65.6
France	36.4	45.5	47.4
Germany	36.3	42.3	43.0
Greece	34.2	62.6	85.8
Ireland	79.8	108.5	110.1
Italy	59.9	86.5	98.6
Luxembourg	14.4	13.5	8.5
Netherlands	50.3	71.6	78.3
Portugal	47.3	70.9	72.0
Spain	21.6	45.2	44.2
UK	53.3	58.9	45.1

Source: EC

achieved, the record so far is not satisfactory and displays a striking variation in public debt policies. Table 2.1 reports data on the accumulation of gross public debt in the member states during the 1980s. In 1989 the debt to GDP ratio ranged from 9% in Luxemburg to 128% in Belgium. In Italy and Greece the public debt-to-GDP ratio is rapidly rising and nearing (Greece) or almost breaching (Italy) the 100% threshold. In Belgium, Ireland, the Netherlands and Portugal public indebtedness remains at high to very high levels. In Belgium the debt ratio has been stabilised at by far the highest ratio in the Community. In Ireland net borrowing has been reduced considerably, followed by a steep decline in the debt-to-GDP ratio. In the Netherlands the debt ratio has been stabilised, however with the debt ratio significantly above the EU average. In Portugal the public debt ratio is now declining, but it also is still above the EU average. Denmark, Germany, Spain, France, Luxembourg and the UK had reasonably sound budgetary positions during the period under consideration.

We describe three main features of the political systems of the EU member countries: (a) the type of government; (b) the durability of governments; and (c) the share of cabinet portfolios or seats in parliament held by social democratic and other leftist parties. It has been argued by various authors that the kind of government (coalition, majority government or minority government) may also influence government debt accumulation (Grilli et al., 1991). To capture possible effects of divided versus single party governments, and following Roubini and Sachs (1989a,b), we have constructed an index of power dispersion (*POL*) which measures the size of the governing coalition, ranging from 0 (smallest coalition) to 3 (minority government):[7]

Index 0   one-party majority parliamentary government;
1   coalition parliamentary government with two-to-three coalition partners;
2   coalition parliamentary government with four or more coalition partners;
3   minority government.

Our second variable *CHANGE* traces the frequency of government changes. A government change occurs after each election and if a change takes place with respect to the parties participating in the governing coalition.[8] For example, when the social democrats left the three-party coalition in the Netherlands in 1982 and the remaining parties formed a minority government, we consider this a change of government. After the elections took place, a new centre-right government was formed, and this we consider as another change of government.

Our third variable is the share of cabinet portfolios held by social democratic and other leftist parties (*LEFT*). This variable is constructed following the approach outlined by Cameron (1985). The total number of months that left-wing politicians held cabinet portfolios is divided by the total number of cabinet members, multiplied by twelve. For their sample of fourteen industrial countries Roubini and Sachs (1989b) concluded that this variable helps explain cross-country differences in government spending.[9] We have also constructed the variable *LEFTP*, which measures the proportion of seats in parliament held by left-wing parties. This variable has also been used in the literature (see for example Solano, 1983). The appendix to De Haan and Sturm (1994) contains detailed information on our political variables.

Our final institutional variable is based upon the work of Von Hagen (1992). On the basis of an assessment of national budgeting procedures, Von Hagen has constructed a number of budgetary process indices. He distinguishes various characteristics which are grouped under five large items: the structure of negotiations within government; the structure of the parliamentary process; the informativeness of the budget draft; the flexibility of the budget execution and the existence of long-term planning constraints. For each characteristic numbers ranging from zero to four are used to describe its quality, with a low number indicating a quality conducive to a small degree of fiscal discipline. In case of missing information a number equal to the average of the available numbers for the other characteristics of the same item is assigned. In our empirical analysis we will use an index (*BUDGET*), which is based upon the characteristics that Von Hagen distinguishes.[10]

II.2.3 Explaining government debt growth in the EU
This section presents the estimation results of a pooled time-series regression in which the growth of the debt–GDP ratio is the dependent variable. Our basic model is borrowed from Roubini and Sachs (1989a). As pointed out by

Roubini and Sachs, the specification of this model is consistent both with elements of optimising approaches to budget deficits (such as the tax-smoothing model of Barro (1979), discussed in section II.1) and with traditional Keynesian models of fiscal deficits. Indeed, both theories imply that budget deficits are countercyclical. Suppressing time indices the estimated equation is:

$$DBY = a_0 + a_1 DBYL + a_2 DUB + a_3 DRB + a_4 DGR + a_5 P + v \quad (2.1)$$

where the dependent variable (*DBY*) is the change in the public debt–GDP ratio and the explanatory variables are: the lagged change in the debt-ratio (*DBYL*),[11] the change in the unemployment rate (*DUB*), the change in debt-servicing costs (*DRB*)[12] and the change in the GDP growth rate (*DGR*), and our political-institutional variables (*P*).[13] Finally, *v* denotes the error term.

The lagged deficit is included to allow for slow adjustment of budget deficits. The adverse shocks of slow growth and high unemployment resulted in increasing deficits; a process which was aggravated by the rise in real interest rates, which significantly and often unexpectedly raised most governments' costs of debt servicing. See Roubini and Sachs (1989a) for a further discussion of the model.

Table 2.2 contains our estimation results. The first row of Table 2.2 presents the outcomes of the basic Roubini and Sachs model. All coefficients have the right sign and most of them are significantly different from zero. Row 2.2.2 shows the outcomes when the power dispersion index *POL* is added as an explanatory variable. In sharp contrast to the results reported by Roubini and Sachs (1989a,b), we find that the coefficient of *POL* is not significantly different from zero. As Edin and Ohlsson (1991) have pointed out, the construction of *POL* places a very restrictive form on its effects. Why should the increase of public debt under a minority government be three times as large as under a two-party majority coalition? Row 2.2.3 therefore reports the results when *POL* is replaced by a dummy variable for each 'political class'. In contrast to the results reported by Edin and Ohlsson (1991), the coefficient of the *POL3* dummy (minority governments) is not significantly different from zero. Closer inspection of fiscal policy in individual countries indeed suggests that minority governments are often able to reduce budget deficits, as the Danish experience clearly demonstrates. The coefficients of *POL1* and *POL2* are also not significantly different from zero.

Next, we have examined whether the number of government changes may help explain cross-country differences in public debt growth. Row 2.2.4 presents the outcomes adding *CHANGE* as explanatory variable. It is very interesting that the frequency of government changes apparently does matter. This result is broadly in accordance with the conclusions of Grilli et al. (1991). Note, however, the differences between the findings of Grilli et al. (1991) and our results. First, Grilli et al. only consider political-institutional

Table 2.2: Explaining cross-country differences in public debt growth in the European Union, 1981–89

	DBYL	DUB	DRB	DGR	POL	POL1	POL2	POL3	CHANGE	LEFT	BUDGET	R²
2.2.1	0.59 (7.7)	1.19 (4.5)	0.24 (1.2)	-0.33 (1.6)								0.52
2.2.2	0.60 (7.5)	1.19 (4.5)	0.24 (1.2)	-0.34 (1.6)	-0.14 (0.4)							0.51
2.2.3	0.57 (7.0)	1.24 (4.6)	0.25 (1.2)	-0.29 (1.4)		-0.16 (0.2)	0.79 (0.7)	-0.78 (0.7)				0.52
2.2.4	0.59 (7.8)	1.12 (4.3)	0.25 (1.2)	-0.33 (1.6)					1.19 (2.4)			0.54
2.2.5	0.58 (7.5)	1.13 (4.2)	0.26 (1.3)	-0.35 (1.7)					0.86 (1.2)			0.52
2.2.6	0.58 (7.5)	1.15 (4.3)	0.25 (1.2)	-0.31 (1.5)						1.13 (1.5)		0.52
2.2.7	0.56 (7.1)	1.22 (4.6)	0.25 (1.2)	-0.31 (1.5)							-0.03 (1.5)	0.52
2.2.8	0.48 (5.4)	1.25 (4.8)	0.27 (1.4)	-0.21 (1.0)							-0.06 (2.4)	0.54
2.2.9	0.49 (5.7)	1.18 (4.6)	0.28 (1.4)	-0.22 (1.1)					1.05 (2.1)		-0.06 (2.3)	0.55

Notes: Absolute values of t-statistics in parentheses. A constant is included in all regressions. R²: R²-adjusted.

27

variables in their cross-section model of government deficits in twelve countries. Second, Grilli et al. do not find support for the view that the frequency of government changes has led to higher deficits during the 1980s. For three other decades, in which debt ratios were often on a downward trend, Grilli et al. report similar results as the present study.

Our conclusion does not change when the constant term is replaced by country dummies (not shown). We have also experimented with a variable which has the value one only in case of a substantial government change and zero otherwise.[14] The coefficient of this variable is not significantly different from zero (row 2.2.5). The next variable included in the model is *LEFT* (row 2.2.6). As can be seen, the coefficient of this variable is not significantly different from zero, which is in accordance with the results that De Haan and Zelhorst (1993) report for Germany. Similar results are found when the proportion of seats in parliament held by left-wing parties (*LEFTP*) is used instead of *LEFT* (not shown).

Finally, in row 2.2.7 we have added the variable *BUDGET* in our model. Although the coefficient of *BUDGET* has the 'right' sign, it is not very significant. So at first sight there is only limited support for the view that budgetary procedures are very important. Closer inspection of the data suggests, however, that the inclusion of Luxembourg severely influences the outcome. Luxembourg not only has the lowest value for *BUDGET*, but also the lowest government deficit of all EU member countries (Table 2.1).[15] Re-estimating the model with a dummy included for Luxembourg reinforces this impression (row 2.2.8): the coefficient of *BUDGET* is now significantly different from zero. Note, however, that the significance of the coefficient of the economic growth variable is reduced. Although maybe not a sufficient condition for stable fiscal policy, there are strong indications that budgetary procedures are relevant in explaining cross-country differences in fiscal policies pursued.

In conclusion, we find that the growth of government debt is positively related to the frequency of government changes and negatively to sound budgetary procedures. Row 2.2.9 shows the regression in which both *CHANGE* and *BUDGET* are included as explanatory variables. Inclusion of both variables at the same time does not affect our conclusions. This implies for example that countries with unstable governments may have more difficulties to satisfy the Maastricht criteria for fiscal policy. The introduction of these criteria may, on the other hand, be an important external impetus, which may compensate for the lack of internal political stability.

III   On the consequences of budget deficits
III.1   Ricardian equivalence
In traditional IS/LM analysis, a change from tax to debt finance for a given level of government expenditure raises disposable income and reduces national saving, thereby stimulating aggregate demand. However, public debt competes

with private debt for available funds, thus driving up interest rates and changing the composition of output, in particular crowding out private capital formation. If the economy were in disequilibrium, unemployment might also fall. Although many Monetarists and Neoclassicals dismissed the empirical relevance of fiscal policy actions, in Keynesian as well as both Monetarist and Neoclassical models the financing of government expenditure by taxes or debt exerts different real effects. The Ricardian equivalence, or debt neutrality hypothesis – as revitalised by Barro (1974) under the aegis of the 'rational expectations revolution' – persuasively challenges this point of view. Deficit finance is interpreted as an intertemporal reallocation of taxes which does not alter the consumption possibilities of rational subjects, who will therefore not change their optimal consumption plans.

The central observation of Ricardian equivalence is that deficits merely postpone taxes. A rational individual should be able to see through the intertemporal veil and realise that the present discounted value of taxes depends only upon real government spending, not on the timing of taxes. This foresight gives rise to a 'Say's law' for deficits (Bernheim, 1989, p.63): the demand for bonds always rises to match government borrowing. Since the timing of taxes does not affect an individual's lifetime budget constraint, it cannot alter his consumption decisions. As a result, both temporary and permanent budget deficits have no real effects, regardless of the degree of employment of resources.

The logic of this reasoning can readily be shown. Suppose that a subject's life is known with certainty and divided into two parts. During the first part of his life the subject consumes Co_1, whereas consumption in the second part of life is denoted by Co_2. The subject derives utility from this consumption and his optimisation problem reads:

$$Max \quad U = \sum_{t=1}^{2} \beta^{t-1} \, U[Co_t], \qquad (2.2)$$

where β denotes the personal discount rate. The optimisation problem is subject to:

$$Y_1 + \frac{Y_2}{1+r} - \left\{ T_1 + \frac{T_2}{1+r} \right\} = Co_1 + \frac{Co_2}{1+r}, \qquad (2.3)$$

where Y denotes income, r is the interest rate, and T is a lump-sum tax liability. Equation (2.3) simply states that the present value of the available earnings stream must equal the present value of consumption. Suppose now that T is lowered in period 1 by the amount of ΔT. The resulting deficit D ($=\Delta T$) is financed by issuing government debt with interest rate r, which is redeemed in period 2. The present value of the necessary taxes to pay for the amortisation and interest payments is, of course, $(1+r)D/(1+r)$, which equals ΔT. Hence, the consumption possibilities for a rational subject have not changed and he will therefore not change his consumption plans.

Debt neutrality implies that individuals incorporate the government's intertemporal budget constraint in their consumption decisions. Therefore, it also does not make any difference whether the debt is owned by foreigners or domestic residents. In fact, only the amount of government spending determines private consumption possibilities. For the sake of illustration the government's budget constraint in the first period of a two-period economy can be given as:

$$G_1 + (1+r)B_0 = T_1 + B_1, \qquad (2.4)$$

where G denotes government spending and B is the stock of government debt. Assuming that debt is repaid entirely in the second period, the government budget constraint reads:

$$G_2 + (1+r)B_1 = T_2. \qquad (2.5)$$

Consolidating (2.3), (2.4), and (2.5) yields:

$$T_1 + \frac{T_2}{1+r} = (1+r)B_0 + G_1 + \frac{G_2}{1+r}, \qquad (2.6)$$

which, in turn, corresponds to the term between brackets in (2.3). So, government purchases matter for private sector decisions, but the debt/tax mix is irrelevant.

Barro (1974) has shown that this result also holds in case of finite lifetimes – which implies that taxes might be raised at such a moment that presently living economic subjects are not harmed – provided that an intergenerational transfer mechanism is operational. If the present generation cares about future generations, it may offset the higher tax burden for future generations implied by the issuance of government debt, for instance by increasing bequests. The strict irrelevance of fiscal policy (or, to be more precisely, debt policy) then depends upon a variety of strong assumptions (Bernheim, 1989, De Haan, 1989, Seater, 1993). These include: 1) agents have infinite planning horizons as successive generations are linked by altruistically motivated transfers; 2) capital markets are either perfect, or fail in specific ways so that liquidity constraints do not necessarily destroy equivalence; 3) consumers are rational and farsighted (no myopia); 4) postponement of taxes does not redistribute resources across families with systematically different marginal propensities to consume; 5) taxes are lump-sum and non-distortionary; 6) the use of deficits cannot create value (not even through bubbles); and 7) the availability of deficit financing does not modify the political process. Careful examination of these factors suggests that exact Ricardian equivalence is implausible. Nevertheless, it is highly controversial whether debt neutrality holds as a close approximation of the role of public debt in a market economy, despite its nearly certain invalidity as a literal description.

Thus far, empirical evidence on Ricardian equivalence must be dubbed 'rather mixed' at best. Testing theories on the potential effects of fiscal policy on the economy has never been trivial. Estimation is sensitive to the treatment of specification, simultaneity, and data stationarity, as well as simple measurement of the quantities involved, so that careful attention to the econometric methodology would seem essential. Much of the published evidence on Ricardian equivalence, both favourable and unfavourable, fails to attend to these issues and is sufficiently flawed to be uninformative (Seater, 1993, p.143). Notably Chapters 3 and 4 of this study will provide a European impetus to this lively debate.

III.2 A Neoclassical perspective
The Neoclassical view of budget deficits and the Ricardian proposition share the common feature that both paradigms should be interpreted as a straightforward generalisation of the permanent income/life cycle hypothesis (see for instance Hall, 1978). Unlike Ricardian equivalence, however, the Neoclassical model envisions farsighted individuals planning consumption exclusively over their *own* life cycles; they act as though they are finite-lived instead of infinite-lived. Budget deficits raise total lifetime consumption by shifting taxes onto subsequent generations. If economic resources are fully employed, increased consumption necessarily implies decreased saving; interest rates must then rise to return capital markets into balance. Hence, persistent deficits crowd out private capital accumulation. However, it is important here to subdivide the deficit into permanent (long run average) and temporary (deviation from long run average) components, where the economic effects of the permanent part evidently prevail.

This more or less standard Neoclassical model has three central features (Bernheim, 1989). First, the consumption of each individual is determined as the solution to an intertemporal optimisation problem, where both borrowing and lending are permitted at the market rate of interest (King, 1983, and Hayashi, 1985). Second, individuals are aware of their finite lifespans. Each consumer belongs to a specific cohort or generation, and the lifespans of successive generations overlap. Finally, market clearing is generally assumed in all periods. Taken together, these assumptions imply that permanent deficits significantly depress private capital accumulation, whereas temporary deficits have either a negligible or perverse effect on most economic variables. If many consumers are either liquidity constrained or myopic, the impact of permanent deficits remains qualitatively unaltered. However, under these circumstances temporary deficits should also depress national saving and raise interest rates in the short run.

While the second feature defines the central difference between the Neoclassical and Ricardian frameworks, the third characteristic (full employment) represents the primary distinction between the Neoclassical and Keynesian theories. If the economy will constantly be drawn to some full employment equilibrium, the permanent deficit will essentially affect the level of national saving and interest rates. By manipulating temporary deficits, it may only be possible to stabilise fluctuations around this equilibrium, due to the various macroeconomic shocks occurring. Nevertheless, Neoclassical economists tend to be very sceptical about the value of fiscal policy as a tool for macroeconomic stabilisation. It is argued that the immediate impact of deficits on aggregate demand is probably much smaller than envisioned by most Keynesians and the ability of policy makers to fine tune fiscal policy to the needs of the business cycle is also seriously questioned (Bernheim, 1989; see also section II.1).

III.3   A resurrection of Keynes: Do real deficits matter?

In a series of papers Eisner and Pieper (1984, 1988a,b, 1992) and Eisner (1986, 1989a,b, 1994) have argued that only real (that is inflation-adjusted) deficits are relevant in analyzing the effects of fiscal policy on the level of economic activity. Since inflation wipes out the real value of public debt, thereby nullifying any increase in private sector real wealth, it is necessary to correct budget deficits accordingly. Eisner and Pieper have first presented estimates of inflation-corrected federal deficits in the United States, a measurement issue that will be dealt with more extensively in section IV. Correcting both for the 'inflation tax' and cyclical influences, federal budgets even appeared to produce surpluses during the 1970s. Eisner and Pieper have then estimated a simple equation in which the growth rate of real GNP is regressed on two constant terms, the inflation-adjusted high-employment deficit and the change in the real monetary base. They found that federal budget deficits had a major impact on economic growth and that the results over the years 1956–84 were overall better when using the inflation-adjusted deficit measure. Eisner argues that '. . . the demand-oriented explanation of stagnation re-emerges. The less the inflation-adjusted surplus or the greater the deficit, the data confirm, the greater the subsequent growth, or the less the decline, in real gross national product. And the greater that deficit, the greater the reduction, or the less the increase, in unemployment' (Eisner, 1986, p.6). In other words, even during and after the era of stagflation, fiscal policy – properly measured – is still a very effective instrument to influence aggregate demand.

The work of Eisner and Pieper has stimulated subsequent research. Various authors have, for different theoretical reasons, questioned the usefulness of the inflation adjustment. For one thing, it is assumed that investors in government debt are totally free of money illusion.[16] Even if the inflationary component of the deficit does not change the behaviour of the bond holder as a consumer, it may very well influence him as an investor as argued by Tanzi et al. (1987). As these authors point out, full bond refinanceability of inflation-induced interest service would require, first, a stable demand for bonds in real terms, and second, that the rate of inflation is not an argument in that function. It is not so obvious either that deficits stimulate economic growth as Eisner and Pieper claim. Fischer (1993) argues, for example, that deficits should be negatively associated with capital accumulation and, hence, negatively with economic growth, for two reasons. The first is crowding-out. The second is that, like the inflation rate, the deficit may serve as an indicator of a government that is losing control of its actions. Indeed, Fischer (1993) presents cross-sectional and panel regressions showing that economic growth is negatively associated with budget deficits through lower capital accumulation and lower productivity growth. Similarly, Easterly and Rebelo (1993) report a consistently negative relationship between growth and budget deficits.

On empirical grounds the conclusions of Eisner and Pieper have also been questioned (see for instance Tullio, 1987, and De Haan and Zelhorst, 1988). Despite diverging opinions the empirical issues at stake are very clear. First, has fiscal policy any effect on real economic growth, and, second does it matter whether the deficit is corrected for inflation or not? The debate has centred on two issues, namely the specification of the model to test for the effects of fiscal policy and the specification of the deficit variable. With respect to the specification of the model, Darrat and Suliman (1992) criticise both the work of Eisner and Pieper and that of De Haan and Zelhorst, arguing that the basic model estimated by these authors is conceptually misspecified for it does not consider several other exogenous factors that could potentially influence real GDP.[17] Variables which, according to these authors, should be included are the inflation rate and long- and short-term interest rates. Furthermore, Darrat and Suliman argue that previous studies have ignored possible feedbacks from changes in real GDP to the policy variables. This argument is, however, not entirely correct. To take the effect of GDP growth on fiscal policy into account, previous work has used the high-employment deficit. Nevertheless, Tullio (1987) has pointed out that this is a very dubious approach as the high-employment deficit is only a hypothetical concept which has little or no relationship with the theoretically relevant change in private sector wealth. Furthermore, estimates of the high-employment deficit are very sensitive with respect to the way trend income is estimated.

With respect to the specification of the deficit variable, De Haan, Goudswaard and Zelhorst (1990) conclude that the inflation correction does not make much of a difference: the impact of inflation-adjusted and unadjusted deficits is generally the same in their sample of ten OECD countries. More recently, Darrat and Suliman (1992) have argued that preceding empirical work is plagued with some estimation problems that make the models unreliable to test the hypothesis that budget deficits should be corrected for inflation changes. They suggest to employ a multi-equation vector autoregressive (VAR) model. Using data for the 1956–84 period for the US they conclude that regardless of whether or not deficits are corrected for inflation they exert a significant positive impact upon real GDP. Their results also suggest that the inflation-corrected deficit yields more reliable estimates. However, applying long-run data for the US to a similar VAR model, De Haan and Sturm (1995) find that both the inflation adjusted and the unadjusted deficit exert a *negative* influence on real growth.

IV   Measurement of debt and deficits

Before we can start our empirical analyses of the consequences of government debt and deficits on financial markets, the concepts of government budget deficits and government debt must be specified. This final part of Chapter 2 deals with various measurement issues, using figures for the Netherlands for illustrative purposes. The following issues are of particular relevance in this respect:

- the comprehensiveness of the public sector;
- is the deficit measured on an accrual or cash basis?;
- is the budget deficit (debt) defined as net borrowing (net debt) or financial deficit (gross debt)?;
- is government's gross borrowing requirement the proper concept for certain purposes?;
- is the budget deficit corrected for cyclical fluctuations in economic activity?;
- is the budget deficit adjusted for inflation?; and
- what is the relationship between a government deficit and government's balance sheet?

Section IV.1 will deal with the first four issues whereas separate sections will consider the last three issues (IV.2–IV.4).

IV.1   Debt and deficits: Concepts and calculations

What does 'public' mean if one discusses public debt? This question, simple as it may seem, is not answered unanimously by economists. Varying answers are largely explained by different institutional settings in various countries. In the United States, for instance, state and local governments are financially far more independent from the federal government than the provinces and municipalities in the Netherlands are from Dutch central government. Therefore, in the Netherlands these lower echelons of government are often included in analyses of government debt and deficits, while in the US oriented

Table 2.3: Government net borrowing, The Netherlands, 1990–94 (% GDP)

Year	Central government	Local government	Social security funds	General government
1990	5.1	–0.1	0.1	5.1
1991	3.4	–0.1	–0.4	2.9
1992	4.3	–0.1	–0.2	3.9
1993	2.9	–0.1	0.4	3.2
1994	3.1	–0.2	0.4	3.2

Minus sign indicates surplus. Source: Ministry of Finance (1996), p.223.

literature federal government is given centre stage. Similarly, what should be done with funds that are responsible for various social security schemes? According to the Maastricht Treaty the deficit of these funds should be included in calculating the deficit relevant as a convergence criterion. The size of the deficit that accords with various concepts of the public sector is presented in Table 2.3. In most chapters of the present study data on government deficits provided by the International Monetary Fund (IMF) will be used. These figures refer to consolidated central government (that is including off-budget agencies and social security funds).

Demand raising effects of government deficits are probably better reflected by a deficit measured on an accrual-basis. The central bank is primarily interested in the financial and monetary consequences of government deficits and these are better accounted for if the deficit is measured on a cash-basis. The differences between both deficit concepts are sometimes quite large, as De Haan (1989) has demonstrated for the Netherlands. For the analyses of the impact of budget deficits on financial markets in the remainder of the book we will employ the more common deficit on cash-basis.

The Dutch Treasury always had a clear preference for the financial deficit (in Dutch: 'financieringstekort') instead of net borrowing ('vorderingentekort') because of considerations with regard to the management of government finance. Net borrowing is the deficit concept upon which one of the convergence criteria of the Maastricht Treaty referred to above is based upon. The main difference between both concepts consists of net loans granted by government which are excluded in net borrowing. For managing the public finances, loans are as important as other expenditures in determining the gross needs for Treasury financing through taxes or borrowing. Those who advocate to include loans when sizing up the financial deficit, point out that when the government issues a loan, it is not just acting as a financial intermediary, because if financial intermediation were all that were required, the private sector could probably take care. Without government being involved, it seems likely that these loans would not have been granted, at least not at conditions which government can accomplish. One might, however, object that

Figure 2.1: Net borrowing versus financial deficit, 1987–95

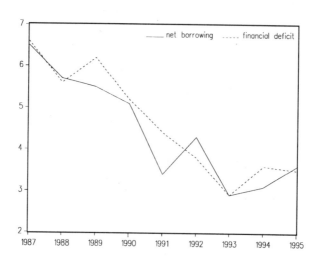

government's borrowing and lending of equal amounts wash out in net economic effects, depending of course on the purpose for which the loan was raised. The choice for one particular concept is not always based on economic grounds only. Casual observation suggests that those who think government spending should be kept in as tight a check as possible are more inclined to prefer a comprehensive budget concept which includes loans. Figure 2.1 illustrates the gap between both concepts for central government in the Netherlands. Over the last years the differences between both concepts are very minor, due to the fact that central government no longer acts as an intermediary for local building societies and local governments. However, in the past the differences between both concepts were sometimes quite large. The deficit figures of the IMF which will mainly be used in the present study refer to net borrowing.

Similarly, one can distinguish between gross and net government debt. The first two columns of Table 2.4 present data on gross and net government debt in the Netherlands. The latter consists of gross debt (both long- and short-term debt) minus the short- and long-term claims. These long-term claims consist primarily of loans to building-corporations.

Finally, some authors have argued that amortisation payments, which are excluded from the conventional definition of the deficit should be taken into account, because of reasons related to the management of public finances. Moreover, if one examines the consequences of deficits on financial markets the gross borrowing requirement (in Dutch: 'begrotingstekort') may be the

Table 2.4: Debt, borrowing, and amortisation payments, 1990–94

Year	Gross financial liabilities	Net financial liabilities	Gross borrowing	Of which: amortisation*
1990	76.5	56.8	43.5	20.2
1991	76.4	56.0	44.6	26.5
1992	77.1	57.7	48.0	27.3
1993	78.5	59.8	38.0	29.4
1994	79.0	60.3	43.0	34.0

Debt figures in % GDP. *: billions of Dutch guilders. Sources: OECD (1995) and Ministry of Finance (1996), p.222 (*).

concept to be preferred. One may argue that portfolio holders may not automatically reinvest their received amortisation payments. First, the growth of the government debt ratio may erode portfolio holders' willingness to invest in government debt. Second, a considerable amount of Dutch government debt is held by foreigners who may not be willing to keep their investments in guilders. Finally, portfolio holders may consume part of the amortisation payments. The final columns of Table 2.4 picture the importance of amortisation payments in total gross borrowing.

IV.2 Structural (cyclically-adjusted) deficits

The cyclically adjusted (or structural) government budget deficit (or surplus) is the deficit (or surplus) which remains after some corrections have been made that reflect the impact of short-run economic fluctuations on government receipts and expenditures. In constructing a cyclically adjusted budget four essential steps can be distinguished:

1) choosing a reference GDP which is free from cyclical fluctuations;
2) determining the responsiveness of receipts and expenditures to cyclical fluctuations;
3) applying this responsiveness to gaps between actual and reference GDP; and
4) adding the adjustments to the actual deficit.

The first of these steps is of crucial importance for the eventual outcome. Various methods are used to determine reference GDP. Often a high employment or potential GDP trend is constructed. This concept has been criticised because potential output is not a well-defined concept and because it implies some arbitrary features (see for example Fellner, 1982). If the structural deficit is to provide information on the financial position of government it is important that agreement is reached on a reasonable estimate of what the economy can accomplish.

Table 2.5: Cyclically adjusted deficits

Year	Structural deficit	Unadjusted deficit
1990	6.3	5.0
1991	3.8	2.8
1992	4.0	3.8
1993	1.9	3.2
1994	1.9	3.0

Deficits in % GDP. Source: OECD, Economic Outlook, June 1995.

Table 2.6: Structural deficit, 1990

Economic Outlook		Cyclically adjusted deficit
June	1993	7.6
December	1993	6.7
June	1994	6.5
December	1994	5.5
June	1995	6.3
December	1995	6.4

Source: OECD, Economic Outlook.

The OECD publishes information on cyclically adjusted budget deficits (see Table 2.5). As follows from this table the differences between actual and cyclically adjusted deficits are sometimes quite substantial, indicating that the financial position of the public sector is heavily influenced by cyclical factors. However, according to Wolswijk (1991), who applied a more detailed analysis, the financial position of the Dutch central government is less influenced by cyclical factors than the OECD estimates suggest.

The difficulties in calculating cyclically adjusted deficits can be illustrated by comparing the figure for the cyclically adjusted deficit for a particular year in various issues of the OECD's Economic Outlook. As follows from Table 2.6, the estimate of the cyclical adjustment appears anything but structural itself, fluctuating between 5.5% and 7.6% of 1990 GDP!

Sometimes cyclically adjusted deficits are used as indicators of discretionary policy measures. It should however be recalled that the cyclically adjusted deficit as such has some serious drawbacks. First, the underlying assumption about the nature of the cycle, namely that there are regular fluctuations around a slowly changing trend, have become increasingly challenged. Various authors have argued that there is little evidence for a tendency for the economy to return to any stable underlying trend (see, however, Zelhorst and De Haan, 1994). Furthermore, not all changes in the structural budget balance are caused by autonomous fiscal policy measures (for example inflation induced fiscal drag). Similarly, not all autonomous decisions lead to structural budget changes (for instance balanced budget changes). Moreover, if the relationship between the structural budget deficit (surplus) and national income is not constant, the change in the cyclically adjusted deficit may not correctly indicate the direction of fiscal policy. Indeed, Buiter (1985, p.54) concludes that 'there is no existing model of the economy that yields the cyclically corrected (full employment) deficit, the change in this deficit, its share in GDP or the change in its share in GDP as a measure of fiscal impact on aggregate demand in any run'. Still, the concept has been used in many empirical studies on the consequences of government budget deficits on economic growth. Also studies examining whether budget deficits raise interest rates often use the cyclically adjusted deficit, albeit for a somewhat different reason. In a simple reduced form model of interest rates, the use of the actual deficit may be problematic since it is not exogenous. Therefore, the cyclically adjusted deficit is often used, as will also be done in our estimates of a reduced form model of interest rates in Chapter 3.

IV.3   Real (inflation-adjusted) deficits

In times of inflation the real value of nominally denominated debt is eroded. As a result, conventionally measured sectoral income and expenditure flows are distorted by a measurement error, the size of which is directly related to the (accumulated) borrowing or lending of the sector concerned. The government deficit also suffers from an inflation-induced measurement error (see for example Siegel, 1979). The inflation-corrected deficit is regarded as the relevant deficit by many authors. Eisner (1986) argues, for instance 'Since federal deficits add to federal debt, which thus adds to private wealth, they can be expected to increase aggregate demand, or spending . . . But for deficits to matter, they must be real deficits. A real deficit is one which increases the real net debt of the government to the public and hence increases the public's perception of its own real wealth' (Eisner, 1986, p.5).

We may clarify this as follows. The real deficit (*rd*) is defined as the change in the real value of outstanding government debt (*B*):

$$rd_t = \frac{B_t}{P_t} - \frac{B_{t-1}}{P_{t-1}} \tag{2.7}$$

where *P* is the general price level. According to the government budget constraint (identity) deficits have to be financed by the issue of interest and non-interest bearing debt. If we assume for the sake of simplicity that deficits are entirely financed by interest-bearing government debt, we can write:

$$B_t = B_{t-1} + P_t G_t + i_{t-1} B_{t-1} - P_t T_t \tag{2.8}$$

where G is real government spending on goods and services, *T* represents real government receipts net of transfers, and *i* is the nominal rate of interest. We define inflation as:

$$\pi_t = \frac{P_t - P_{t-1}}{P_{t-1}} \tag{2.9}$$

Combining the previous equations (2.7), (2.8), and (2.9) gives:

$$rd_t = G_t - T_t + \frac{B_{t-1}}{P_t}(i_{t-1} - \pi_t) \tag{2.10}$$

In nominal terms:

$$P_t rd_t = P_t G_t - P_t T_t + i_{t-1} B_{t-1} - \pi_t B_{t-1} \qquad (2.11)$$

The first three terms at the right hand side of equation (2.11) denote the conventionally measured deficit; the final part is the inflation correction.

There are, however, some problems with this reasoning (Catsambras, 1988). First, it is assumed that investors in government bonds are totally free of money illusion. Second, there is no difference made between expected and unexpected inflation. According to some authors (see for example Cagan, 1983) the deficit should, in principle, be corrected for anticipated inflation which is reflected in higher nominal interest rates. This part of interest payments should not be regarded as income for the bondholders, but be treated as a return of capital. A somewhat different position has been taken by Tanzi et al. (1987) who pose that '. . . although it might be reasonably argued that a high conventional deficit that results mainly from the effect of inflation on nominal interest payments may not have any direct effect on the bondholder as a consumer, it is very likely to influence him as an investor. A high conventional deficit will increase the nominal payments the government makes to bondholders . . . exactly at the time when their perception of expected rates of returns on different assets and of the risks associated with those returns are changing rapidly. Thus, it is unlikely that, under such circumstances, the government will be able to refinance the inflation-induced component of interest expenditure under the same real conditions (that is, equal real rate for identical maturity) as it would have in the absence of inflation. Full bond refinanceability of inflation-induced interest service would require, first, that there is a stable demand for bonds in real terms, and second, that the rate of inflation is not an argument in that function' (Tanzi et al., 1987, p.723).

Various authors have argued that the inflation correction should be applied to the market value of government debt. If government deficits affect aggregate demand through its wealth raising effects, it is, of course, the market value of the assets that matter. As Eisner states 'The market values of government securities fall when market interest rates rise, and rise when interest rates fall just as do those of the private sector. Holders of government securities take a double beating, when inflation further eats away at real value, just as do holders of private securities. And the real market value of government debt correspondingly declines with rising interest rates and inflation . . . So it is the market value of debt with which we are properly concerned. And finally, what matters is what that market value is worth in goods or purchasing power, that is, its real value' (Eisner, 1986, pp. 11–12).

Although only an accounting correction is involved, policy conclusions reached on the basis of the uncorrected deficit may differ widely from those that are reached on the basis of the inflation-corrected deficit. Sargent (1983), for instance, argues that the Thatcher government faced a problem of credibility regarding its anti-inflation policy since it was running a deficit, yet, the inflation-corrected deficit for the United Kingdom as estimated by Cukierman and Mortensen (1983) appears to be in surplus most of the time. As already pointed out in section III.3, Eisner and Pieper (1984) have argued that the conventional view of US policies during the 1970s and 1980s was also distorted by measurement errors. Eisner argues, for instance, that '. . . in the years of the Carter Administration, the real value of outstanding public debt declined sharply. Higher interest rates reduced the market value of Treasury securities and higher prices further cut their real worth . . . In real terms, corresponding to the total change in the real market value of debt, the federal budget was not in deficit but in surplus. The false perception of a real deficit led to restrictive monetary and fiscal policies and the worst recession since the Great Depression of the 1930s' (Eisner, 1986, p.177). Whether the view that only properly adjusted budget deficits matter with respect to the impact of fiscal policy on financial markets is still under dispute. In Chapter 3 we will provide some evidence for the European Union.

IV.4 The public sector balance sheet

A government deficit can be created by either keeping government spending at the same level and reducing taxes, or by increasing government spending while keeping taxes constant. In the latter case it makes a difference whether a deficit is caused by higher government consumption or higher government investments. A government deficit as such provides little or no information with respect to changes in government's net worth, while net worth indicates what legacy the current generation provides to future generations. If government, for instance, increases its spending on capital formation at the expense of current spending, there is no impact on the deficit. There is, however, a clear impact on the public sector's net worth and the size of the assets which may benefit future generations. Similarly, if government sells some of its assets its deficit is reduced correspondingly, but this sale has no impact on net worth of the public sector, provided that the asset is sold at a fair price.

Accordingly, one should supplement figures on government deficits with a public sector balance sheet. As Hills puts it 'The aims and objectives of the public sector may be completely different from those of a private company, but it is hard to see why information considered central to the assessment of a private company's performance should be virtually non-existent in the presentation of public sector budgetary policy' (Hills, 1984, p.6).

Various authors have presented estimates of a government balance sheet. Two issues have to be dealt with in constructing such a balance sheet. First, which assets and liabilities are to be included – especially: are implicit assets and liabilities also taken into account? – and, second, how are these various assets and liabilities to be valued? (see Boskin et al., 1987).

Table 2.7: Central government's balance sheet in the Netherlands, 1993 and 1994 (billions of Dutch guilders)

Assets	1993	1994	Liabilities	1993	1994
Currency and deposits	9.3	10.4	Short-term liabilities	23.5	28.7
Short-term claims	51.5	40.9	Liabilities w.i. claims	17.4	14.0
Claims w.i. liabilities	17.4	14.0	Participations in I.O.	18.1	16.9
Long-term claims	53.7	40.2	Long-term debt	365.6	360.3
Loans to I.O.	24.1	23.3	Reserve valuation ch.	102.4	101.6
Public enterprises*	55.2	52.9	Miscellaneous	3.3	3.3
Dwellings and stocks	145.2	147.8			
Miscellaneous	1.2	1.2	Balance	−172.7	−193.9
Total	357.6	330.8	Total	357.6	330.8

: including share holdings; w.i: which imply; ch.: changes; I.O: International Organisations. Source: Ministry of Finance (1996).

In the Netherlands central government publishes its balance sheet each year. Table 2.7 presents this confrontation of assets and liabilities for 1993 and 1994. By comparing this balance sheet with the one presented by Boskin et al. (1987) for the United States some differences come to the fore. It may be useful to discuss these differences in some detail, to inform the reader of the problems that have to be dealt with in constructing a balance sheet for the public sector. First, Boskin et al. include the Federal Reserve as part of central government, whereas in the Dutch practice the net worth of the central bank is included. This is related to the delineation of the public sector, already referred to above. In this case, it should in principle not make much of a difference, but, unfortunately, net worth of the central bank has not been treated consistently. Until 1985 the so-called 'valuation differences of gold and foreign exchange' were excluded and this explains why the central bank's net worth was only 1.886 billion in 1984, while in 1985 it was 36.898 billion. De Haan (1989) has corrected this inconsistency and has calculated the change in central government's net worth as a percentage of GDP. He concludes that the information content of the change in net worth differs sometimes remarkably from the information content of the budget balance. Whereas the deficit showed, for instance, an improvement of the financial position of government, the change in net worth indicated the opposite.

Second, Boskin et al. (1987) use the perpetual inventory method to calculate government's capital stock: real gross investment is cumulated and estimated accumulated depreciation is subtracted. At the balance sheet of central government in the Netherlands as shown in Table 2.7, the data are presented in nominal terms; valuation differences due to inflation are included under reserve valuation changes, which, however, also includes changes in the market value of public sector enterprises and share holdings. Depreciation is as follows: the depreciation rate of road improvements is 50%, for roads, canals and buildings it is 1%, while land – which is included under dwellings and stocks – is not depreciated.

Third, at the balance sheet as presented by Boskin et al. (1987) financial assets reflect market, rather than the par value. There exist no estimates of the market value of government debt, not to mention the market value of governments financial assets. It comes, therefore, as no surprise that, with the exception of share holdings, financial assets and liabilities are valued at par in Table 2.7.

Fourth, Boskin et al. (1987) present their estimates in constant prices. The Dutch balance sheet includes the 'reserve valuation changes' item, but this refers only to the valuation changes due to inflation of dwellings and stocks. So the impact of inflation on financial assets and liabilities is not taken into account.

Finally, Boskin et al. (1987) include oil and gas mineral rights, which they calculate as the sum of three components: future royalties of proven reserves, future royalties of estimated undiscovered reserves, and future bonuses on unleased land. One may, however, wonder whether this approach is satisfactory: why not also include implicit assets and liabilities. Some authors – notably Buiter – have argued that by integrating the public sector budget constraint forward in time, the government's present value budget constraint is obtained, which may provide useful information with respect to the sustainability of fiscal policy. Following Buiter (1984) we may clarify this as follows. Public sector real net wealth (RW), which should equal the present value of real government consumption C_g, is defined as:

$$RW = P_k K + P_n N - \frac{(B + P_c C - sF)}{P} + T_{pv} + S_{pv} + Z_{pv} \qquad (2.12)$$

where P_k is the real value of 1 unit public sector capital goods; K is the public sector capital stock; P_n is the real price of 1 unit N where N is the amount of property rights of natural resources; B is the amount of outstanding debt having a fixed market value; C is the amount of outstanding consols; P_c is the price of consols; s is the exchange rate; F is the stock of foreign currency denominated assets of the government; P is the general price level; T_{pv} is the present real value of present and future taxes net of transfers; S_{pv} is the present real value of current and future seigniorage and Z_{pv} is the present real value of future investment programmes.

From this stock a number of different deficit concepts can be derived which emphasise various aspects of 'sustainability' of fiscal and financial policy. If the present value of the government's consumption plan (C_g) exceeds its net worth, for instance, something has to adjust – be it C_g, RW or both – to reestablish the equality. The annuity value of the present value of the difference between C_g and RW is called 'permanent deficit' (or surplus) by Buiter (1984). It represents the permanent adjustment that has to be made. Buiter has, for illustrative purposes, estimated the public sector's permanent deficit in the UK and concludes that in 1981–82 there was in fact a permanent surplus.

Does the concept of net worth as outlined above make sense? The most important objection which has been raised against the concept, is its use of certainty equivalence. The amount of knowledge assumed to be present is enormous – empirical calculations depend, for instance, on forecasts of economic and demographic developments – and this may be considered highly unrealistic, even though a similar assumption is, of course, made in standard life cycle models with respect to human and non-human wealth.

As a concept to analyse the sustainability of fiscal policy the concept lacks empirical applicability. Blanchard (1993) has suggested some alternative indicators of sustainability. One of them is the primary gap, that is the primary surplus minus the debt to GDP ratio multiplied by the difference between the real interest rate and the economic growth rate. A second indicator of sustainability is called the 'medium-term tax gap', which is the average over the current and the next two years of spending and transfers as ratios to GDP, plus the ratio of debt to GDP times the interest rate miuns the growth rate, minus the current tax rate.

V   Concluding remarks

In this chapter we have reviewed the theory of fiscal policy and some related measurement issues. First we have dealt with the question of what factors may justify the existence of budget deficits. It appeared that deficits can be useful if they result from automatic (that is passive) stabilisation policies or (observationally almost equivalent) tax-smoothing arguments. The case for budget deficits seeems more weakly founded if they are mainly the result of political and institutional factors as stressed in the 'public choice' literature. Nevertheless, we have also provided some empirical evidence that variables proxying for this class of arguments can indeed explain some developments of public debt growth in the European Union.

Subsequently we have contemplated the effects budget deficits may have on financial markets and the economy. These effects crucially depend on the question whether public indebtedness increases private agents' perception of their relative wealth. According to Barro's resurrection of the Ricardian equivalence theorem people do not regard government bonds as real net wealth, since economic subjects fully understand that government debt issue requires additional future taxation proceeding from the need to finance interest and amortisation payments. Keynesians, Monetarists, and Neoclassicals alike all reject the equivalence hypothesis since individuals may not always be able to remove the intertemporal veil of public debt. Given the objections raised against the full equivalence of debt and taxes, the extreme Ricardian view is indeed not very plausible. However, exclusively discounting the 'inflation tax' in the assessment of private wealth positions as Eisner and Pieper propose, would seem the other polar case. Perhaps the proper way to proceed is not to '. . . adopt either of the foregoing two extremes but assume instead that the proper wealth variable is . . . ($k \times$ (real government debt) + real money stock), where k is a constant (greater than zero and less than one) reflecting the degree to which individuals do not discount the future tax liabilities connected with government bonds' (Patinkin, 1965, p.289).

Notes

1. The classification of the tax-smoothing argument under the heading of normative theories instead of positive ones (section II.2) may be disputed, as tax-smoothing may also merely provide a description of actual government behaviour without an explicit awareness of its pros and cons. However, Barro's (1979) derivation of the case for tax-smoothing from first principles (that is optimising behaviour) has led us to emphasise its normative aspects here.
2. Friedman captured his arguments mainly in IS/LM terms, the same model which formed the (often implicit) basis for a demand oriented fiscal policy. Judgements about the slope of the IS-curve and not merely of the LM-curve led him to argue that the effects of fiscal policy are likely to be minor (Friedman, 1976, p.313). It should be noted that not even all Monetarists were equally convinced by his point of view. In a series of papers Brunner and Meltzer (1972, 1976) and Brunner (1976) have developed an analytical framework which they regard as an alternative for IS/LM analysis. Although the short and intermediate run effects of fiscal policy will not affect the level of economic activity substantially, government policy may affect normal (that is long-run) output, because its level depends on (1) the amount of labour absorbed by the government and (2) the amount of taxes and subsidies, which decrease incentives to acquire skill and knowledge. According to Brunner 'this linkage between fiscal policy and normal output involves a long-run "crowding-out" effect substantially more important than the much discussed short-run effects' (Brunner, 1976, p.38).
3. A Dutch policy variant of this principle has become known as the 'golden rule' (in Dutch: 'gulden financieringsregel').
4. See Aschauer (1988) for a review.
5. Note, however, that it is very difficult to distinguish empirically between passive stabilisation policies and tax-smoothing motives of budget deficits, as both arguments imply anti-cyclical behaviour of budget deficits.
6. Sections II.2.2 and II.2.3 are based upon De Haan and Sturm (1994).
7. Note, however, that for some countries some minor differences exist between our index and the power dispersion index as presented by Roubini and Sachs (1989a). The Roubini and Sachs index for the Netherlands for the period 1983–85 (2) is, for instance, clearly wrong as the government coalition consisted of two parties during that period. See the appendix to De Haan and Sturm (1994) for further details.
8. This variable intends to measure the chance of being thrown out of office and therefore all elections are included even if the government is re-elected.
9. Roubini and Sachs (1989b) have used Cameron's (1985) variable in their regressions on the growth of government spending. Note, however, that Cameron's period of observation (1965–81) is rather different from the one used by Roubini and Sachs (1973–85), which casts considerable doubt on their conclusion.
10. With respect to the *structure of negotiations* the following characteristics that Von Hagen distinguishes are included in *BUDGET*: a) existence of general constraints (like golden rule); b) agenda setting for budget negotiations; c) scope of budget norms in the setting of the agenda and d) the way cabinet members are involved in the negotiations. Concerning the

structure of the parliamentary process the following characteristics are included: a) possibility of amendments; b) whether it is required that they are offsetting; c) whether all expenditure is passed in one vote and d) whether there is an initial global vote on budget size. With respect to the *informativeness of the budget* the following characteristics are taken into account: a) are special funds included?; b) are government loans to non-government entities included in the budget? Concerning *flexibility of budget execution* the following characteristics are included: a) Minister of Finance can block expenditures; b) spending ministries subject to cash limits; c) disbursement approval required from Minister of Finance; d) are transfers of expenditures between chapters allowed?; e) changes in budget law during execution and f) carry-over of unused funds to next year. As to *long-term planning constraints* the following characteristics are taken into account: a) multiannual target; b) length of planning horizon; c) the nature of the forecasts and d) the degree of commitment implied by the forecasts. Three characteristics that Von Hagen distinguishes are left out in constructing *BUDGET*: 1) the issue whether parliamentary amendments can cause the fall of the government, because Von Hagen himself indicates that this issue does not unambiguously strengthen the budgetary process; 2) the assessment of budget transparency, and 3) the link of the budget draft to the national accounts, since that information is of little use from the viewpoint of fiscal discipline.

11. In contrast to Roubini and Sachs we have used data on gross government debt, which are more reliable than those on net debt.

12. This variable is defined as $d(i-\pi-n)BY_{t-1}$, where i denotes interest payments on government debt divided by government debt, π is the rate of inflation and n is the GDP growth rate. This variable is very similar to the one used by Roubini and Sachs (1989a). Whenever the real interest rate exceeds the rate of real output growth – as was the case in many countries during the 1980s – the outstanding debt imposes a burden on the public finances. If this rising debt burden is transitory, it should be accommodated by a temporary rise in the budget deficit as argued by Roubini and Sachs. We have also experimented using actual interest payments in nominal terms, expressed as a percentage of GDP instead of *DRB*. This yielded very similar results (not shown).

13. Since the growth of government debt may affect both the GDP growth rate and the change in the unemployment rate there may be a simultaneity problem.

14. When a government is not replaced after elections this dummy has the value one. Similarly, when the same coalition of political parties remains in power after some political crisis this dummy is also one.

15. This low value of *BUDGET* for Luxembourg does not seem to be influenced so much by the budgetary process as well as by the absence of information on the elements on which the index is used.

16. See, for example, Catsambras (1988) and Tanzi et al. (1987).

17. De Haan, Goudswaard and Zelhorst (1990) include import prices, real wage costs, a fiscal impulse measure, real money supply, and total export in their regressions.

3   European capital markets: Deficits and interest rates

. . . investors are overly fixated on the size of a country's budget deficit. In Europe at least, bond markets are more or less substitutable: investors switch between them. Increased supply from one simply adds a bit more to the pot . . .

The Economist, 24 September 1994, p.88

I   Introduction

As has been shown in the introductory Chapter 1, in the aftermath of the oil crises interest rates rose simultaneously in most Western European countries. The link between (real) interest rates in various countries is of crucial importance to our understanding of open economy macroeconomics. In models with costless international arbitrage in goods and financial assets, real interest rates of comparable securities should be equal across countries. Following this line of argument, movements in interest rates should be studied via attempts to explain the common elements in those rates across countries, as has been done for the main industrialised countries by Blanchard and Summers (1984) and Barro and Sala-i-Martin (1990) for real interest rates as well as by Tanzi and Lutz (1993) for nominal interest rates. However, many other authors have argued that real interest rates among OECD countries do not only differ significantly in terms of levels, but also in terms of time patterns (see for example Mishkin, 1984a,b, and Cumby and Obstfeld, 1984). Above all, the assumption of costless arbitrage seems to be at odds with empirical evidence for most of the industrialised countries. Bhandari and Mayer (1990) and Lemmen and Eijffinger (1995), for example, show that financial markets are not very well integrated internationally, except for countries participating in the European Monetary System (EMS).

Many empirical studies have looked into the role fiscal policy plays in determining interest rates in an open economy.[1] Aside from these aggregate studies, most studies are performed at the individual country level. In general, the evidence presented in the latter (country-specific) studies is far from conclusive, mainly because it appears that the relationship between government budget deficits and interest rates is not very stable over time. Similar difficulties have arisen when researchers tried to estimate money demand functions for the countries under investigation here. Kremers and Lane (1990) argue that due to increased currency substitution resulting from the process of liberalising capital movements within the EMS area, the demand for money in individual countries may have become more volatile, while at the same time the demand for money in the EMS area as a whole may have become more stable. Indeed, these authors conclude that a stable and well-behaved money demand function can be specified for the EMS as a whole and that this function has properties that are more satisfactory than those of similar money demand functions for single countries.[2]

In this chapter we combine both lines of argument and estimate an IS/LM model and a separate model of investment demand and desired saving for the determination of interest rates on the level of individual countries, as well as for the EMS area as a whole. Specific attention will be paid to the stability of the aggregate model as compared to country-specific models. Data have been collected for five economies of the European Union (France, Germany, Italy, the Netherlands, and the United Kingdom) which in 1985 constituted over 85% of total EU-GDP. First, we will analyse the determination of nominal long-term interest rates in our sample of countries along the lines of the reduced-form of an IS/LM model, which is quite similar to the model that Modigliani and Jappelli (1988) have estimated for Italy. Although we cannot identify all structural parameters of the model in this manner, we consider it rich enough to discriminate between the conventional view that deficits push up interest rates and the alternative view based on the Ricardian equivalence theorem, as laid out in Chapters 1 and 2. The IS/LM setting is chosen here, since a separate Investment–Savings (IS) model would in fact require the construction of expected (ex-ante) *real* interest rates, those rates being the relevant instruments to equate demand and supply in such a setting. As is well known, however, sufficiently precise measurement of inflationary expectations in the very long run is all but impossible.

The second part of the chapter deals with the determination of short-term interest rates, which will be analysed in the setting of a (more partial) IS model. Although the IS/LM model and the IS model are presented and estimated separately in the present chapter, it will become clear that both types of models are very much interrelated and lead to very similar empirical specifications. As has already been argued, special attention needs to be paid to the construction of an adequate measure of inflationary expectations. For interest rates of a sufficiently short maturity, we should be able to cope with this complication in a satisfactory manner, following a slightly modified version of the Barro and Sala-i-Martin (1990) procedure.

This chapter proceeds as follows. Section II will discuss the determination of (nominal) long-term interest rates. After having presented a small structural model for an open economy, its reduced form will be estimated using data for a sample of five European countries. Section III presents a (similar) analysis for short-term expected real interest rates. Each section briefly concludes.

II Long-term interest rates
II.1 The model
We use a simple, structural model of the economy which specifies the main determinants of interest rates. The model is similar to the one used by Modigliani and Jappelli (1988), and contains the following equations:

$$Co_t = a(Y_t^n - T_t) + bD_t + dW_{t-1} - eB_{t-1} + u_{1t} \tag{3.1}$$

$$I_t^n = jCU_t - k(i_t - \pi_t^e) + u_{2t} \tag{3.2}$$

$$M_t = mY_t^n - pi_t + nW_{t-1} + u_{3t} \tag{3.3}$$

$$NX_t = q(i_t^* - i_t) + u_{4t} \tag{3.4}$$

$$S_t^T = Y_t^n - Co_t - (G_t - GI_t^n) = I_t^n + GI_t^n + NX_t. \tag{3.5}$$

The endogenous variables in the model are: net national income Y^n, private consumption Co, net private investment I^n, net capital outflows NX, and the nominal interest rate i. The government deficit D $(=T-G)$, total government spending G, net government investment GI^n, taxes T, private sector wealth W, government debt B, money supply M, expected inflation π^e, the capacity utilisation rate CU, and our measure of world interest rates i^* are assumed to be exogenous to the model. All uppercase variables should be interpreted in real terms. All parameters of the model are presumed to be positive. The terms $u_{1,2,3,4}$ represent the error components of the corresponding behavioural functions, respectively. For the sake of notational simplicity, the 't' subscript will be dropped hereafter.

Equation (3.1) is a very general consumption function, in which private consumption depends on disposable income $(Y^n - T)$, the government deficit $(D=T-G)$, initial private sector wealth inclusive of government debt (W_{-1}), and government debt at the beginning of each period itself (B_{-1}). This equation reduces to the standard specification of the consumption function if $b=e=0$. When individuals regard a tax cut as equivalent to a future tax liability (compare section III.3 of Chapter 2), $a=b$, $d=e$, and equation (3.1) becomes:

$$Co = a(Y^n - G) + d(W_{-1} - B_{-1}) + u_1. \tag{3.6}$$

Any value of $e>0$ will point to a certain degree of discounting future tax liabilities from the part of the private sector.

Equation (3.2) is a formulation of the investment function akin to the putty-clay approach.[3] New investment is assumed to be proportional to the desired addition to capacity, with the factor of proportionality being a function of the relative cost of capital. Equation (3.2) is a linear approximation of such a model, with the current capacity utilisation rate (*CU*) as a proxy for the change in desired capacity, and the expected real interest rate ($i-\pi^e$) proxying for the relative cost of capital. Equation (3.3) is a linear approximation of a standard *LM*-function based on Keynesian liquidity preference theory. Money supply (*M*) is assumed to be exogenous. Unlike Modigliani and Jappelli (1988), we allow the demand for money to be also affected by private sector wealth.

Equation (3.4) represents the foreign sector of an open economy by means of net capital outflows (*NX*). As substitution evolves between financial assets with differential yields, the latter can be specified as an increasing function of the differential between the world interest rate, corrected for the expected depreciation of the foreign currency, and the domestic interest rate (i^*-i). It is common in the literature to express the net capital outflow as a linear function of this differential, with the factor of proportionality (*q*) depending positively on international capital mobility.[4] A low value of *q* either hints at the existence of capital controls, or indicates that domestic assets are not considered good substitutes for foreign assets.

Net national saving is equal to the difference between current income and the aggregate of private and government consumption (equation 3.5). In equilibrium the supply of saving also equals the sum of the demand for total investment and net capital outflow. Equations (3.1), (3.2), (3.3), (3.4), and (3.5) make up a model of 5 equations in the endogenous variables. Solving for the nominal interest rate yields:

$$i = \alpha_1 \pi^e + \alpha_2 M + \alpha_3 D + \alpha_4 G + \alpha_5 W_{-1} + \alpha_6 B_{-1} + \alpha_7 CU + \alpha_8 i^* + v, \quad (3.7)$$

where v is a composite error term. Table 3.1 presents the relation of the reduced form coefficients to the structural parameters of the model. Columns (2) and (3) indicate the reduced form and the structural coefficients of equation (3.7), respectively. Each coefficient in column (3) has to be divided by Δ, which is reported in the final row of the table.

Considering the role of the exogenous variables, equation (3.7) predicts a positive response of the nominal interest rate to expected inflation ($\alpha_1>0$), though not necessarily equal to one. The coefficient of π^e would be smaller than one, unless $k/[k+q+(1-a)p/m]=1$, that is, under the implausible assumption of total capital immobility, together with a zero elasticity of money demand with respect to interest rates ($p=0$), or an infinite interest sensitivity of investment ($k\rightarrow\infty$). An increase in the money supply shifts the *LM*-curve to the right, increasing income and pushing down the interest rate ($\alpha_2<0$).

As far as the role of fiscal policy is concerned, the following effects are predicted. An increase of the government deficit (−*D*) or government expenditures (*G*) will stimulate aggregate demand, thereby crowding out

Table 3.1: Relation between reduced-form coefficients and structural-form coefficients of equation (3.7)

Variable (1)	Coefficient (2)	Structural Form[a] (3)
π^e	α_1	k
M	α_2	$[a-1]/m$
D	α_3	$b-a$
G	α_4	$1-a$
W_{-1}	α_5	$d+[1-a]n/m$
B_{-1}	α_6	$-e$
CU	α_7	j
i^*	α_8	q
v		$u_1+u_2+u_4+\{[1-a]/m\}u_3$
Δ		$k+q+[1-a]p/m$

[a] *The structural form coefficients in column (3) have to be divided by Δ which is given in the final row. The term v is the composite error of equation (3.7).*

national saving and exerting upward pressure on interest rates ($\alpha_3<0,\alpha_4>0$). A rise in the budget deficit is thus expected always to increase i, except when $a=b$ (that is the Ricardian case), whereas a rise in government expenditure unambiguously increases i. It follows, that a crucial test of the standard theory versus the Ricardian proposition is $\alpha_3<0$; any negative and significant value of α_3 is sufficient to reject the extreme Ricardian proposition.

The coefficient of the stock of wealth of the public sector (α_5) should be fairly small, but positive, given that the propensity to consume out of total wealth (d) as well as the elasticity of money demand to wealth (nM/W_{-1}) are presumed to be small. The effect of government debt on i (α_6) is equal to $-e/\Delta$. Since standard consumption theory predicts a value for e – the extent to which the private sector regards debt as a future liability – very close to zero, we expect α_6 to be negative but small, or even insignificantly different from zero. Strict Ricardian equivalence implies a higher negative value for α_6.

According to the investment function (3.2), coefficient α_7 of the capacity utilisation rate (CU), used to proxy for changes in desired productive capacity, should be positive. Finally, coefficient α_8 of the world interest rate (i^*) enables us to gauge international capital mobility. When domestic and foreign assets are perfect substitutes, q tends to infinity, α_8 tends to one, and all other coefficients tend to zero. In that case it is impossible to distinguish between the Ricardian proposition and the hypothesis of perfect capital mobility.

To summarise, although we make a number of simplifying assumptions, the model presented here is rich enough to discriminate between various competing hypotheses. In particular, we should be able to address the two following issues:

i.   The neutrality of deficit financing. As we have shown, a crucial test for this hypothesis lies in the value of α_3, which is presumed zero if agents fully discount future tax liabilities ($a=b$), and positive and significant if the standard consumption function holds.
ii. The hypothesis of a high degree of capital mobility would be supported by a coefficient of world interest rates (α_8) close to unity, together with the coefficients of other variables close to zero.

II.2   Country-specific analysis

This section presents estimates of the reduced form of the model presented in section II.1 for the five individual countries over the period 1960–91. The dependent variable in each of the regressions is the nominal long-term interest rate i^l, measured as the yield on corresponding government bonds taken from the *IFS*-database.[5] As a proxy for world interest rates we use the corresponding German interest rate (if appropriate) as well as the United States interest rate, the latter corrected for the expected depreciation of the US dollar vis-à-vis the currency in question. Before 1970 (Bretton–Woods) this expectation is assumed to be zero, for later years it has been estimated by means of a rolling forecast from a regression of the actual depreciation on two own lags and one lag of the inflation differential against the US. Variables like D, G, W, and B are expressed as a percentage of nominal GDP. Money supply is included as the growth rate of money and quasi-money, since the flow of money is generally considered to be of much more importance for the level of activity and inflation than the money stock itself. For the sake of comparison with other research we substitute the liquidity ratio for the rate of money growth in some of the regressions. However, tests on stationarity of the time series concerned have convinced us that the emphasis should be put primarily on the rate of money growth.

Government budget deficits have been corrected for the influence of the business cycle, more in particular by removing the cyclical component from tax revenues. It seems likely that over the business cycle the error term of the investment equation (u_2) is correlated with the deficit variable, so that $cov(v, D/Y)>0$, inducing upward bias in coefficient α_3 of the deficit. Moreover, correlation may also exist between lagged errors and the current budget deficit, due to the fact that past long-term interest rates influence present and future deficits through interest payments on debt issued in previous periods (Nunes-Correia and Stemitsiotis, 1993). Ideally, we should use a measure of the structural budget deficit, but unfortunately such series were not available for the countries in question. Nevertheless, wanting to account for possible endogeneity of the deficit, we have resorted to an instrumental variables procedure, with lagged components of the deficit used as instruments.

Expected inflation for each country is approximated by an $AR(2)$ forecast of actual CPI inflation, a backward looking procedure which has the advantage that it uses information available to economic subjects at the time of the forecast. In order to solve for autocorrelation in the error term due to potential measurement errors in expected inflation, we have chosen to employ two-step two-stage least squares (2S2SLS) estimation of the model containing unobserved rational expectations (see Cumby, Huizinga, and Obstfeld, 1983, and Nijman, 1990). This method can be seen as a linear variant of the generalised method of moments (GMM, see Hansen, 1982), and allows for serially correlated and heteroscedastic errors. Newey and West's (1987) modification of the variance-covariance matrix has been used, to ensure that its estimate is positive semi-definite.

Before employing the variables in the regression analysis, all of them were checked on stationarity by means of the augmented Dickey–Fuller test. It is a well-known fact that estimating a model with non-stationary time series can lead to spurious regressions and, therefore, does not make much sense (Granger and Newbold, 1977). However, it turned out that all variables defined in this way were (trend-)stationary. The results of some different specifications of the reduced form (3.7) for the various countries are reported in Table 3.2. For each country we chose as a starting point regression 3.3 of Modigliani and Jappelli (1988, p.25), including the main significant variables.[6] For none of the countries under investigation we were able to find a positive and significant coefficient on our wealth variable, regardless of the other variables included; therefore this variable was omitted in Table 3.2. To avoid multicollinearity disturbances, we first consider the effects of fiscal policy sufficiently captured by only two variables, D and B_{-1}, thereby excluding G.

From the first two rows of Table 3.2 it may be inferred that in France long-term interest rates have mainly been affected by movements in inflationary expectations and government budget deficits. In addition, the capacity utilisation rate has some explanatory power, as well as foreign interest rates, if measured by the corresponding German counterpart (row 3.2a3 and row 3.2a5). The role of money supply is insignificant, measured either as growth rate or as liquidity ratio (not reported). Similar results are reported by Knoester and Mak (1994). Presumably the expected inflation rate already captures the money supply effect on nominal long-term interest rates. With respect to the fiscal variables we can conclude that budget deficits have unambiguously raised long-term interest rates;[7] its coefficient seems to be somewhat large and not very robust with respect to the other variables included, however. Government debt comes in with the right sign, but the degree to which the French have discounted future tax liabilities appears to be insignificant, nevertheless (rows 3.2a4 and 3.2a5).

For Germany we cannot discern a significant impact of budget deficits on interest rates, in contrast to findings of Nunes-Correia and Stemitsiotis (1993) and Knoester and Mak (1994). Movements in German long-term interest rates

Table 3.2: Single country estimates of equation (3.7)

	C.T.	π^e	DM	D/Y	CU	i^*	B/Y_{-1}	R^2	DW	Q(4)	Sign.	$\chi^2(2)$	Sign.
a) France:													
3.2a1	-0.18 (1.1)	0.55 (4.6)	-0.01 (0.1)	-1.23 (2.3)	0.27 (1.5)	0.08 (1.8)		0.69	1.92	1.02	0.91	2.39	0.30
3.2a2	-0.20 (2.1)	0.54 (4.5)		-1.31 (4.5)	0.29 (2.6)	0.07 (1.6)		0.67	1.90	0.88	0.93	2.35	0.31
3.2a3	-0.22 (1.8)	0.34 (2.3)		-1.82 (4.7)	0.24 (1.7)	0.95# (3.8)		0.65	2.15	0.67	0.96	0.01	1.00
3.2a4	-0.17 (1.8)	0.33 (1.3)		-1.89 (2.9)	0.28 (2.7)	0.08 (1.9)	-0.14 (1.3)	0.57	2.07	2.30	0.68	2.46	0.29
3.2a5	-0.19 (1.5)	0.25 (1.0)		-2.10 (3.6)	0.22 (1.6)	0.99# (4.0)	-0.09 (1.0)	0.60	2.29	1.77	0.78	0.76	0.68
b) Germany:													
3.2b1	-0.09 (1.0)	0.86 (7.0)	-0.11 (2.3)	-0.21 (0.5)	0.17 (1.7)	0.03 (1.3)		0.67	1.48	3.13	0.54	5.31	0.07
3.2b2	-0.08 (0.9)	0.86 (8.1)	-0.13 (2.4)	-0.24 (0.6)	0.16 (1.7)			0.66	1.46	5.13	0.27	3.56	0.17
3.2b3	-0.03 (0.3)	0.84 (9.6)	-0.09 (1.3)	-0.11 (0.3)	0.09 (1.0)		0.04 (1.1)	0.66	1.67	4.41	0.35	3.18	0.20

Table 3.2: Single country estimates of equation (3.7) continued

	C.T.	π^e	DM	D/Y	CU	i^{l*}	B/Y_{-1}	R^2	DW	Q(4)	Sign.	$\chi^2(2)$	Sign.
c) Italy:													
3.2c1	-0.16 (1.8)	0.47 (4.8)	-0.01 (0.3)	-0.28 (3.8)	0.21 (2.2)	0.16 (2.9)		0.89	0.99	12.59	0.01	2.69	0.26
3.2c2	-0.23 (2.2)	0.54 (5.2)	-0.00 (0.0)	-0.31 (3.7)	0.27 (2.3)	0.22# (0.7)		0.85	0.78	20.59	0.00	3.00	0.22
3.2c3	-0.23 (2.1)	0.42 (3.6)	-0.03 (0.7)	-0.45 (2.7)	0.29 (2.4)	0.13 (2.2)	-0.03 (1.4)	0.88	0.95	12.93	0.01	3.91	0.14
3.2c4	-0.44 (3.3)	0.09 (0.7)	-0.26& (3.1)	-1.62 (4.5)	0.76 (4.5)	0.01 (0.2)	-0.25 (3.5)	0.82	1.53	1.22	0.87	1.88	0.39
3.2c5	-0.44 (2.4)	0.15 (1.0)	-0.2@ (1.7)	-2.1@ (2.9)	0.57 (2.7)	0.08 (1.3)	-0.2@ (2.4)	0.81	1.18	5.36	0.25	3.89	0.14
d) The Netherlands:													
3.2d1	-0.18 (1.6)	0.41 (3.7)	0.01 (0.1)	-0.93 (3.3)	0.24 (2.0)	-0.03 (0.4)		0.41	0.91	12.80	0.01	6.34	0.04
3.2d2	-0.19 (3.2)	0.17 (1.9)	0.03 (0.4)	-0.60 (4.2)	0.19 (3.4)	0.96# (7.2)		0.79	0.97	14.70	0.01	4.85	0.09
3.2d3	-0.18 (4.1)	0.20 (2.7)		-0.56 (6.5)	0.19 (3.8)	0.96# (7.8)		0.80	0.91	16.13	0.00	4.64	0.10

Table 3.2: Single country estimates of equation (3.7) continued

	C.T.	π^e	DM	D/Y	CU	$i^{l,*}$	B/Y_{-1}	R^2	DW	Q(4)	Sign.	$\chi^2(2)$	Sign.
d) The Netherlands (continued):													
3.2d4	-0.32 (6.4)	-0.21 (1.4)	-0.06 (0.6)	-0.85 (6.5)	0.41 (6.6)	1.04# (10.3)	-0.09 (3.9)	0.75	1.55	6.82	0.15	4.70	0.10
3.2d5	-0.34 (7.2)	-0.23 (1.4)		-0.90 (8.7)	0.41 (6.8)	1.07# (11.2)	-0.09 (3.3)	0.72	1.58	8.40	0.08	3.75	0.15
e) The United Kingdom:													
3.2e1	-0.11 (2.6)	0.56 (9.0)	-0.03 (1.4)	-0.29 (2.1)	0.18 (3.5)	0.29 (6.4)		0.83	1.81	1.63	0.80	2.49	0.29
3.2e2	-0.15 (2.9)	0.47 (5.3)	0.02 (0.4)	-0.41 (2.5)	0.21 (3.1)	0.71# (4.3)		0.79	1.00	12.68	0.01	7.30	0.03
3.2e3	-0.04 (1.1)	0.33 (3.5)	-0.06 (2.2)	-0.55 (5.2)	0.17 (4.4)	0.17 (2.8)	-0.06 (3.2)	0.88	1.54	4.30	0.37	0.26	0.88
3.2e4	-0.07 (1.4)	0.24 (3.9)	-0.06 (1.4)	-0.62 (6.3)	0.20 (4.0)	0.44# (2.6)	-0.07 (4.8)	0.85	0.93	14.81	0.01	3.14	0.21

Sample: 1960–91 (#Obs.=32). t-statistics in parentheses. Critical values: t(5%|26)=2.06, t(1%|26)=2.78. Dependent variable: long-term government bond yield. 2S2SLS estimation with Newey–West (1987) standard errors; # off-diagonal (nonzero) elements of the residual covariance matrix has been set at two. Instruments: C.T., π^e, DM, $(G/Y)_{-1}$, $(T/Y)_{-1}$, CU, $i^{l,*}$, $(B/Y)_{-1}$, and (a time) Trend. C.T.: Constant Term; DW: Durbin Watson; Q(4): Ljung–Box (1978) statistic; Sign: Significance level; $\chi^2(2)$: Hansen's (1982) test of overidentifying restrictions. $^{\#}$: German interest rate; $^{\&}$: M/Y; $^{@}$: in real (GDP-deflated) levels where coefficients have been $\times 1000$.

56

can for a large part be explained by corresponding movements in expected inflation. Germany is the only country in our sample for which we cannot invalidate the Fischer effect (implying $\alpha_1=1$). Also, some influence of monetary policy on long-term interest rates can be detected. Like Knoester and Mak (1994), we included the liquidity ratio in our set of regressors, but it turned up with the wrong sign. The capacity utilisation rate, US interest rates (row 3.2b1), and the debt ratio (row 3.2b3), all appear to be insignificant.[8]

Part c of Table 3.2 reports our estimations for Italy. In line with results reported by Modigliani and Jappelli (1988), long-term interest rates appear to be determined predominantly by expected inflation, budget deficits, the capacity utilisation rate, and US interest rates, as opposed to German interest rates (compare the first two rows of part c of Table 3.2). At first sight, monetary policy does not affect long-term interest rates over and above its effect on inflationary expectations (rows 3.2c1–3). If the liquidity ratio is substituted for the rate of money growth (row 3.2c4), as in Modigliani and Jappelli (1988), monetary policy does seem to exert a separate influence, albeit at the expense of expected inflation and the US interest rate. In contrast to Modigliani and Jappelli (1988), we conclude that this specification yields evidence of partial discounting of future tax liabilities in the plans of Italian consumers. The latter result is confirmed in case the equation is estimated in real ((GDP-) deflated) levels, as is done in row 3.2c5 following Knot and De Haan (1995a). Notwithstanding the overall significance of budget deficits in the determination of Italian interest rates, we must again conclude that this relationship is far from stable with respect to the other determinants.

For the Netherlands (section d of Table 3.2) we were not surprised to find that the German interest rate represents the appropriate foreign interest rate, given the tight link between the guilder and the Deutschemark that has prevailed during a large part of the sample period. Apart from these external influences, Dutch long-term interest rates seem to have been affected domestically by inflationary expectations, government budget deficits, and the capacity utilisation rate. If the debt ratio is also plugged into the specification (last two rows of part d), its coefficient turns up negatively and significantly so. Once more, this result would suggest a certain degree of discounting of future tax liabilities. Note however, that here again a considerable number of coefficients seem to be afflicted by multicollinearity problems, which result in a substantial degree of parameter instability depending on the other regressors included.

Finally, long-term interest rates in the United Kingdom seem to be affected in a similar fashion by US interest rates (rows 3.2e1/3) as well as German interest rates (3.2e2/4). Furthermore, expected inflation, budget deficits, capacity utilisation, and the public debt ratio all have contributed significantly to the development of long-term nominal interest rates, while the influence of money growth appears to be ambiguous. The latter result could not be improved upon by substituting the liquidity ratio for *DM* (not reported).

Table 3.3: (In)Stability of the single country estimates

	C.T.	π^e	DM	D/Y	CU	i^{l*}	B/Y_{-1}	IR-α_3	R^2	DW	Q(4)	Sign.	$\chi^2(2)$	Sign.
3.3a1 60–87	−0.18 (2.4)	0.47 (6.1)	−0.15 (2.1)	−0.90 (2.6)	0.30 (3.0)	0.17 (6.0)		0.62	0.79	1.87	0.99	0.91	4.49	0.11
3.3a1 60–83	−0.11 (1.1)	0.52 (6.4)	−0.09 (1.4)	−0.52 (1.6)	0.20 (1.6)	0.19 (5.5)		1.34	0.84	2.07	2.70	0.61	5.41	0.07
3.3b1 60–87	0.13 (1.1)	0.58 (5.7)	−0.25 (5.1)	0.58 (1.5)	−0.05 (0.4)	0.03 (0.8)		1.82	0.74	1.52	4.14	0.39	7.07	0.03
3.3b1 60–83	0.31 (1.7)	0.30 (1.4)	−0.32 (4.9)	1.12 (2.1)	−0.24 (1.3)	0.02 (0.5)		3.06	0.66	1.41	9.39	0.05	5.11	0.08
3.3c1 60–87	−0.30 (3.0)	0.38 (4.2)	0.01 (0.2)	−0.39 (4.9)	0.36 (3.3)	0.19 (3.7)		1.51	0.90	1.00	8.18	0.09	2.11	0.35
3.3c1 60–83	−0.21 (2.1)	0.19 (1.5)	−0.08 (1.3)	−0.66 (4.8)	0.27 (2.5)	0.22 (3.8)		5.09	0.90	0.95	11.62	0.02	4.47	0.11
3.3d4 60–87	−0.24 (3.3)	−0.25 (1.6)	−0.09 (0.8)	−0.72 (4.6)	0.34 (4.5)	0.89# (6.9)	−0.13 (5.8)	1.03	0.82	1.42	5.95	0.20	3.59	0.17
3.3d4 60–83	−0.30 (3.1)	−0.37 (2.0)	0.07 (0.6)	−0.90 (5.0)	0.38 (3.8)	1.04# (6.8)	−0.12 (4.0)	0.39	0.91	2.63	4.77	0.31	1.19	0.55
3.3e3 60–87	−0.04 (0.9)	0.38 (3.3)	−0.06 (2.0)	−0.46 (2.2)	0.17 (3.2)	0.17 (2.6)	−0.06 (3.1)	0.86	0.89	1.56	3.78	0.44	0.98	0.61
3.3e3 60–83	−0.05 (0.7)	0.31 (1.7)	−0.05 (1.2)	−0.77 (2.0)	0.15 (1.6)	0.19 (2.2)	−0.04 (2.0)	2.08	0.85	1.56	3.29	0.51	2.52	0.28

Table 3.4: Summary statistics of the main variables

Variable	i^l	π^e	DM	D/Y	G/Y	W/Y_{-1}	B/Y_{-1}	CU	$i^{l,*}$
Mean (%)	8.98	5.84	7.68	−2.74	31.79	175.58	28.42	82.98	4.47
Std. dev.(%)	2.28	2.63	4.38	1.62	6.15	45.80	8.83	2.94	5.39
Correlation coefficients									
i^l	1	0.84	−0.24	−0.77	0.74	−0.74	−0.33	−0.51	0.54
π^e	0.84	1	−0.16	−0.65	0.49	−0.47	−0.57	−0.72	0.41
DM	−0.24	−0.16	1	0.15	−0.24	0.22	−0.02	−0.01	−0.19
D/Y	−0.77	−0.65	0.15	1	−0.91	0.83	0.02	0.59	−0.39
G/Y	0.74	0.49	−0.24	−0.91	1	−0.96	0.16	−0.28	0.32
$(W/Y)_{-1}$	−0.74	−0.47	0.22	0.83	−0.96	1	−0.05	0.16	−0.27
$(B/Y)_{-1}$	−0.33	−0.57	−0.02	0.02	0.16	−0.05	1	0.45	0.04
CU	−0.51	−0.72	−0.01	0.59	−0.28	0.16	0.45	1	−0.37
$i^{l,*}$	0.54	0.41	−0.19	−0.39	0.32	−0.27	0.04	−0.37	1

Notes: Sample 1960–91. All variables are specified in the appendix.

To sum up, one is tempted to conclude from Table 3.2 that widening deficits in most of the countries under investigation have unambiguously pushed up long-term interest rates. Nevertheless, the relationship between budget deficits and interest rates appears to be highly sensitive to multicollinearity problems in most of the countries. Apart from this kind of parameter instability, we also checked some key results on parameter instability over time, that is arising from changes in the sample period. Table 3.3 replicates one regression for each of the countries from Table 3.2 for the sample periods 1960–83 and 1960–87 (labelling identical to that in Table 3.2).[9] For each coefficient α_3 of the corresponding government budget deficit we have calculated a so-called 'instability-ratio' (IR) which is defined as the absolute difference between the coefficients originating from full sample (FS) estimation and subsample (SS) estimation, respectively, divided by its standard error (SE) in the full sample. It can easily be seen that for each country the relationship between budget deficits and interest rates appears to be quite unstable, in the sense that the coefficients change by more than a standard error away from the reference estimate of Table 3.2. As has already been mentioned in the introduction, it is our contention that a more aggregate analysis will yield more satisfactory results. In the remainder of section 3.2 we therefore analyse the model assuming an integrated European capital market.

II.3 Net national saving in Europe: Uses and sources
For the intended aggregated analysis we will use annual data over the period 1960–91, mainly originating from the International Monetary Fund. Table 3.4 contains the first two moments of all variables used in the empirical analysis.

Figure 3.1: Deficits (% GDP) and long-term interest rates in the European Union

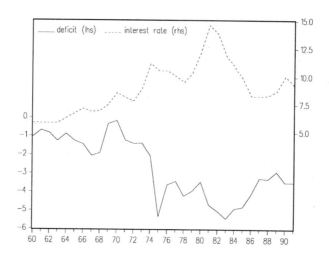

Sources and definitions of the variables are specified in the appendix. European aggregates like T, G, D, W_{-1}, B_{-1}, I^n, M, and NX are calculated in (German) Deutschemark using actual nominal exchange rates and have, subsequently, been divided by nominal GDP (Y, aggregated similarly).[10] European indices like the nominal interest rate and the capacity utilisation rate are computed by weighing the five country-specific values by the share of each country's real GDP (1985 prices) for that year in aggregate real GDP of all five countries, using base-year nominal exchange rates. Figure 3.1 plots the development of the resulting European index of nominal interest rates as well as the aggregate deficit–income ratio (in % of GDP). Expected inflation is computed similarly, but now with private consumption as a weighing factor. Foreign interest rates are measured by US interest rates, corrected for the expected depreciation of the dollar vis-à-vis the Deutschemark. Finally, tests on stationarity show that all variables defined in this manner are (trend) stationary.

Chapters 1 and 2 and section II.1 already spelled out that there are two competing explanations as to why budget deficits may not affect interest rates: the capital inflow hypothesis and the Ricardian equivalence theorem. Under the first hypothesis a decrease in government saving would be compensated by an inflow of foreign capital, while under the second private saving would

Table 3.5: Net national saving in Europe: Uses and sources

Period	I^n/Y (1)	GI^n/Y (2)	NX/Y (3)	S^T/Y (4)	S^P/Y (5)	S^G/Y (6)	$S^{P,*}/Y$ (7)	$S^{G,*}/Y$ (8)
1960–91	0.107	0.025	0.004	0.136	0.138	-0.002	0.124	0.012
1960–66	0.130	0.030	0.005	0.165	0.145	0.020	0.134	0.031
1967–73	0.133	0.032	0.006	0.171	0.151	0.020	0.143	0.029
1974–79	0.107	0.025	0.003	0.135	0.148	–0.012	0.133	0.002
1980–85	0.078	0.018	0.002	0.098	0.127	–0.029	0.105	–0.007
1986–91	0.078	0.017	0.003	0.098	0.116	–0.017	0.100	–0.002

Notes: $S^{P,*}=S^P-\pi^e B_{-1}$; $S^{G,*}=S^G+\pi^e B_{-1}$. *Definitions and sources of the variables are in the appendix. The sums of the columns (1), (2) and (3), of columns (5) and (6), and of columns (7) and (8) are identical to column (4).*

increase to compensate for lower government saving (see also Monadjemi and Kearney, 1991).

Table 3.5 shows the development of national saving and its components as a percentage of GDP in the European Union during our sample period. One of the most remarkable trends is the decline in European 'national' saving (S^T/Y in column 4) by almost seven percentage-points over the last three decades. The breakdown of net national saving by net private investment (I^n), net government investment (GI^n) and net capital outflow (NX) is in columns (1) to (3). As can readily be inferred, the current account remained in surplus during the whole sample period, thereby offering hardly any compensation for the reduction in national saving. Although government investment also decreased, private investment bore the bulk of the adjustment.[11] Net private investment shrank dramatically from the early 1970s onwards, only to affirm that an inflow of foreign capital did *not* offset downward trends in national saving.

Columns (5) and (6) report on net national private (S^P) and public saving (S^G). At first sight, private saving and government saving seem to have gone down in tandem, with government dissaving responsible for the largest part of the overall decline in national saving. However, private as well as public saving have not been corrected for the inflation-induced depreciation of the stock of public debt. In order to assess the impact of government dissaving on the economy, one should calculate a measure of the real increase in the government's net liabilities. In times of inflation, as experienced for example in the late 1970s, this correction tends to increase government saving and to decrease private saving by the amount of the so-called 'inflation tax' (columns 7 and 8; compare Eisner and Pieper, 1984). Including this correction, private and government dissaving each seem to explain about half of the decline in national saving. Our finding that increased budget deficits have resulted in a reduction of private and national saving is not compatible with the Ricardian proposition.

II.4   Estimation results for the European Union

This section presents estimates of the reduced form of the model presented in section II.1 for the European Union in the aggregate. The dependent variable is the European index of nominal long-term interest rates as defined in the previous section. Estimation again proceeds by two-step two-stage least squares (2S2SLS) with Newey and West's (1987) modification of the residual covariance matrix. Table 3.6 reports on a number of different specifications of equation (3.7). Like in the country-specific estimates, our measure of aggregate wealth did not exert any significant and positive effect on nominal interest rates; therefore, we also left this variable out of Table 3.6 (compare Knot and De Haan, 1995a).[12]

At the start, regression 3.6.1 is similar to the first regression for each individual country reported in Table 3.2. The first thing to note about row 3.6.1 is that expected inflation is significant while the growth of money supply is not. More or less the same conclusion holds if the liquidity ratio is substituted for the growth rate of money, as can be inferred from row 3.6.2. Presumably, its effect is already largely discounted in the coefficient of expected inflation. The latter is high, but nevertheless differs significantly from unity (the Fischer effect), even at the 1% level. This outcome would confirm that inflationary expectations have reduced ex-ante real interest rates during our sample period. However, insofar as investors use other variables, besides past inflation, which are also included in Table 3.6, to forecast future inflation, such effects may be captured by those variables. Furthermore, π^e is correlated with i^{k*} (0.41), since past inflation rates are likely to be correlated with the expected rate of depreciation of the exchange rate included in our measure of world interest rates.

Aside from expected inflation, budget deficits, capacity utilisation, and foreign interest rates all come in significantly and with the predicted signs. The coefficient of D/Y is negative (implying $a>b$), significant, and consistent with the consumption function (3.1), but not with its Ricardian counterpart equation (3.6). This result provides fairly strong evidence against the Ricardian equivalence theorem (Chapters 1 and 2). From the value and significance of the coefficient α_7 of the capacity utilisation rate CU we conclude that the investment function (3.2) is not contradicted by data for the European Union, in accordance with the case for individual countries in Table 3.2. The coefficient on foreign interest rates is positive and significant, but much smaller than what might have been expected under the hypothesis of overall perfect capital mobility. This result can perhaps be explained by the widespread controls of capital movements that have been in vogue in several countries in the Union (France, Italy) during various episodes within our sample, and it is in line with the proposition that extra-EMS asset

Table 3.6: Aggregated European estimates

	C.T.	π^e	DM	D/Y	CU	i^{l*}	B/Y_{-1}	G/Y	R^2	DW	Q(4)	Sign.	$\chi^2(2)$	Sign.
3.6.1	-0.14 (2.9)	0.62 (6.6)	-0.01 (0.3)	-0.59 (4.8)	0.21 (3.8)	0.09 (2.9)			0.87	1.55	3.03	0.55	3.41	0.18
3.6.2	-0.18 (2.7)	0.62 (7.1)	0.05& (1.4)	-0.51 (5.1)	0.21 (2.8)	0.10 (3.0)			0.87	1.64	2.62	0.62	1.78	0.41
3.6.3	-0.16 (3.6)	0.48 (5.5)	-0.03 (1.0)	-0.74 (6.8)	0.26 (4.7)	0.10 (3.2)	-0.05 (2.8)		0.88	1.61	3.72	0.45	2.46	0.29
3.6.4	-0.20 (3.3)	0.48 (5.5)		-0.82 (6.7)	0.30 (4.1)	0.10 (3.3)	-0.06 (2.8)		0.88	1.59	3.75	0.44	1.29	0.52
3.6.5	-0.16 (3.5)	0.63 (8.1)	-0.05 (1.6)	-0.78* (7.1)	0.26 (4.3)	0.12 (3.6)	-0.03 (1.5)		0.86	1.52	3.91	0.42	3.47	0.18
3.6.6	-0.22 (3.1)	0.65 (8.1)		-0.89* (6.8)	0.32 (3.7)	0.12 (3.5)	-0.03 (1.7)		0.86	1.50	3.45	0.48	1.66	0.44
3.6.7	-0.20 (2.7)	0.51 (5.5)		-0.17@ (4.0)	0.30 (3.3)	0.10 (3.5)	-0.01@ (2.3)		0.89	1.67	2.53	0.64	5.67	0.06
3.6.8	-0.19 (1.3)	0.42 (4.1)		-0.75 (0.8)	0.29 (1.3)	0.13 (4.5)	-0.06 (2.6)	0.03 (0.1)	0.88	1.65	4.23	0.38	1.91	0.39

Sample 1960–91 (#Obs.=32). t-statistics in parentheses. Critical values: t(5%|26)=2.06, t(1%|26)=2.78. Dependent variable: European index of long-term government bond yields. Estimation by 2S2SLS with Newey–West (1987) standard errors; # off-diagonal elements of the residual covariance matrix has been set at two. Instruments: C.T., π^e, DM, (G/Y), (T/Y)$_{-1}$, CU, i^{l*}, (B/Y)$_{-1}$, and (a time) Trend. C.T.: Constant; DW: Durbin Watson; Q(4): Ljung–Box (1978) statistic; Sign.: Significance level; $\chi^2(2)$: Hansen's (1982) test of overidentifying restrictions. &: M/Y; *: corrected for $\pi^e B_{-i}$; @: in real (GDP-deflated) levels where coefficients have been × 1000.

63

substitutability and (hence) capital mobility have been much lower than intra-EMS counterparts. Consequently, we doubt whether it is allowed to consider linkages between fiscal policy and interest rates from a global perspective, as Tanzi and Lutz (1993) and Barro and Sala-i-Martin (1990) do.

Regressions 3.6.3 and 3.6.4 add to the set of regressors the debt ratio $(B/Y)_{-1}$, in order to measure the degree by which private agents have discounted future tax liabilities in forming their consumption plans. The clearly significant coefficient α_6 suggests that at least some partial discounting has taken place ($d>0$), albeit to a limited extent. A somewhat disturbing result of 3.6.3 is the increase in the coefficient α_3 of the budget deficit; a phenomenon that is strengthened further by the elimination of (insignificant) money growth in regression 3.6.4. Apparently, the aggregation of individual-country data has not completely resolved the multicollinearity problems that afflicted the individual country estimates of Table 3.2 (compare also Table 3.4). It should be noted, however, that the degree to which the coefficient α_3 changes is less pronounced than in most of the country-specific estimates. Although we intuitively believe that this relative parameter stability strengthens the case for an aggregated analysis, it is not easy to come up with a theoretical explanation for this empirical phenomenon arising from the process of economic and monetary integration. Towards the end of this section we will investigate whether similar observations can be made with respect to the other dimension of parameter instability distinguished here, that is instability over time.

Regressions 3.6.5 and 3.6.6 replicate rows 3.6.3 and 3.6.4, respectively, but now with the deficit variable corrected for the inflation-induced depreciation of the stock of government debt owned by the private sector. As explained in Chapter 2, Eisner and Pieper (1984, 1988a,b, 1992), and Eisner (1986, 1989a,b, 1994) claim that conventionally measured government budget deficits overstate actual deficits. In order to judge the impact of deficits on the economy, one should calculate a real budget deficit, which requires a measure of the real increase in government debt. According to Eisner and Pieper it is of vital importance that the deficit be corrected for inflation, because it wipes out the real value of government debt and, hence, should not exhibit any real effects. This correction, however, hardly changes our earlier estimates; at most they increase by less than half a standard error. The finding that the impact of both measures on the economy is about equal is in accordance with the experience of other authors.[13]

As in Knot and De Haan (1995a), regression 3.6.7 estimates the link between fiscal policy and interest rates where the fiscal variables are now measured in real ((GDP-) deflated) levels instead of as ratios. It can readily be seen that this modification does not change our previous results in any qualitative sense. In regression 3.6.8 we try to trace the separate impact of government spending (G/Y) on nominal interest rates. The extremely high correlation between government spending and deficits in Table 3.5 (-0.91)

Table 3.7: Stability of the aggregate model

	C.T.	π^e	DM	D/Y	CU	i^{l*}	B/Y_{-1}	IR-α_3	R^2	DW	Q(4)	Sign.	$\chi^2(2)$	Sign.
3.7.1 60–87	-0.25 (4.7)	0.63 (6.6)	-0.00 (0.0)	-0.65 (4.5)	0.34 (5.6)	0.13 (4.3)		0.48	0.88	1.49	2.12	0.71	6.15	0.05
3.7.1 60–83	-0.30 (5.2)	0.63 (6.2)	-0.02 (0.8)	-0.76 (4.1)	0.40 (6.2)	0.13 (4.1)		1.44	0.89	1.52	3.30	0.51	5.87	0.05
3.7.3 60–87	-0.23 (6.5)	0.46 (4.7)	-0.02 (0.5)	-0.79 (6.4)	0.34 (8.5)	0.14 (4.2)	-0.05 (3.4)	0.44	0.89	1.60	3.29	0.51	4.08	0.13
3.7.3 60–83	-0.26 (11.3)	0.49 (4.9)	-0.03 (1.0)	-0.80 (4.6)	0.38 (14.4)	0.15 (4.7)	-0.04 (3.6)	0.56	0.90	1.66	3.07	0.55	4.54	0.10
3.7.4 60–87	-0.27 (5.3)	0.49 (5.2)		-0.83 (7.5)	0.38 (6.5)	0.14 (4.8)	-0.05 (3.5)	0.12	0.89	1.61	3.75	0.44	3.27	0.19
3.7.4 60–83	-0.31 (6.8)	0.50 (5.0)		-0.90 (5.2)	0.43 (8.1)	0.16 (5.1)	-0.05 (3.3)	0.75	0.90	1.66	3.54	0.47	3.41	0.18
3.7.5 60–87	-0.23 (5.2)	0.61 (8.2)	-0.04 (1.3)	-0.85* (6.7)	0.34 (6.4)	0.16 (5.3)	-0.03 (2.0)	0.59	0.88	1.60	3.27	0.51	4.62	0.10
3.7.5 60–83	-0.25 (8.3)	0.66 (9.7)	-0.04 (1.0)	-0.73* (3.8)	0.35 (10.2)	0.16 (5.3)	-0.02 (2.0)	0.47	0.89	1.59	2.86	0.58	4.50	0.11

Notes: See Table 3.6. t-statistics in parentheses. IR: Instability Ratio (= $|\alpha(FS)-\alpha(SS)|/SE(\alpha;FS)$); *: corrected for $\pi^e B_{-r}$.

makes it virtually impossible to distinguish any such impact of government spending, and we were not all too surprised to find that its impact seemed negligible. At the same time, the standard error of the deficit coefficient rises enormously, even so much that it loses significance. We therefore reran regression 3.6.8 without both D/Y and G/Y, and performed an F-test as to whether it would be allowed to omit both fiscal variables. Straightforward calculation showed that this is clearly not the case $(F_{[2,25]}=9.74)$, confirming once more the influence of fiscal policy on interest rates.

To summarise, we can conclude from all these regressions that budget deficits in the European Union have undoubtedly raised the level of long-term interest rates. The estimated impact of an increase in the deficit–GDP ratio of 1 percentage-point varies from a rise of approximately 0.5 to 0.8 percentage-points in the European index of nominal interest rates. Apart from the variation in this elasticity with respect to the other regressors included, we also investigated its relative performance over different sample periods. Table 3.7 reproduces a number of regressions from Table 3.6 that are similar in specification to the ones considered in Tables 3.2 and 3.3. Again, these regressions are re-estimated over the sample periods 1960–87 and 1960–83, and the outcomes were used to calculate instability ratios (*IR*, see section II.2) with respect to the coefficient α_3 of the government budget deficit.

It can immediately be seen from Table 3.7 that in sharp contrast to the results obtained for individual countries, the coefficients on the European deficit–income ratio hardly change. In only one case (row 3.7.1) an instability ratio higher than one is reported, implying that in all other cases the estimated coefficient for the subsample is altered by less than one standard deviation relative to the full sample estimate. Similar results were obtained by Knot and De Haan (1995a) by means of an analysis in real levels instead of ratios. A potential explanation for this result could be the appearance of 'debt substitution' between various national government bonds, analoguously to the concept of currency substitution in money demand functions. Anyhow, we conclude that the analysis of the linkage between fiscal policy and interest rates at a European level yields more satisfactory (stable) results than analyses performed at the national level.

II.5   Concluding remarks

In this section we have estimated a reduced-form equation of long-term nominal interest rates in the European Union. Our findings support the conventional view that movements in nominal interest rates can accurately be explained by changes in expected inflation, government budget deficits, government debt, capacity utilisation rates, and foreign interest rates. The major results of this section may be summarised as follows:

Table 3.8: Breakdown of nominal interest rates by sources of variation

Period	i^l (1)	$\alpha_1\pi^e$ (2)	$\alpha_3 D/Y$ (3)	$\alpha_6(B/Y)_{-1}$ (4)	$\alpha_7 CU$ (5)	$\alpha_8 i^{l,*}$ (6)	v (7)
1960–91	8.98	2.81	2.23	−1.59	2.48	0.47	−19.79[#]
1960–66	−2.73	−1.03	−1.37	−0.35	0.31	−0.10	−0.19
1967–73	−1.14	−0.59	−1.25	0.40	0.30	−0.20	0.21
1974–79	1.41	1.38	0.84	0.56	−0.71	−0.24	−0.43
1980–85	3.25	1.28	1.63	−0.02	−0.84	0.80	0.41
1986–91	−0.15	−0.76	0.58	−0.59	0.84	−0.21	−0.01

Notes: All variables in percentages. Actual values of the nominal interest rate, in deviation from its mean, are in column (1). The other variables are subtracted from their means and multiplied by their coefficients of regression 3.6.4. The full sample means – also multiplied by their coefficients – are given in the first row. The last column displays the unexplained residual, being column (1) minus the sum of columns (2) to (6). #: Constant term of 3.6.4.

i. The analysis of the linkage between fiscal variables and interest rates at a European level yields more satisfactory (that is stable) results than analyses performed at the national level.
ii. In the European Union persistent deficits have exercised an upward pressure on long-term interest rates, thereby contradicting the Ricardian proposition of the neutrality of deficit-financing. However, our outcomes also suggest that the private sector partially discounts future tax liabilities.
iii. The effect of world long-term interest rates on corresponding European interest rates is unmistakably confirmed. However, the rather low coefficient points at substantial impediments to extra-EMS capital mobility over the sample period.

To illustrate our results, Table 3.8 offers a decomposition of the nominal interest rate by its sources of variation. For selected subsample periods we report the averages of the variables that, according to our model, have contributed to the movements of the nominal interest rate. Table 3.8 is based on regression 3.6.4. Each variable is subtracted from its mean and multiplied by its coefficient of regression 3.6.4. The upper line of the table shows the means for the sample period as a whole, also multiplied by their coefficient. Column (7) displays unexplained residuals, that is the difference between the deviations of the actual values of the nominal interest rate shown in column (1) and the sum of the columns (2) to (6), which represent our fitted values.

It follows from Table 3.8 that the overall high European interest rates in the early 1980s have been caused mainly by increases in expected inflation, mounting budget deficits and high world interest rates. Starting from the beginning of our sample, budget deficits rose by over 3.5 percentage-points of GDP, causing approximately half of the rise in the nominal interest rate (1.63+1.37=3.00 out of 3.25+2.73=5.98 percentage-points). Inflationary expectations rose by more than 5 percentage-points which made nominal interest rates rise by about 2.5 points. Higher foreign interest rates accounted for a 0.8-point increase of the European nominal interest rate, whereas the combined effect of spare capacity and increased discounting of future tax liabilities somewhat moderated rising rates.

III   Short-term interest rates
III.1   Introduction

The previous section sought to investigate the determinants of long-term nominal interest rates in the European Union. Although the expected *real* interest rate is the relevant magnitude, if testing for crowding out in a loanable funds setting is the goal, nevertheless *nominal* interest rates were analysed there, since it is very difficult to construct an adequate measure of inflationary expectations in the very long run. In this section we analyse the development of short-term interest rates in our sample of European countries. It is our contention that with a limited horizon like a three-months period, we will be in a better position to compute relatively well-performing measures of inflationary expectations, so that (after-tax) expected real interest rates can be approximated. Besides, given the ease with which participants in financial markets can switch among maturities, persisting patterns in expected real short-term rates would also be reflected in medium- and long-term rates.

As in section II.4 the model is estimated with aggregate or weighed European data. Following the argument of the previous sections, we think that estimating an aggregate model will yield more stable results than estimating country-specific ones. Because of the lack of reliable data on three-month interest rates prior to the early 1970s, Italy had to be excluded from our sample of countries. The analysis is organised as follows. The reduced form of an IS model of real interest determination is derived and presented in section III.2. Section III.3 discusses the methodology and the aggregate data, which have been used to estimate the reduced-form model in section III.4. Section III.5 extends the model by concentrating on the potential impact of movements in the relative price of crude oil. Section III.6 offers some concluding remarks.

III.2   A model of real interest determination

In this section we will present a simple Investment–Savings model of real interest determination. The model consists of four equations in which the expected real interest rate is determined by investment demand, desired saving, and net capital outflows. Following Barro and Sala-i-Martin (1990), the relation for gross private investment demand can be approximated by:

$$I_t^g = \beta_{10} + \beta_{11} STOCK_t - \beta_{12}[r_t^e - r_{t-1}^e] + I_{t-1}^g + u_{1t}. \qquad (3.8)$$

This expression can be derived from a q-type model of investment demand, where the shadow price of capital is determined by the present discounted value of future profits. In equation (3.8) the real rate of return on the stock market $STOCK_t$ in conjunction with the first difference of the real interest rate $r^e - r_{-1}^e$, together proxy for the first difference of this discounted profitability. The relevant interest rate for household and firm expenditure decisions is the expected real after-tax rate, defined as:

$$r_t^e = (1-\kappa_t)i_t - \pi_t^e, \qquad (3.9)$$

where κ is the tax rate, i the nominal interest rate, and π^e denotes expected inflation. National saving is assumed to be determined by:

$$S_t = \beta_{30} + \beta_{31} YT_t + \beta_{32} r_t^e + \beta_{33}\pi_t^e + \beta_{34}S_{t-1} + \beta_{35}DM_t + \beta_{36}D_t + u_{3t}. \qquad (3.10)$$

Desired national saving is thought to be a function of temporary income YT, assuming that temporary changes in income are more important for saving decisions than are permanent ones. Besides, saving also responds positively to the expected after-tax real interest rate and inflationary expectations. Higher inflation is associated with greater uncertainty here, which leads to postponement of purchases of durables and hence to an increase in desired saving. Furthermore, according to the so-called 'Mundell effect', the supply of funds available for investment will also increase as rational agents will transform part of their liquid wealth into interest-bearing assets, in order to avoid the (nominal) interest loss (Mundell, 1963).[14] The variable S_{-1} picks up persisting influences on the saving rate. Finally, the saving function is expanded to include the effects of monetary and fiscal policy. In models where money is nonneutral, a higher rate of monetary expansion DM raises income and increases saving. With respect to fiscal variables it is often argued that increases in public borrowing D reduce desired national saving (Blanchard, 1985; Allen, 1990). Like in section II, the foreign sector of the economy is represented as:

$$NX_t = \beta_{40} + \beta_{41}[r_t^{e,*} - r_t^e] + u_{4t}. \qquad (3.11)$$

In equilibrium the supply of saving is equal to the sum of the demand for investment and the net capital outflow. Together with the equations (3.8),

(3.10), and (3.11), this makes up a model of four equations in I^g, S, NX, and r^e. Solving for the latter yields:

$$r_t^e = \frac{1}{\beta_{12}+\beta_{32}+\beta_{41}} \left\{ [\beta_{10}-\beta_{30}+\beta_{40}] + \beta_{11}STOCK_t + \beta_{12}r_{t-1}^e - \beta_{31}YT_t \right.$$

$$\left. -\beta_{33}\pi_t^e + [1-\beta_{34}]I_{t-1}^g - \beta_{34}NX_{t-1} + \beta_{41}r_t^{e,*} - \beta_{35}DM_t - \beta_{36}D_t \right\} + v_t,$$

(3.12)

where $v = (u_1-u_3+u_4)/[\beta_{12}+\beta_{32}+\beta_{41}]$ is the composite error term, which is assumed to be white noise.

It follows from equation (3.12) that improved stock returns, higher foreign real rates, and more government borrowing raise the expected real interest rate. On the other hand, higher temporary income, increasing inflationary expectations, and accelerating monetary expansion all raise desired saving and thereby reduce real interest rates. The implications for the lagged variables r^e, I^g, and NX will depend on the dynamics of the model. The effect of lagged investment demand is positive if persistence in investment demand exceeds persistence in desired saving, that is if $\beta_{34}<1$. Finally, the coefficient on the world real interest rate $r^{e,*}$ enables us to gauge international capital mobility. When domestic and foreign assets are considered perfect substitutes, β_{41} tends to infinity, $\beta_{41}/[\beta_{12}+\beta_{32}+\beta_{41}]$ tends to one, and all other coefficients tend to zero.

III.3   Data and methodology

The previous section illustrated that investment demand and desired saving depend on expected after-tax real interest rates. Only information on before-tax nominal interest rates exists, together with average (broad) tax rates, and realised inflation rates. Because gaps between actual and expected inflation are likely to be substantial in some periods, utilising actual inflation rates would yield rather imprecise estimates of expected real interest rates. Therefore, we will start by estimating expected inflation rates based on regression forecasts for actual inflation. To get reliable forecasts and, hence, an accurate measurement of the resulting expected real interest rate series, we have constrained maturity to a three-month horizon, despite the well-known fact that investment and saving decisions are primarily based on medium- and long-term considerations. However, the patterns in short-term expected real interest rates reveal a good deal of persistence; given the ease with which participants in financial markets can switch among maturities, those patterns would for the main part also be reflected in longer-term rates.

We use quarterly data on inflation for each country from 1952.Q2 up to the quarter prior to the date for which the forecast was constructed.[15] The functional form for the inflation regressions depends on the time-series characteristics of the inflation rate in the various countries, including

Table 3.9: Quarterly regressions for inflation

Country	France	Germany	Netherlands	United Kingdom	United States
S1	0.067 (1.2)	0.035 (2.2)	0.081 (5.1)	0.100 (6.6)	0.047 (3.2)
S2	0.062 (1.1)	0.032 (2.1)	0.004 (0.3)	0.048 (3.2)	0.055 (3.8)
S3	0.077 (1.3)	0.012 (0.7)	0.053 (3.4)	0.047 (3.1)	0.042 (2.9)
S4	0.075 (1.3)	0.053 (3.4)	0.030 (2.0)	0.065 (4.3)	0.034 (2.3)
AR(1)	0.904 (7.7)	0.655 (4.1)		0.340 (4.4)	0.252 (3.2)
AR(2)		−0.397 (2.9)		0.395 (5.1)	0.376 (4.8)
AR(3)		0.573 (3.9)			0.238 (2.9)
SAR(4)	0.423 (4.4)		0.529 (7.8)		
MA(1)	−0.568 (4.6)	−0.594 (3.5)			
MA(2)		0.415 (2.6)			
MA(3)		−0.408 (3.4)			
SMA(4)	−0.351 (3.4)				
R^2	0.48	0.33	0.44	0.49	0.61
SEE	0.038	0.029	0.046	0.046	0.024
DW	1.74	1.99	1.90	2.09	2.04
Q(4)	4.43	1.98	2.04	2.53	3.71

Notes: t-statistics in parentheses. Dependent variable is the inflation rate, expressed at annual rates. AR(p) is a p-order autoregressive term and MA(q) a q-order moving-average term. SAR and SMA denote seasonal AR and MA, respectively. S1 is a dummy for quarter 1 and so on. R^2: R-squared. SEE: Standard Error of Equation. DW: Durbin Watson statistic. Q(4): Ljung–Box statistic. Sample: 1952.Q2–90.Q4.

deterministic seasonals for each quarter and a number of autoregressive as well as moving-average terms.[16] Subsequently, these (rolling) regressions were used to construct one-period-ahead forecasts. Table 3.9 shows the estimated equations for the four European countries and the United States over the sample 1952.Q2–90.Q4.

Next, annual measures of expected inflation have been computed by averaging the quarterly values from the regression forecasts. We then calculated after-tax expected real interest rates on a quarterly base for each country by subtracting the constructed value for π^e from the corresponding after-tax nominal interest rate $(1-\kappa)i^s$ (for example the three-month interest rate in January matches up with expected inflation from January to April). The tax rate κ was proxied by the amount of taxes on income and profits as a percentage of GDP for each country on an annual base and, subsequently, assumed constant over all four quarters. The complexity of modern tax systems is such that we do not pretend to be able to incorporate all the effects of taxation by the use of this simple proxy, but we consider these taxes to be most relevant from the individual shareholders' point of view.[17] We then form annual series for the real interest rates according to equation (3.9) by averaging the four quarterly values. Finally, we construct a European index of the after-tax expected real interest rate for each year as a weighed average of the four individual country indices, based on real (1985 prices) GDP weights. The resulting series for the after-tax expected real interest rate as well as the one for the after-tax actual real interest rate are shown in Figure 3.2 (in percentages). Applying the same weighing procedure, we have also constructed series for the index of real stock returns and for actual as well as expected inflation in Europe; the latter two are shown in Figure 3.3.

To construct a series for temporary income (*YT*) we employ the method developed by Beveridge and Nelson (1981) and Miller (1988) to decompose a non-stationary time series into its permanent and transitory parts. We opt for this method, because it allows for a stochastic trend component. The alternative of a deterministic trend would imply that shocks do not influence the permanent part at all. The Beveridge and Nelson approach uses the time series behaviour of the first differences of the series, which are assumed to be stationary. Denote the actual series by z and the first differences as w ($=\Delta z$). The first step is to estimate an *ARMA* model for the first differences w. The transitory and permanent parts of z are then given by:

$$\begin{cases} a_t = \lim_{k \to \infty}[w_t(1)+w_t(2)+\ldots+w_t(k) - k\mu] \\ z_t^P = z_t - a_t, \end{cases} \tag{3.13}$$

where $w_t(j)$ is the forecast of $w(t+j)$ made on time t, and μ denotes the long-run mean of w. In practice the limit in equation (3.13) can be replaced by a

Figure 3.2: After-tax real interest rates in the EU

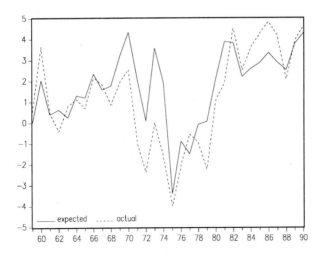

Figure 3.3: Actual and expected inflation in the EU

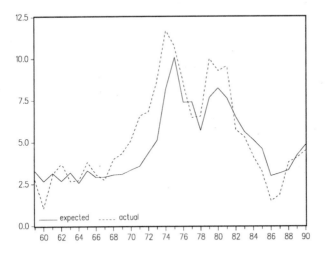

Table 3.10: Summary statistics of the main variables

Variable	$r^{s,e}$	STOCK	YT/Y	π^e	I^g/Y_{-1}	NX/Y_{-1}	$r^{s,e,*}$	DM	D/Y
Mean (%)	1.73	2.33	2.73	4.75	21.12	0.49	1.00	4.36	−1.51
Std. dev.(%)	1.80	18.79	0.85	2.09	2.23	0.58	2.18	3.81	1.15
Correlation coefficients									
$r^{s,e}$	1	0.33	−0.30	−0.34	0.02	0.08	0.54	−0.37	0.27
STOCK	0.33	1	0.05	−0.36	−0.09	0.47	0.46	−0.27	0.09
YT/Y	−0.30	0.05	1	−0.51	0.76	−0.11	0.01	0.20	0.37
π^e	−0.34	−0.36	−0.51	1	−0.48	−0.16	−0.55	−0.14	−0.63
$(I^g/Y)_{-1}$	0.02	−0.09	0.76	−0.48	1	−0.50	0.09	0.06	0.47
$(NX/Y)_{-1}$	0.08	0.47	−0.11	−0.16	−0.50	1	0.08	0.03	0.01
$r^{s,e,*}$	0.54	0.46	0.01	−0.55	0.09	0.08	1	−0.15	0.07
DM	−0.37	−0.27	0.20	−0.14	0.06	0.03	−0.15	1	−0.00
D/Y	0.27	0.09	0.37	−0.63	0.47	0.01	0.07	−0.00	1

Notes: Sample 1959–90. All variables are specified in the appendix.

large number of forecasts. The representation of the first difference of the log of real GDP (*dy*) is:

$$dy = 0.035 + 0.466AR(1), \qquad R^2 = 0.23, \qquad Q(4) = 3.45$$
$$(6.9) \quad (3.4)$$

Table 3.10 contains the first two moments of all variables used in the empirical analysis. European (nominal) aggregates like M, I^g, NX, and D are expressed in Deutschemark using actual nominal exchange rates (see also note 10); in the regression analysis variables like I^g, NX, YT, and D enter as ratios to corresponding GDP. The world after-tax expected real interest rate is again proxied by the corresponding variable for the United States. Before employing the variables in the regression analysis of the next section, all have been checked on stationarity by means of the augmented Dickey–Fuller test. It appeared that all variables constructed in this manner were (trend) stationary.

III.4   Reduced-form estimates

This section presents estimates of the reduced form of the model presented in section III.2 over the sample 1959–90. The dependent variable is the European index of the after-tax expected real interest rate as defined in section III.3. Table 3.11 reports results obtained for a number of different specifications of equation (3.12).

Regression (3.11.1) represents equation (3.12) with virtually all variables included; for the moment we abstain from both policy variables. Despite the relatively large number of regressors in (3.11.1), most coefficients are significant and exhibit the predicted signs. Clear exceptions are the variables representing 'abroad': the US after-tax expected real interest rate $r^{s,e,*}$ and the current account balance $(NX/Y)_{-1}$.[18] In line with results reported by Mark (1985) and Cumby and Mishkin (1986), and complementary to our findings for long-term interest rates in the previous section, we also have to reject the hypothesis of equality of (real) interest rates between our sample of European countries and the United States for a short maturity. As has already been indicated in section II, extra-EMS capital mobility is usually thought to be much lower than intra-EMS capital mobility (Bhandari and Mayer, 1990). So we think that also in the case of short-term interest rates, any aggregation among OECD countries should be confined to the European level instead of taking the 'global view', as has nevertheless been done by Barro and Sala-i-Martin (1990).

In order to determine whether the European Union can be regarded as a completely closed economy for the purpose of this section, we have performed an F-test on the omission of the two variables representing the foreign sector of our economy. Somewhat surprisingly, the value of the test statistic $(F_{[2,24]}=0.37)$ indicates that it is indeed allowed to eliminate these variables from this specification,[19] as is done in regression (3.11.2). As the intercept also remained insignificant during the entire analysis, we refrain from it hereafter. However, the estimated coefficients of our measure of profitability, *STOCK*, and the lags on the real rate itself as well as investment demand are all positive and significant. It appears that persistence in investment demand is greater than persistence in desired saving. As predicted by the model, temporary income enters negatively and significantly so, as does expected inflation.[20] From the magnitude and significance of the latter coefficient in most regressions here as well as in the next section, we may conclude that disregarding its influence in the explanation of expected real interest rates would have reinforced the misspecification problem already present, as indicated by Ramsey's *RESET* test-statistic. Apparently, even at a short horizon, nominal interest rates and inflationary expectations do not move together in a one-for-one fashion. Mishkin (1984a) already demonstrated that for the countries in question this so-called Fischer effect is also invalidated at the individual-country level.

In regression (3.11.4) we add a measure of monetary policy and a measure of fiscal policy. Since the analysis applies to short-term interest rates, we are not really surprised to find that the index of money growth enters negatively and significantly (DM), while the coefficient of the aggregate deficit–income ratio turns out to be insignificant.[21] As in the analysis of long-term interest rates in the previous section we have also tried to account for the possible endogeneity of the deficit, and have resorted to the same instrumental variables procedure. Despite this cyclical correction, the results remain unaltered. Finally, we have tried to construct a measure of temporary

Table 3.11: After-tax expected real interest rates in the EU

Regression	(3.11.1)	(3.11.2)	(3.11.3)	(3.11.4)	(3.11.5)
C.T.	1.170	−1.159			
	(0.2)	(0.4)			
STOCK	0.036	0.033	0.030	0.025	0.023
	(2.0)	(2.4)	(2.6)	(2.1)	(2.0)
$r^{s,e}_{-1}$	0.430	0.393	0.380	0.423	0.412
	(2.4)	(2.8)	(2.8)	(3.3)	(3.3)
YT/Y	−1.304	−1.540	−1.505	−1.322	−1.342
	(2.5)	(3.6)	(3.6)	(3.3)	(3.4)
π^e	−0.268	−0.264	−0.297	−0.237	−0.300
	(1.6)	(1.8)	(2.6)	(1.6)	(2.8)
$(I^g/Y)_{-1}$	0.227	0.361	0.310	0.305	0.314
	(0.9)	(2.3)	(4.0)	(4.1)	(4.3)
$r^{s,e,*}$	0.034				
	(0.2)				
$(CA/Y)_{-1}$	−0.486				
	(0.7)				
DM				−0.119	−0.126
				(2.1)	(2.3)
D/Y				0.149	
				(0.6)	
R^2	0.64	0.63	0.63	0.70	0.69
SEE	1.22	1.19	1.17	1.10	1.09
SSR(/100)	0.36	0.37	0.37	0.30	0.31
LM–1	0.10	0.07	0.17	0.87	0.34
LM–4	1.65	1.67	1.64	1.54	1.16
ARCH–1	1.58	0.86	1.34	2.02	1.90
ARCH–4	1.28	0.62	0.75	0.86	0.50
RESET–1	3.49[#]	3.61[#]	4.05[#]	2.49	2.47
J–B(2)	0.64	1.40	0.62	0.53	0.22
CHOW–79	1.56	1.76	1.98	2.85	2.25

Notes: t-statistics in parentheses. Sample: 1959–90 (N=32). C.T.: Constant Term. LM–p: Lagrange-multiplier F-test on serial correlation (p lags). ARCH–p: Auto Regressive Conditional Heteroskedasticity F-test. RESET: Ramsey's RESET F-test (only squared fits). J–B(2): Jarque–Bera normality χ^2-test. CHOW–79: Breakpoint–Chow F-test for 1979. [#]: Significant at 10%.

government spending in the European Union, employing the Beveridge–Nelson approach.[22] However, we were unable to isolate important temporary variations in aggregate as well as individual real government spending.

As one might expect from standard monetary theory, money growth and real interest rates are negatively correlated. But from regressions (3.11.4) and (3.11.5) it may also be inferred that aggregate European money growth has explanatory power over and above its association with expected inflation. Mishkin (1984a) already noted that at the individual-country level the same independent connection between money growth and real rates over and above its association with expected inflation also holds in most of the European countries considered here. It is possible that money growth helps forecast future inflation in a way that is complementary to the construction of our backward-looking π^e variable.

III.5 The impact of oil prices

Section III.4 found a significant impact of movements in real stock returns, temporary income, expected inflation, lagged investment, and money growth on the European index of after-tax expected real interest rates. Various authors have pointed at the role of the relative price of crude oil in the determination of real interest rates, albeit with remarkable ambiguity. Wilcox (1983), for example, reports a significantly negative influence of the oil price on US after-tax expected real interest rates over the sample 1952–79, that is including only the effects of the first oil crisis. To explain this outcome, Wilcox stresses that energy can be regarded as a complementary factor of production. A reduction in its supply or a rise in its price reduces use of that factor and lowers the marginal products of the remaining inputs like capital. This explanation, however, fails to draw a distinction between the average q of installed capital and the marginal q of new potential technologies, the latter being most relevant for investment decisions. In the presence of adjustment costs, Sims (1980b) has shown that the initial effect of an expected decline in future marginal products of capital on the instantaneous interest rate can also be reversed. If it is costly to adjust the capital stock rapidly, it will take a certain period of time before the tight link between interest rates and future yields on capital can be re-established. Indeed, Barro and Sala-i-Martin (1990) find a positive and significant effect of oil prices on a world index of before-tax expected real interest rates over the sample 1959–88, that is including the oil crisis of 1979 as well as the 1973 one. According to these authors, rising oil prices mainly affected temporary income, thereby reducing desired saving and increasing real interest rates.

Since our measure of the relative price of oil (*RPOIL*) clearly exhibited non-stationarity, we employ first differences in regressions (3.12.1) to (3.12.4). The substantial improvement in the overall performance of regressions (3.12.1) and (3.12.2) immediately stands out, including a considerable reduction of the

Table 3.12: The impact of oil prices on real interest rates

Regression	(3.12.1)	(3.12.2)	(3.12.3)	(3.12.4)
STOCK	0.029	0.019	0.017	0.016
	(2.8)	(1.9)	(1.4)	(1.6)
$r^{s,e}_{-1}$	0.450	0.366	0.505	0.313
	(4.0)	(3.4)	(4.0)	(2.8)
YT/Y	−1.452	−1.280		−1.249
	(4.2)	(3.9)		(3.9)
π^e	−0.415	−0.340	−0.111	−0.379
	(4.1)	(3.5)	(1.1)	(3.8)
$(I^g/Y)_{-1}$	0.348	0.298	0.071	0.299
	(5.4)	(4.8)	(2.3)	(4.9)
$r^{s,e,*}$		0.299	0.403	0.307
		(2.5)	(2.7)	(2.6)
DM	−0.130	−0.118	−0.144	−0.114
	(2.7)	(2.7)	(2.6)	(2.6)
ΔRPOIL	0.043	0.063	0.064	
	(2.9)	(4.0)	(3.2)	
ΔRPOIL⁺				0.079
				(4.1)
ΔRPOIL⁻				0.032
				(1.2)
R^2	0.77	0.82	0.70	0.83
SEE	0.96	0.88	1.10	0.86
SSR(/100)	0.23	0.18	0.30	0.17
LM–1	0.06	0.19	0.66	0.99
LM–4	2.71#	1.49	0.28	2.13
ARCH–1	6.02#	0.79	1.78	0.15
ARCH–4	2.78#	1.99	0.84	1.64
RESET–1	1.99	0.84	0.09	0.22
J–B(2)	1.77	0.44	0.37	1.58
CHOW–79	1.75	0.78	1.30	1.36

Notes: See Table 3.11. Sample: 1959–90 (N=32).

misspecification problem indicated by the *RESET* test-statistic. Aside from this, the oil price comes in positively and significantly for our European index of after-tax expected real interest rates. This result can be brought into line with the apparently contradictionary result of Wilcox (1983), once we recall that correlations between US real rates and real rates of European counterparts during the period under consideration were negligible (regression 3.11.1) or at best very weak (regression 3.12.2).[23,24] Moreover, high oil prices were accompanied by high real interest rates especially during the years after the second oil crisis, a period not included in the Wilcox paper. On the other hand, our results could also point at the existence of significant impediments to a rapid and adequate adjustment of the European capital stock to the altered circumstances. Nevertheless, this elucidation cannot explain why, after the second oil crisis of 1979, real interest rates remained so high during the remainder of the 1980s. Despite the strong significance of our coefficient on $\Delta RPOIL$, the coefficient of temporary income remains virtually unaffected, and, as is shown in regression (3.12.3), omission of that variable leads to a serious decline in explanatory power. We therefore conclude that it cannot be the effect on temporary income that is responsible for the positive effect of oil prices on real interest rates, at least in the case of the European Union.

So the question remains what information is represented by the oil price that is not already contained in the other variables of regression (3.12.2). Perhaps, rising oil prices have signalled a contraction of European monetary policy, as Hamilton (1983) witnessed for the US. Additionally, it could be argued that the growth rate of money and quasi-money is not a complete measure of the monetary stance. Immediately after the second oil crisis (1979), rising oil prices led to further increases in already persistent high levels of inflation which were combatted by the monetary authorities by directly raising (nominal) interest rates. In this way, monetary policy was already very contractive without this being reflected in the growth rate of M.[25] Furthermore, one can doubt once more whether all variation in actual expected inflation is captured by our π^e variable, given the representation of our inflation equations based on extrapolations of past inflation (Table 3.9), thereby excluding sudden contemporary shocks. Probably, actual inflationary expectations adapted more quickly to the fast increases in the oil price at the very beginning of the 1980s than our measure of expected inflation, resulting in high nominal interest rates and (too) high levels of our measure of expected real rates. Reversing this mechanism, falling oil prices in the later 1980s resulted in underestimating expected real interest rates. Due to the dummy-like behaviour of *RPOIL* (see Figure 4 in Knot, 1995), the period from 1979 onwards may have been very important for the determination of its coefficient in regression (3.12.2). So, in this interpretation the oil price would contain information about monetary policy and inflationary expectations that is not already present in *DM* and π^e.

In spite of the emerging literature on asymmetric effects of positive and negative shocks on certain macro variables (for instance Neftçi, 1984, and Cover, 1992), the literature on real interest rates thus far fails to draw a distinction between positive oil-price shocks and negative oil-price shocks. We therefore split up our $\Delta RPOIL$ series into a series containing the positive shocks in the oil price (labelled $\Delta RPOIL^+$) and a series containing its negative counterparts ($\Delta RPOIL^-$). From regression (3.12.4) it may be inferred that the effects of oil price movements on real interest rates were indeed asymmetric in Europe. Predominantly, upward movements in the relative price of crude oil have exerted an important upward pressure on real interest rates at various points in time, while the correlation between negative movements in both variables appears much weaker and not even significantly different from zero.

Finally, we have checked our results on stability by performing a series of Breakpoint–Chow tests on the last row of Tables 3.11 and 3.12. Cumby and Mishkin (1986) report evidence of a major shift in the underlying stochastic structure of real interest rate movements in Europe sometime around the beginning of the European Monetary System. Using 1979 as the breaking date, we found hardly any evidence of model instability for the regressions reported in Tables 3.11 and 3.12. Furthermore, we have re-estimated equation (3.12.2) for various subsamples of the period under consideration, where the starting and ending date varied between 1959 and 1967, and between 1982 and 1990, respectively. Again this exercise did not modify our results, neither qualitatively nor quantitatively. So we conclude that once again the aggregate model seems to be remarkably stable over the period considered.

III.6   Concluding remarks
In this section we have investigated the determinants of after-tax expected real interest rates with a maturity of three months in four European countries: France, Germany, the Netherlands, and the United Kingdom. From a model of investment demand, desired saving, and net capital outflows, a reduced-form equation for the expected real interest rate was derived. We computed series for expected inflation in the four countries and subsequently employed them in computing measures for the after-tax expected real interest rates. Estimating the reduced form over the sample 1959–90 it was found that our European index of expected real interest rates was mainly driven by changes in real stock returns, temporary income, expected inflation, lagged investment, money growth, oil prices, and US real rates. The last coefficient differed significantly from unity, indicating that capital mobility between the EU and the US was far from perfect during the period considered. This result justified again our choice for a European point of view instead of a global one. With respect to the role of oil prices we found that the after-tax expected real interest rate was mainly affected by upward movements in the relative price of crude oil, suggesting that its impact was asymmetric. Overall, our aggregate model of short-term interest rates appears to be remarkably stable.

Table 3.13: Decomposition of real interest rates by sources of variation

	Period	1971–75	1976–80	1981–85	1959–90
(1)	$r^{s,e}$	−0.88	−1.79	1.35	1.73
(2)	STOCK	−0.29	−0.05	0.05	0.04
(3)	$r^{s,e}_{-1}$	0.28	−1.02	0.47	0.60
(4)	YT/Y	0.23	0.64	0.87	−3.49
(5)	π^e	−0.52	−0.86	−0.39	−1.61
(6)	$(I^g/Y)_{-1}$	0.14	−0.60	−0.40	6.30
(7)	$r^{s,e,*}$	−0.68	−0.80	0.85	0.30
(8)	DM	−0.10	0.04	0.27	−0.52
(9)	$\Delta RPOIL$	0.48	0.75	−0.37	0.09
(10)	ν	−0.40	0.14	−0.00	0.02

Notes: Actual values of the after-tax expected real interest rate (in %), in deviation from its mean, are given in the first row. The other variables (also in %) are subtracted from their means and multiplied by their coefficient of regression (3.12.2). The sample means, also multiplied by the coefficients, are reported in the last column. The last row displays the unexplained residual, that is the difference between row (1) and the sum of the rows (2) to (9).

As opposed to the analysis of long-term interest rates, variables capturing the impact of fiscal policy were found to be of no importance in the determination of short-term interest rates. It would seem that government deficits matter for the level of those interest rates that are more relevant for intertemporal decision making from the part of the private sector. In a growing economy with capital accumulation, for example, increasing budget deficits may create a shortage of funds available for investment in the long run, in anticipation of which long-term interest rates will rise. The main transmission mechanism here is the term structure of interest rates. As in a simple model presented by Blanchard and Fischer (1989, p.134), the effect of the present budget deficit on present short-term interest rates is small, while long-term interest rates will rise in anticipation of higher future short-term rates.

To illustrate our results we will use the estimated model (3.12.2) to simulate some of the movements in expected real interest rates over the sample. To this end Table 3.13 reports average values of variables that, according to our model, have contributed to the movements of the after-tax expected real interest rate, for selected subsample periods. Each variable is subtracted from its mean and multiplied by its coefficient of regression (3.12.2). The means for the sample period as a whole, also multiplied by their coefficient, are reported in the last column of the Table. Row (10) displays the unexplained residuals, that is the differences between the deviations of the actual values (row 1) and our fitted values (rows 2 to 9).

As can be learned from Table 3.13, the fall in real interest rates during the 1970s of about 1 percentage point was mainly caused by differences in initial conditions (the lagged investment ratio and real interest rate) and increasing inflationary expectations, whereas decreases in temporary income, slowing money growth, rising oil prices and higher stock returns moderated this fall somewhat. In the first half of the 1980s real interest rates recovered about three percentage points, predominantly due to higher US rates (which explain more than half of the rise), in addition to divergent initial conditions, falling inflation, and contractive monetary policy. Here, the only variable that moderates this rise is again the relative price of oil. Furthermore, Table 3.13 demonstrates that real interest rates in Europe rose sharply at the beginning of the 1980s, because nearly all its determinants moved it (coincidentally?) in the same direction.

Appendix: Definitions and sources of variables used
(Annual frequency unless indicated otherwise)

---

i^s

Nominal interest rate on three-month loans for January, April, July, and October (quarterly), except money-market rate for France, from *International Financial Statistics* line 60 (IMF) and *Main Economic Indicators* (OECD).

i^l

Long-term government bond yield from *IFS* line 61.

CPI

Consumer price index (1985=100), *IFS* line 64. Annual in section II; seasonally unadjusted, for January, April, July, and October (quarterly) in III.

π

Actual CPI-inflation is $\log(CPI_{+1}/CPI)$, annual (section II), or $4\log(CPI_{+1}/CPI)$, quarterly (section III).

π^e

Constructed measure of expected inflation. Computed as an $AR(2)$ forecast of actual inflation in section II. Quarterly in section III by means of Table 3.9.

κ

Average tax rate on income and profits (% GDP), from *Revenue Statistics of OECD Member Countries* (OECD).

$r^{s,e}$

After-tax expected real short-term interest rate as in equation (3.9), quarterly.

Y

Nominal GDP from *IFS* line 99b. For the construction of (weighed) European indices we use real (1985 prices) GDP (*IFS* line 99b.r).

The European measure of real GDP (in Deutschemark) is computed by aggregating the country-specific measures, using base-year nominal exchange rates (*IFS* line rf).

YT   Temporary income, constructed employing the Beveridge–Nelson approach to real GDP.

STOCK   Real rate of return on stock market. Nominal returns were computed from *IFS* data on industrial share prices from January$_{-1}$ to January. The corresponding CPI inflation (also January to January) was subtracted in order to calculate real returns.

M   Money supply, that is money plus quasi-money (*IFS* lines 34+35).

DM   Growth rate of *M*, equal to $\log(M/M_{-1})$.

CU   Capacity utilisation rate, OECD, *Main Economic Indicators*. For Italy this series has been kindly provided by Mr. Guiso of Banca d'Italia.

D   Government budget deficit (–) or surplus (+), from *IFS* line 80.

B   Stock of government debt owned by the private sector (*IFS* lines 88a+89a–12a). For the United Kingdom lines 88a and 89a have been substituted by the series for government debt from the *Annual Abstract of Statistics* edited by the Central Statistical Office.

G   Government spending, *IFS* line 82.

GI^n   Net government investment, that is gross investment minus depreciation from OECD, *National Accounts* 2 (Detailed Statistics).

T   Government revenue, *IFS* line 81.

I^g   Gross domestic capital formation (1985 prices) from *IFS* line 93e.c.

I^n   Net investment, that is gross domestic capital formation minus depreciation (OECD, *National Accounts* 2, Detailed Statistics).

NX   Net capital outflows, proxied by the current account, *IFS* line 77a.d.

W   Total wealth of the private sector, equal to *K+NFW*.

K   Capital stock. As usual we assume $K(1960)=2.5\times$GDP (see among others Dramais, 1986). Thereafter $K=K_{-1}+I^n$.

NFW   Net financial wealth of the private sector. This series was not available for the countries in question but could be constructed in the following manner: Current account balance (*NX*) = increase in *NFW* + increase in net financial wealth public sector (=*D*), so that $\Delta NFW = NX - D$. Now *NFW*(1959) is the only missing factor of our variable W_{-1}; its influence, however, is captured by the constant term.

$r^{s,e,*}$ US after-tax expected real interest rate (quarterly), computed in the same way as interest rates of the European counterparts.

$i^{l,*}$ US long-term government bond yield (*IFS* line 61), corrected for the expected devaluation of the US dollar vis-à-vis the currency in question. Before 1970 (Bretton–Woods) this correction is assumed to be zero; afterwards it is the forecast of a rolling regression of the actual rate of depreciation on two own lags and one lag of the inflation differential between the country in question and the US.

RPOIL   Relative price of Saudi Arabian crude oil, being the ratio of the price of crude petroleum from *IFS* line 76 to the (German) GDP deflator.

Notes

1. See De Haan (1989) for a comprehensive overview of such studies.
2. Note that these conclusions have been challenged by Barr (1992) and Arnold (1994). See, however, also Kremers and Lane (1992) and Artis, Bladen-Hovell, and Zhang (1993).
3. A very similar relation can also be derived from a Jorgenson-type model of optimal investment under adjustment costs (Blanchard and Fischer, 1989, pp. 296–301). Empirical evidence suggests that investment behaviour in most of the countries under consideration here is well-described by putty-clay-like models (Bischoff, 1971, and Bekx et al., 1989).
4. See for example Stevenson, Muscatelli, and Gregory (1988).
5. Exact sources and definitions of the variables are in the appendix to this chapter.
6. Like Modigliani and Jappelli (1988), we first included the US interest rate as measure of world interest rates. In contrast to their approach, the growth rate of *M* is included here, instead of the liquidity ratio.
7. A similar result is reported by Nunes-Correia and Stemitsiotis (1993).
8. Knoester and Mak (1994) used a mixture of Swiss, Dutch, and British interest rates as a proxy for the foreign interest rate relevant to Germany. Despite its clear significance, there is every reason for serious doubt with respect to its exogeneity, however. Furthermore, the theoretical foundation of this variable remains unclear.
9. If appropriate, we took the first regression for each country, for the sake of comparison and in conformity with Modigliani and Jappelli (in case of Italy). For the Netherlands (German instead of US interest rate) and the UK (strong significance of B/Y_{-1}) this was clearly not the case.
10. Alternative conversion rates could be purchasing power parity (PPP) exchange rates or fixed base-year exchange rates. A drawback of the former procedure is that PPP exchange rates are notoriously difficult to construct and frequently rely upon assumptions concerning the nature of the underlying economies that are often violated. The obvious disadvantage of fixed-base exchange rates is that the choice of the base-period itself is arbitrary; a problem which seems especially relevant at longer horizons.

11. The correlation coefficient between capital outflows and national saving is a mere 0.21, whereas the correlation between national saving and private investment, and between national saving and government investment amounts to 0.98 and 0.95, respectively.

12. In Knot and De Haan (1995a) the model of section II.1 is also estimated for the European Union over the sample 1960–89. An important difference, however, is the way in which several variables are measured. In Knot and De Haan (1995a) variables like M, D, G, B, and W are measured in real ((GDP-) deflated) levels, whereas stationarity analysis convinced us here that it is more appropriate to insert these variables expressed in percentages of GDP. Despite this difference, the results are strikingly similar in a qualitative sense.

13. The empirical evidence regarding this issue is summarised in Chapter 2.

14. Strictly speaking, the Mundell effect does not affect the flow of new (desired) saving but the stock of previously accumulated savings which are retained in liquidities. What matters in the context of this model, however, is that it does affect the supply of funds available for investment and hence the real interest rate, in case inflation rises.

15. Precise definitions and sources of the variables are specified in the appendix.

16. Here we contrasted the methodology of Barro and Sala-i-Martin (1990), who imposed the $ARMA(1,1)$ specification regardless of the time-series characteristics of the inflation data. When we tried to replicate their findings it appeared that this specification would have yielded a large number of highly unstable coefficients, even depending on the econometric package used!

17. A survey of the effects of taxation on real interest rates in the OECD countries is provided by Atkinson and Chouraqui (1985). The proxy for the tax rate chosen here is comparable to Allen (1990). To assess any potential distortion arising from this approximation we have redone the entire analysis of section III under the competing assumptions that taxes do not matter at all (that is $\kappa=0$) or that the tax-measure should also include social security contributions. Both alternatives yielded quantitatively similar and qualitatively identical results. Hence, one is tempted to conclude that taxes do not matter for the determination of real interest rates in a loanable funds setting. However, given the simple character of both tax proxies investigated, it could also well be that the most important effects of taxes are too complex to be covered by such simple proxies.

18. As the partial correlation between the US real interest rate and expected inflation is rather high (Table 3.10), we have investigated whether insignificance of the US rate is due to multicollinearity. However, omission of expected inflation from this specification does not render significant the coefficient of $r^{s,e,*}$.

19. However, the simple correlation between EU and US after-tax expected real interest rates is 0.54 over the period 1959–90.

20. The presence of expected inflation on both the left hand side (in $r^{s,e}$) and the right hand side of (3.12) produces automatic correlation between the left and right side variables (correlation is −0.34). Circumventing this by redefining the dependent variable to be the nominal (after-tax) interest rate would only affect the coefficient on π^e, which would be augmented by one.

21. Empirical evidence regarding the impact of budget deficits on short-term real interest rates is also very mixed. Take for example the US, for which negative estimated effects were reported by Plosser (1987), whereas positive *and* significant effects have been reported by Allen (1990).

22. In an intertemporal equilibrium setting, only temporary government purchases affect the real interest rate. A temporary change in the level of government spending does not affect the optimal intertemporal allocation of rational consumers, who will therefore try to maintain their consumption plans. The resulting excess demand for goods will lead to upward pressure on interest rates. See amongst others Aschauer (1988) and De Haan and Zelhorst (1992).

23. It may be noted that inclusion of the oil price also renders significant the effect of foreign interest rates on the European one. Presumably due to multicollinearity inherent to this type of specification, including the oil price variable seems to be a necessary condition for the US real rate to become significant (partial correlation between $\Delta RPOIL$ and $r^{s,e,*}$ is −0.66!).

However, its coefficient in (3.12.2) still differs from unity very significantly (*t*-value 5.7) and its effect is much weaker than comparable estimates would suggest (Cumby and Mishkin, 1986, Table 2B).

24. Sims (1980b) has noticed a tendency for postwar US recessions to be preceded by an increase in interest rates, while Hamilton (1983) concludes that all but one of those recessions have also been preceded by a dramatic increase in the price of crude oil. So this would suggest a positive contemporaneous correlation between oil prices and interest rates also for the US.

25. Sims (1980b) also found evidence for this proposition for the US. As mentioned in the previous footnote, he witnessed a tendency for postwar recessions to be preceded by an increase in interest rates, which *also* seems to have predated the decline in the rate of growth of the money supply known to be associated with the first stages of an economic downturn.

4 Deficit announcements and interest rates in Germany

As recent experience in several countries shows, early announcement and legislation of credible medium-term deficit reduction measures have immediate beneficial effects on long-term interest rates and on economic confidence, even when recessionary conditions make it difficult to undertake significant deficit cuts in the short run.

International Monetary Fund (1993), p.3

I   Introduction

In Chapter 3 the relationship between government budget deficits and interest rates has been investigated for a number of countries. Using a methodological framework that is very common in this kind of research, we found no evidence that budget deficits have raised long-term interest rates in Germany over the last three decades. Despite this and related evidence, as yet, no consensus exists among economists whether deficits raise interest rates, neither in general nor more specifically in the case of Germany.[1]

Recently, several authors have examined this relationship employing a conceptually different framework, the so-called 'announcement effect methodology'.[2] The idea behind this approach is that in an efficient market, information about any determinant of interest rates will be quickly incorporated into observed rates. As a consequence, if an increase in the deficit is associated with higher interest rates, unanticipated announcements of a growing deficit should trigger an immediate response in financial markets. One of the advantages of the announcement effect approach is that it precludes the necessity to specify a structural model for interest rates.[3] Another advantage is that many of the econometric problems that afflict interest rate–deficit regressions as presented in Chapter 3 (like simultaneity and temporal aggregation problems) are circumvented.[4] Consequently, this approach may also yield different results as compared to the more standard analysis of Chapter 3, possibly providing some complementary insights.

Wachtel and Young (1987) have applied this method to the case of the United States. The authors employ projections of current and future deficits as provided by the Office of Management and Budget (OMB) and the

Congressional Budget Office (CBO). They conclude that on the day that these government agencies release information about projected federal deficits, financial markets respond to those announcements. An increase in projected deficits drives up interest rates. This announcement effect is evident for government securities of all maturities, but it is most significant in influencing longer-term yields. Additionally, employing so-called 'intervention analysis' as developed by Box and Tiao (1975), Quigley and Porter-Hudak (1994) have corroborated the results of Wachtel and Young (1987) and found them to be fairly robust. Building on Wachtel and Young's findings, Thorbecke (1993) has tried to discriminate between various explanations for the positive association of unexpected deficits and interest rates. He concludes that news of larger deficits makes the dollar appreciate and also causes a rise in interest rates, whereas news (innovations) of changes in government spending leaves interest rates unaffected. Taken together, this evidence indicates that financial markets expect deficits to crowd out investment. Ederington and Lee (1993) find that monthly announcements from the Treasury Department have a significant effect on the Treasury bond futures market.

In this chapter we apply the announcement effect methodology to the Federal Republic of Germany (FRG), using data covering the period 1987–93. Our choice is motivated both by the size of the German economy and the rapid increase in government budget deficits after the unification of the FRG and the former German Democratic Republic (GDR). Furthermore, Germany can be regarded as the anchor country of the European Monetary System (EMS), whose functioning will be analysed in detail in Chapters 5 and 6. The remainder of this chapter is organised as follows. Section II discusses the methodology that we will use. This is followed by a description of German fiscal policy and the resulting data for our analysis in section III. Section IV presents the empirical results and, finally, section V offers some conclusions.

II   Methodology

Following Wachtel and Young (1987), the basic framework is given by:

$$\Delta i^l = \alpha_0 + \alpha_1 (Z - Z^e) \tag{4.1}$$

where Δi^l is the change in long-term nominal interest rates which takes place at the time of the announcement, Z is an information announcement, and Z^e is the expected announcement. Thus, $(Z - Z^e)$ is the unanticipated component (the 'news' or 'innovation'). An announcement effect is present if α_1 differs significantly from zero.

It is possible to test whether financial markets also react to the anticipated part of the announcement – to test whether the market is efficient – by using:

$$\Delta i^l = \alpha_0 + \alpha_1 (Z - Z^e) + \alpha_2 Z \tag{4.2}$$

Market efficiency implies that $\alpha_2 = 0$.

As set out by Plosser (1982) there are at least three possible explanations for a positive association of deficit news and nominal interest rates. First, expected deficits may crowd out investment and raise real interest rates. According to the Ricardian approach, deficit effects can only be due to temporary government expenditure increases that affect interest rates (see previous chapters, Barro, 1987, and De Haan and Zelhorst, 1992). Finally, government deficits may be expected to be monetised in the future. Following Thorbecke (1993) we try to discriminate between these various explanations by estimating equations (4.3) and (4.4). In equation (4.3) news about government outlays is added as an additional explanatory variable:

$$\Delta i^{\,l} = \alpha_0 + \alpha_1 (Z_d - Z_d^e) + \alpha_3 (Z_g - Z_g^e) \qquad (4.3)$$

The subscripts indicate whether the innovation is related to the government deficit (d), or to government spending (g). Under the Ricardian approach, α_1 is expected to be zero, whereas α_3 will differ significantly from zero. In equation (4.4) the dependent variable is the US dollar–Deutschemark exchange rate:

$$\Delta s = \beta_0 + \beta_1 (Z - Z^e) \qquad (4.4)$$

where Δs denotes the change in the US dollar–Deutschemark exchange rate. The idea behind this equation is that news about an inflationary increase in the money stock will elicit a capital outflow and depreciate the currency (Deutschemark), whereas news of an increase in the real interest rate will result in a capital inflow, and lead to a currency appreciation (Engel and Frankel, 1984, and Thorbecke, 1993). So equation (4.4) allows to discriminate between the monetisation view and the other two hypotheses.

III   Data

Chapters 1 and 3 sketched the development of the deficit–income ratio in Germany since the early 1960s. This chapter focuses more specifically on the development of the German public finances in the period surrounding the unification of 1990. From Figure 1.5 we can see that before unification, the budget of Germany's public sector profited substantially from the strong economic upswing of the late 1980s. Since unification in 1990, however, government transfers to the new East-German 'Länder' amounted yearly to 4–5% of West-German GDP, which more or less wiped out the steady improvement in its public finances of the preceding years and pushed Germany's public sector borrowing requirement to 5.2% of GDP in 1993 (about DM 160 billion); the equivalent of roughly half domestic private savings. Uncertainty about the precise impact of such an unprecedented shock on the government budget led to a nose-to-tail sequence of deficit forecasts from various sources.

We focus on the effect of government deficit announcements in the period from 1987 to 1993 on the long-term interest rate (that is the domestic bond yield as published in the *Wall Street Journal*), for which data were kindly provided by Auke Koopal of Lombard Odier Asset Management. The rates are daily closing yields to maturity; so the dependent variable consists of the difference between the observation on the announcement day and the day before. With respect to deficit announcements, we have used public releases of three organisations. First, the Federal Ministry of Finance (Bundesministerium der Finanzen, BF) makes regular announcements of deficit projections in either Finance News (Finanznachrichten) or in formal Press Statements (Pressemitteilungen). These have been kindly provided by the Bundesministerium der Finanzen. Furthermore, we have gathered press statements from Bundesministerium officials (generally, the minister) as published in *Het Financieele Dagblad*. Second, the Bundesbank (BU) in its Monthly Bulletin (Monatsberichte) also publishes deficit projections. Finally, the Council of Economic Advisers (Sachverständigenrat, S) presents in its Annual Report (Jahresgutachten) deficit projections.

In our empirical analysis we use three deficit news variables: deficit innovations constructed on the basis of projections of all three institutions, innovations based on forecasts of the Bundesministerium der Finanzen only, and those based on projections of the Bundesbank and the Sachverständigenrat taken together. The first variable gives us 93 observations, which can be subdivided into 67 deficit projections from BF and 26 from BU/S. We concentrate on announcements concerning the budget deficit of the so-called Gebietskörperschaften, that is the deficit of consolidated government, excluding social security (central, state and local governments). The innovation is constructed as follows. Very often the announcement itself contains information about both the previous and the current projection in which case the innovation is the difference between these projections. In case the announcement only contains a new projection, we have calculated the innovation as the difference between the current and the previous projection of the deficit. The appendix describes the data used in greater detail.

Following Thorbecke (1993), we also try to discriminate between various explanations for a positive association of unexpected deficits and interest rates. For this approach we have used data on innovations in government spending, which have been constructed in a similar way as the deficit innovations, and data on 3-month Euromarket interest rates and the dollar/Deutschemark exchange rate, which are from Datastream and have been kindly provided by Bas van Aarle. As explained in the previous section, under this approach equations (4.3) and (4.4) are estimated. However, multicollinearity problems may arise as government spending and budget deficit innovations may be correlated.[5] The partial correlations between deficit and spending innovations for the various categories of our data set are 0.07 (all), 0.10 (BF), and −0.01 (BU/S), respectively; this does not indicate that multicollinearity is much of a problem.

IV   Empirical results

Table 4.1 presents our estimation results of equations (4.1) to (4.4). The first row shows the outcomes for equation (4.1), using the projections of all three institutions to construct the 'deficit news' variable. It follows that unexpected increases of the deficit raise nominal long-term interest rates.[6] Regression 4.1.2 adds the deficit variable itself in order to test market efficiency in the sense of equation (4.2). The variable is significant at conventional levels, while the coefficient α_1 of the news variable remains virtually unaffected. On the basis of this equation we have to reject the efficient market hypothesis for German long-term bond yields, a result that contrasts with the findings reported by Wachtel and Young (1987) for the United States. As regression 4.1.3 demonstrates, the positive association between deficit news and interest rates is not caused by innovations in government outlays, since the coefficient of innovations related to government outlays is not significantly different from zero. In this respect it may also be noted that the number of observations on innovations in government outlays is limited to 55, since the dataset contains less observations regarding these innovations.

So far, we have not taken up announcements of the money growth rate in our analysis. To examine whether this has influenced our results, we have re-estimated regression 4.1.1, including 'money surprises' $(Z-Z^e)_m$ as additional explanatory variable. A problem here is how to construct such a variable. Various studies have examined the response of asset markets to weekly money supply announcements in the US. A few studies have used fitted values from time-series models to represent expected changes in the money supply (see Cornell, 1983a, for a discussion). The more common procedure in American studies has been to assume that market expectations can be represented adequately by the median response to the weekly Money Market Services survey (see for instance Grossman, 1981, and Cornell, 1983b).[7] As far as we know, such survey data are not available for Germany. Therefore we have estimated ARIMA-models for the expected money (M3) growth rates.[8] Despite all this, it follows from regression 4.1.4 that our previous conclusions are not modified by the inclusion of this additional variable. In accordance with the results of Clark et al. (1988) for the US, we do not find evidence that money growth innovations affect interest rates.

In rows 4.1.5 and 4.1.6 of Table 4.1 we report the regression outcomes of equation (4.1), now differentiating between 'deficit news' of the Ministry of Finance on the one hand and the Bundesbank and the Sachverständigenrat on the other. It is very interesting to note that 'deficit news' from the Bundesministerium der Finanzen does not raise long-term interest rates, in

Table 4.1: Deficit news and interest rates

Data	C.T.	$(Z-Z^e)_d$	Z_d	$(Z-Z^e)_g$	$(Z-Z^e)_m$	Δi^s	R^2	F
4.1.1 all	−0.0003	0.0012						0.003	5.49#
(93)	(0.4)	(2.4)						
4.1.2 all	0.0078	0.0012	0.0001					0.012	12.15#
(93)	(3.8)	(2.4)	(4.3)					
4.1.3 all	−0.0003	0.0012		0.0001				0.003	2.77
(93)	(0.4)	(2.3)		(0.2)				
4.1.4 all	−0.0003	0.0013			−0.0008			0.003	2.82
(93)	(0.3)	(2.4)			(0.4)			
4.1.5 BF	−0.0003	0.0002						0.000	0.80
(67)	(0.4)	(0.3)						
4.1.6 BU/S	−0.0003	0.0027						0.006	11.20#
(26)	(0.4)	(3.3)						
4.1.7[1] all	0.0002	0.0000						0.000	0.24
(93)	(0.3)	(0.5)						
4.1.8 all	−0.0004	0.0011					0.1839	0.124	130.0#
(93)	(0.5)	(2.3)				(15.9)		
4.1.9 BU/S	−0.0005	0.0027					0.1843	0.127	134.4#
(26)	(0.6)	(3.6)				(16.0)		

Notes: Dependent variable is daily change in long-term nominal interest rate. Total number of observations in each regression is 1827; the number of non-zero observations on the deficit innovation variable is given in the Data column. C.T.: Constant; [1]: Dependent variable is DM/dollar exchange rate; R^2: Adjusted R-squared; F: F-statistic of regression; #: Significant at the 5%-level. Positive innovations in Z_d represent expected increases in the deficit.

contrast to deficit innovations based on projections from the Bundesbank and the Council of Economic Advisors. Likewise, Wachtel and Young (1987) and Thorbecke (1993) both found higher coefficients for CBO announcements than for OMB announcements.[9] Wachtel and Young suggest that this may be due to the fact that market participants have greater confidence in the economic assumptions made by CBO than those made by OMB, since CBO has a reputation for independence and integrity, whereas OMB tends to reflect the political views of the administration. Apparently, something similar must be the case with respect to the credibility of deficit announcements from the various sources in Germany.

Our results so far suggest that deficit news raises interest rates and that this positive association is not due to deficit financing of temporary government outlays. To test for two possible explanations of the positive relationship between government deficits and interest rates, we have finally estimated equation (4.4). As has been explained in section II, a negative impact of deficit news on the exchange rate is in accordance with the monetisation view, whereas a positive relationship corroborates the crowding out view. In regression 4.1.7 the coefficient of the deficit news variable turns out to be not significantly different from zero. So on the basis of this regression it is not possible to discriminate between the monetisation and the crowding out hypotheses.

Regressions 4.1.8 and 4.1.9 add changes in short-term (3-month Euromarket) interest rates to the regressors of 4.1.1 and 4.1.6, respectively, so that in fact the effect of deficit-news on the term structure of interest rates is tested. As might be expected, projections on deficits still to arise and to be financed in the relatively far future predominantly affect the longer end of the term structure.[10] In addition, Jorion and Mishkin (1991) present evidence that the German term structure provides better information on the future path of inflation than on the future path of short-term interest rates. Taken together this would imply that our evidence points at market perceptions concerning future monetisation of public deficits. Another line of research, however, leads us to believe that the monetisation view is not likely to be correct. It is well known that the Bundesbank is one of the most independent central banks. Research by Grilli et al. (1991), Cukierman (1992), and De Haan and Sturm (1992) has shown that relatively independent central banks are less inclined to monetary finance government budget deficits. Furthermore, Demopoulos et al. (1987) report that the Bundesbank did not accommodate government deficits in either the fixed or the flexible exchange rate period during their sample period. Similar findings are reported by Burdekin and Wohar (1990).

V   Conclusions

To the best of our knowledge the government budget deficit announcement effect methodology has, so far, only been applied to the case of the United States. Wachtel and Young (1987), Thorbecke (1993), Ederington and Lee (1993), and Quigley and Porter-Hudak (1994) report a positive financial market response to unexpected announcements of the federal budget deficit, which is especially strong for longer-term yields. In this chapter we have followed the same approach for Germany. The period surrounding unification with the former GDR forms an interesting test-case since government deficits have increased rapidly and, to a large extent, also unexpectedly. Using information on deficit projections from the Ministry of Finance, the Bundesbank and the Council of Economic Advisors, we find indeed a positive association between 'news' about the consolidated government budget deficit and changes in long-term interest rates. This association is, however, only significant if information comes from the Bundesbank and the Council of Economic Advisors. Our findings do not enable us to determine whether this positive and significant relationship between budget deficits and interest rates is due to the fear that government debt may crowd out private investment, or that it will be monetised in the near future. Other research, however, suggests that the possibility of the latter actually happening must be judged very unlikely.

Appendix: Sources and contents of the news

Definitions:

BF: Bundesministerium der Finanzen/Ministry of Finance.
FN: Finanznachrichten/Finance news.
PM: Pressemitteilung/Press statements.
BU: Bundesbank/German central bank.
MB: Monatsbericht/Monthly Bulletin.
S: Sachverständigenrat (Jahresgutachten)/Council of economic advisors (Annual report).
DB: Defizit der Bund/Federal deficit.
DL: Defizit der Länder/Deficit of the states.
DG: Defizit der Gebietskörperschaften (Abgrenzung der Finanzstatistik)/ Consolidated government deficit: Bund, Länder, Gemeinden, kommunale Zweckverbände, Lastenausgleichsfonds, ERP Sönder-vermogen, EG-Anteile, Kreditabwicklungsfonds, Fonds 'Deutsche Einheit' (seit/since 90/06/25).
G#:   Government spending.
##H1: First half of the year
##Q3: First three quarters of the year
*:   Excluding Berlin

From 90/07/30 onwards all definitions including the former German Democratic Republic.

Date	Source	Deficit	Innovation	Spending	Innovation
87/01/15	BF/FN	DB(86)=23.0	$\Delta D=-0.7$	GB(86)=261.6	$\Delta G=-1.9$
87/03/12	BF/FN	DL(86)=17.4	$\Delta D=-0.9$	GL(86)=243,6	$\Delta G=+1.5$
87/05/14	BF/FN	DB(88)=30.0	$\Delta D=+4.0$		
87/06/29	BF	DB(87)=26.3	$\Delta D=+4.0$	GB(88)=275.0	$\Delta G= 0$
		DB(88)=29.3			
87/09/18	BF	DB(87)=29	$\Delta D=+2.7$		
87/09/28	BF/PM	DL(87H1)=12.0	$\Delta D=+2.9$	GL(87H1)=120.7	$\Delta G=+2.1$
87/11/23	S	DG(87)=54.5	$\Delta D=-3.6$	GG(87)=651	$\Delta G=-4.6$
		DG(88)=66		GG(88)=671	
87/12/28	BF/FN	DL(87Q3)=14.3	$\Delta D=-0.6$	GL(87Q3)=180.8	$\Delta G=-0.5$
88/01/05	BF	DB(88)=40	$\Delta D=+10.5$		$\Delta G=+2.0$
88/01/14	BF/FN	DB(87)=27.5	$\Delta D=-1.5$	GB(87)=269.1	$\Delta G=+0.5$
88/03/01	BF/FN	DL(87)=19.2	$\Delta D=-3.0$	GL(87)=252.2	$\Delta G=-0.8$

Date	Source	Deficit	Innovation	Spending	Innovation
88/05/30	BF	DB(89)	$\Delta D=-5$		
88/06/10	BF	DB(89)=30	$\Delta D=-1.0$		
88/07/04	BF	DB(89)=32	$\Delta D=+2.0$		
88/07/06	BF/FN	DB(88)=39.2	$\Delta D=-0.8$	GB(88)=275.4	$\Delta G=+0.4$
88/07/07	BF/FN	DB(90)=36.0	$\Delta D=+5.1$	GB(90)=293.8	
88/08/04	BF	DB(88)=37	$\Delta D=-2.2$		
88/08/19	BU	DB(89)	$\Delta D=-5$		
88/08/23	BF/FN	DL(87)=19.4	$\Delta D=+0.2$	GL(87)=252.3	$\Delta G=+0.1$
88/09/19	BU/MB	DG(88)	$\Delta D=-3.25$		
		DB(89)=33			
88/09/28	BF/PM	DL(88H1)=10.5	$\Delta D=-1.9$	GL(88H1)=123.9	$\Delta G=+1.2$
88/11/07	BF	DB(89)=27.5	$\Delta D=-5.5$	GB(89)=290	$\Delta G=+1.8$
88/11/18	S	DG(88)=58	$\Delta D=-10.35$	GG(88)=673	$\Delta G=-1.6$
		DG(89)=45		GG(89)=700	
88/12/21	BU/MB	DG(88)=55	$\Delta D=-3$		
		DB(89)=29			
88/12/22	BF/FN	DL(88Q3)=11.8	$\Delta D=-1.0$	GL(88Q3)=185.6	$\Delta G=+0.5$
89/01/16	BF/FN	DB(89)=27.9	$\Delta D=-1.1$	GB(89)=290.3	$\Delta G=+0.3$
89/02/20	BU/MB	DG(89)=35.5	$\Delta D=-8.4$	GG(89)=700.0	$\Delta G=-0.3$
89/03/03	BF/FN	DL(88)=16.5	$\Delta D=-2.3$	GL(88)=257.8	$\Delta G=-1.7$
89/05/31	BF/FN	DB(89)=27.8	$\Delta D=-0.1$	GB(89)=291.3	$\Delta G=+1.0$
89/06/28	BF	DB(90)=33.6	$\Delta D=-2.4$	GB(90)=301.0	$\Delta G=+7.2$
89/07/05	BF/FN	DB(90)=33.7	$\Delta D=+0.1$	GB(90)=301.3	$\Delta G=+0.3$
		DB(91)=32.2		GB(91)=311.4	
89/09/21	BU/MB	DG(89)=27.5	$\Delta D=-7.9$		
89/11/20	S	DG(89)=27	$\Delta D=-0.5$	GG(89)=695	$\Delta G=-6$
		DG(90)=37		GG(90)=719.5	
89/12/20	BU/MB	DG(89)=20	$\Delta D=-7$		
		DB(90)=28			
89/12/21	BF/FN	DB(90)=26.9	$\Delta D=-1.1$	GB(90)=300.1	$\Delta G=-1.2$
90/01/16	BF	DB(89)=17.9	$\Delta D=-9$	GB(89)	$\Delta G=-1.5$
90/02/19	BU/MB	DG(90)=59.0	$\Delta D=+23.1$	GG(90)=736.7	$\Delta G=+17.2$
90/03/01	BF/FN	DL(89)=7.4	$\Delta D=-0.1$	GL(89)=269.2	$\Delta G=-1.5$
90/06/18	BF	DB(90)=30.9	$\Delta D=-2.6$		
		DB(91)=38		GB(91)=309.1	$\Delta G=-2.3$
90/06/22	BF/FN	DB(90)=31.0	$\Delta D=-1.9$	GB(90)=311.8	$\Delta G=+4.9$
90/06/25	BU/MB	DG(90)=70	$\Delta D=+13.5$		
		DG(91)=86			
90/06/26	BF	DB(91)=31.4	$\Delta D=-6.6$	GB(91)=324	$\Delta G=+14.9$

Date	Source	Deficit	Innovation	Spending	Innovation
90/07/03	BF/FN	DG(90)=79 DG(91)=96	$\Delta D=-1$	GB(92)=334.0	$\Delta G=+14$
90/07/30	BF	DG(90)	$\Delta D=+10$	GG(90)	$\Delta G=+10$
90/08/01	BF	DG(90)	$\Delta D=+2$	GG(90)	$\Delta G=+2$
90/09/27	BU	DG(90)=100 DG(91)=150	$\Delta D=+9$		
90/09/28	BF	DB(90)=66.8	$\Delta D=+5.8$	GB(90)	$\Delta G=+8.1$
90/11/14	BF/FN	DG(91)=140 DB(91)=70	$\Delta D=-10$	GB(91)	$\Delta G=-35$
90/11/15	S	DG(90)=98 DG(91)=160	$\Delta D=-7.8$	GG(90)=768.5 GG(91)=981	$\Delta G=-5.9$
90/12/19	BU/MB	DG(90)=110	$\Delta D=+12$		
91/01/28	BF	DB(90)=50	$\Delta D=-17$		
91/01/30	BF/FN	DL(90Q3)=12.7	$\Delta D=-2.1$	GL(90Q3)=202.2	$\Delta G=-0.8$
91/02/14	BF	DB(91)=69.6	$\Delta D=-0.4$	GB(91)=399.7	$\Delta G=-10$
91/02/19	BU/MB	DG(91)=155	$\Delta D=-4.6$	GG(90)=820	$\Delta G=+51.5$
91/06/19	BU/MB	DG(91)=160 DB(91)=67.5	$\Delta D=+5$	GB(91)=410	$\Delta G=+10.3$
91/06/24	BF	DB(91)=65 DB(92)=50	$\Delta D=-2.5$		
91/07/09	BF/FN	DB(92)=49.7	$\Delta D=-0.3$	GB(92)=422.5	
91/08/19	BF	DB(91)=60	$\Delta D=-6.4$		
91/09/23	BU/MB	DG(91)=140	$\Delta D=-11.1$		
91/09/24	BF	DG(91)=120	$\Delta D=-20$		
91/10/17	BF/FN	DB(91)=66.4	$\Delta D=+6.4$	GB(91)=410.3	$\Delta G=0$
91/11/14	S	DG(91)=135 DG(92)=131	$\Delta D=+8.6$	GG(91)=972 GG(92)=1036	$\Delta G=-9$
91/12/03	BF/FN	DB(91)=60	$\Delta D=-6.4$	GB(92)=422.2	$\Delta G=-0.3$
91/12/18	BU/MB	DG(91)=130 DG(92)=120 DB(92)=46.5	$\Delta D=+1.4$		
92/01/24	BF	DG(91)=127.5 DB(91)=52.1	$\Delta D=-2.5$	GB(91)=401.8	$\Delta G=-8.5$
92/05/05	BF/FN	DB(92)=45	$\Delta D=-1.5$	GB(92)=426.2	$\Delta G=+4$
92/05/13	BF/FN	DB(92)=42.7	$\Delta D=-2.3$	GB(92)=426.0	$\Delta G=-0.2$
92/07/01	BF/FN	DB(92)=40.5 DB(93)=38	$\Delta D=-2.2$	GB(92)=425.1 GB(93)=435.7	$\Delta G=-0.9$
92/07/02	BF/FN	DL*(91)=25.5	$\Delta D=-13.3$	GL*(91)=356.2	$\Delta G=-7.2$
92/07/10	BF/FN	DL(91)=27.2	$\Delta D=-4.3$	GL(91)=390.1	$\Delta G=-4.0$
92/09/14	BU/MB	DG(92)=110	$\Delta D=-4$		

Date	Source	Deficit	Innovation	Spending	Innovation
92/11/04	BF	DB(93)=44	ΔD=+6	GB(93)=435.7	ΔG= 0
92/11/16	S	DG(92)=120	ΔD=+10	GG(92)=1000	ΔG=−36
		DG(93)=137		GG(93)=1059	
92/11/23	BF	DB(93)=43	ΔD=−1	GB(93)=436	ΔG=+0.3
92/12/17	BU/MB	DG(92)=110	ΔD=−10		
93/01/18	BF	DB(93)=48	ΔD=+5		
93/01/20	BF	DB(93)=50	ΔD=+2		
93/01/21	BF	DB(93)=52	ΔD=+2		
		DG(93)=132.5			
93/01/27	BF/FN	DB(92)=38.6	ΔD=−1.9	GB(92)=427.2	ΔG=+2.1
93/02/17	BU/MB	DG(93)=125	ΔD=−7.5		
93/03/16	BF	DB(93)=54.7	ΔD=+2.7		
93/03/19	BF	DB(93)=60	ΔD=+5.3		
93/04/21	BF	DB(93)=67.7	ΔD=+7.7		
93/04/29	BF	DB(93)=70	ΔD=+2.3		
93/05/17	BF	DG(94)	ΔD=+25.8		
93/05/26	BF	DB(94)	ΔD=−20		
93/06/23	BU/MB	DG(93)=150	ΔD=+7		
93/06/29	BF	DB(94)=70	ΔD=−10		
93/07/13	BF	DB(94)=67	ΔD=−3	GB(94)=478.4	ΔG=+26.4
93/11/11	BF/PM	DB(94)=69.1	ΔD=+1.6	GB(94)=479.95	ΔG=+1.6
93/11/15	S	DG(93)=160	ΔD=+10	GG(93)=1071	ΔG=+12
93/12/02	BF/PM	DB(93)=71.5	ΔD=+1.5		
93/12/14	BU/MB	DG(93)=150	ΔD=−11.5		

Note: In case the announcement is from the Bundesministerium der Finanzen (BF) but not from Pressemitteilungen (PM) or Finanznachrichten (FN), or from the Bundesbank (BU) but not from the Monatsberichte (MB), it is taken from Het Financieele Dagblad. *A dotted line is drawn at the time of the (re) unification.*

Notes

1. Compare for example Knoester and Mak (1994) or Nunes-Correia and Stemitsiotis (1993) who both report a weak but significant positive impact of deficits on interest rates in Germany.
2. This approach has been used extensively to examine the effect of new economic statistics (including for example announcements regarding the money stock) on interest rates. See, for instance, Dwyer and Hafer (1989) and Ederington and Lee (1993) and the references cited therein. Similarly, various authors have analysed the effects of new information about firms on bond and stock markets. See, for instance, Datta and Dhillon (1993).
3. However, the announcement effect methodology does not provide insight into the reasons for any observed relationship. Increased deficits may lead to higher interest rates for various reasons, like crowding out of capital accumulation, fear of monetisation (see for example De Haan and Zelhorst, 1990b), or because deficits are due to temporary government expenditure

increases that affect interest rates (see Barro, 1987, and De Haan and Zelhorst, 1992). Following the approach of Thorbecke (1993), we will try to discriminate between these alternative explanations.

4. Simultaneity problems occur because interest rates vary procyclically, whereas deficits vary countercyclically (see Chapter 3). Temporal aggregation problems are due to the fact that if financial markets react to news about deficits, they do so instantaneously, so that regressions in which quarterly or annual data are used may not capture the response appropriately.

5. Indeed, Thorbecke (1993) reports partial correlation coefficients which are quite high and that may cast some doubt on his findings.

6. As with most event studies, the R^2-statistics are low. These low values occur because economists can explain only a small fraction of the tremendous variation in financial data. More important here is the significance of the estimated coefficients on the various innovations.

7. Whether these survey data are rational is contended. Grossman (1981) concludes that these data efficiently embed available information and that unexpected money supply movements increase interest rates. Similar results are reported by Cornell (1983b) for the period after October 1979. In sharp contrast, Clark et al. (1988) conclude that systematic errors occur in these survey data, which are associated with certain weeks when social security payments are made. When the survey data are corrected to eliminate these systematic errors, the apparent negative relationship between interest rates and expected money supply changes disappears. Interest rates are not systematically related to anticipated or unanticipated money supply changes during the period February 1984 to December 1986.

8. Data on M3 are taken from the Monatsberichte of the Bundesbank. We have proceeded as follows. Using each time the 48 previous monthly observations for the growth rate of M3, the best ARIMA-model according to Akaike's Final Prediction Error (*FPE*) criterion, as described in Chapter 1, has been employed to generate a forecast for the money growth rate. The difference between this forecast and the actual money growth rate is the 'money surprise'.

9. Still, in their regressions OMB announcements did exert a significant (positive) effect on long-term interest rates.

10. This obsevation was confirmed by direct regressions of deficit news on the change in short-term interest rates ($\alpha_1 = 0.0007$, $t = 0.7$) and on the change in the term structure of interest rates ($\alpha_1 = 0.0021$, $t = 2.0$). It may be noted, however, that Wachtel and Young (1987) and Thorbecke (1993) report a significant impact of CBO deficit announcements on three month interest rates for the US, while OMB projections only significantly affect interest rates of a maturity of 20 years or more.

5 Interest rate differentials and exchange rate policies in the European Monetary System

The one person in your family who ever asks your advice about economics is your uncle, who is in the import-export business. A while back he called you about a foreign exchange issue. 'Let's suppose I owe a million German marks, payable in one month.' *he said.* 'We have the money to pay the bill in dollars, so the issue is whether to put the money into marks now or later. I figure we should put the money wherever it would earn the highest rate, but my treasurer, one of those MBA hot shots, tells me that this is irrelevant because if the interest rate is high in Germany that means that the mark is expected to go down. When I ask her what we should do, she says that it doesn't matter. *"Flip a coin,"* she says! Is this what I am paying her so much money for? To flip coins?' *You tried to calm your uncle down, and explain the idea of efficient markets to him, but he was unconvinced.*

Froot and Thaler (1990), pp.179–80

I Introduction

In 1978 the countries of the European Union founded the European Monetary System (EMS). Its cornerstone is the Exchange Rate Mechanism (ERM), the agreement to limit bilateral exchange rate fluctuations among participating countries, which became effective 13 March 1979. The ERM limited bilateral exchange rate fluctuations to margins of plus/minus 2.25 percent around predetermined central parities. Italy obtained a margin of plus/minus 6 percent for the lira, which was reduced to the narrow band in January 1990. Greece chose not to participate in the ERM; Spain joined it in July 1989; the United Kingdom in October 1990 and Portugal in April 1992. These countries also entered the ERM with a broad margin. After hefty speculations the Italian lira and the British pound were forced out of the ERM in September 1992. After continuing speculative attacks on most of the remaining participating currencies and subsequent devaluations, the margins of the ERM were widened to plus/minus 15 percent in August 1993.

Monetary policy in member countries of the EMS is to a large extent aimed at a stable exchange rate vis-à-vis the German Deutschemark. Underlying the choice for this so-called 'hard-currency option' is the importance of Germany as a partner in foreign trade for the countries considered and, above all, the pronounced anti-inflation reputation of the German monetary authorities.[1] Despite the proclaimed fixed (but adjustable) exchange rates, small but persistent interest rate differentials vis-à-vis Germany have existed in all countries in the EMS area during the last decade. On average, short-term interest rate differentials were in the order of magnitude of a few percentage points from the start of the ERM onwards, but they clearly shrank in the late 1980s. For some countries positive interest differentials emerged although average inflation had been lower than German inflation during much of the period under consideration.

Four possible explanations have been offered for the existence of these interest differentials. First, they may originate from the existence of formal impediments to international capital movements. In the Netherlands, the last minor barriers to full capital mobility were already removed in July 1983, whereas on the other hand in Ireland similar liberalisation measures did not take place until January 1993. Taking a middle position, countries like Austria, Belgium, Denmark, France, and Italy first also isolated the domestic money market from international financial markets; only in 1990 (1988 in the case of Denmark) were the last exchange controls abolished.[2] As a second potential source of interest differentials, differential tax treatment of interest income in the various countries can play a role.[3] In the third place, interest differentials may reflect that market participants continuously expected a devaluation in spite of the proclaimed (fixed) exchange rate policy. Finally, differentials may be caused by risk premia, due to uncertainty with respect to exchange rate policy as perceived by the market. The announced exchange rate policy may not have been completely credible, since differences in economic fundamentals have persisted, for example in inflation, unemployment, fiscal policy, and current account positions. The sheer proclamation of a fixed exchange rate policy is of course not sufficient to remove the devaluation risk since one would not expect a government to announce that it contemplates a devaluation somewhere in the future.[4]

In this and the next chapter we will direct our attention to the last two possible explanations of interest rate differentials. We consider the complete term structure of interest rate differentials with Germany for the currencies participating in the Exchange Rate Mechanism of the EMS. It is clear that for a small open economy which faces an exogenous term structure of foreign (in case of the ERM: German) interest rates, the domestic term structure will be related to the term structure of expected currency depreciation, that is, if domestic and foreign interest rates are sufficiently integrated.

Recently, Svensson (1991b) has developed a theory of the term structure of interest differentials in a target zone. Svensson has also examined data on the term structure of Swedish interest differentials focusing on a stable period for the Swedish krona and found them to be negatively correlated with the exchange rate, which is broadly consistent with his theory. Other authors, however, have reported positive correlations between devaluation expectations (as measured by drift-adjusted interest differentials)[5] and exchange rates, contradicting Svensson's theory for a considerable number of countries (Caramazza, 1993, Chen and Giovannini, 1993, Cukierman et al., 1993, and Thomas, 1994). In this chapter we will show that the apparently conflicting results in Svensson (1991b) are a consequence of the absence of a time-varying (endogenous) devaluation risk in his model.

We therefore extend Svensson's analysis in three directions. First we present a model for the term structure of interest differentials in a target zone with time-varying devaluation risk; this model is inspired by previous work by Bertola and Svensson (1993) and Lindberg and Söderlind (1993). Secondly, we analyse the term structure of interest differentials in seven countries: Austria, Belgium, Denmark, France, Ireland, Italy, and the Netherlands. Although Austria has not been a formal member of the EMS until 1995, it has pegged its currency to the Deutschemark ever since the late 1970s and can henceforth be regarded as a 'shadow member' of the ERM. The other countries have participated in the ERM right from the beginning, albeit that the Italian currency had, until January 1990, a plus/minus 6 percent band instead of the usual plus/minus 2.25 percent band. Our estimation period is 1983–93, except for the lira, where our sample period ends in August 1992; in September of the same year the Italian lira was kicked out of the ERM. Finally, we explicitly differentiate between stable and unstable periods for the various currencies taken into account.

The chapter is organised as follows. Section II sketches the theoretical background in which the interest rate differential is linked to expected exchange rate movements and uncertainty concerning these changes. We will make a distinction between realignments of central parities and movements of the exchange rate within the band as proposed by Svensson (1993). Section III presents an empirical exploration of the relationship between interest differentials and exchange rates for the countries investigated. The last section summarises and concludes.

II   Theoretical background

This section sketches the theoretical background of the relationship between interest rate differentials and exchange rate movements. First, a portfolio model of interest rate determination in a small open economy is presented (section II.1). An expression for the interest differential vis-à-vis the rest of the world is derived which bears clear resemblance to the well-known uncovered interest parity (UIP) condition. Second, we will briefly review and integrate the theory on target zones with time-varying devaluation risk developed by Bertola and Svensson (1993) and Lindberg and Söderlind (1993). This procedure results in an isomorphic extension of the Lindberg and Söderlind solution (section II.2). Subsequently, we will examine in detail the determination of the term structure of interest rate differentials in such a target zone (section II.3).

II.1   A portfolio model of interest rate determination

In this section we look at the effects of exchange rate risk on the interest rate differential for a small open economy vis-à-vis the rest of the world, assuming perfect capital mobility. Following Giovannini and Jorion (1988) and Andersen and Sørensen (1991), we consider a discrete-time two-asset model in which a representative investor has to decide whether to invest in domestic securities or in foreign securities. Although the nominal return on both assets is known with certainty, the real rate of return may differ due to the risk arising from the possibility of exchange rate adjustments.

A domestic investor is assumed to maximise a utility function defined over the (conditional) expectation (E) and the (conditional) variance (Var) of real wealth in the next period (w_{t+1}):

$$Max\ U\{E_t[w_{t+1}], Var_t[w_{t+1}]\}, \qquad U_1>0,\ U_2<0. \tag{5.1}$$

Furthermore, he allocates a fraction θ of his initial nominal wealth W_t to the domestic security DB, and a fraction $(1-\theta)$ to the foreign security FB, so that:

$$\begin{aligned}\theta_t W_t &= DB_t \\ (1-\theta_t)W_t &= S_t FB_t,\end{aligned} \tag{5.2}$$

where S_t represents the initial price of foreign currency measured in units of domestic currency. Moreover, we assume that the foreign price level is constant and normalised to one and, imposing some form of relative purchasing power parity, that the exchange rate varies proportionally with the domestic price level P.[6] Hence, $P=S$ and next period real wealth w_{t+1} equals nominal wealth divided by S_{t+1}:

$$w_{t+1} = \frac{(1+rr_t)\theta_t W_t}{S_{t+1}} + \frac{(1+rr_t^*)(1-\theta_t)W_t}{S_t}, \tag{5.3}$$

where $1+rr_t$ is the gross nominal rate of return during the time to maturity and an asterisk indicates a corresponding foreign variable. As a result of the assumption of a small open economy without capital restrictions, the foreign (net) rate of return rr_t* is presumed to be exogeneous. Conditions abroad affect the domestic economy, but the economy is too small to have any influence on conditions abroad.

Likewise, the objective function of a representative foreign investor can be written:

$$Max \ U^* \{ E_t[w_{t+1}^*], Var_t[w_{t+1}^*] \}, \qquad U_1^* > 0, \ U_2^* < 0. \qquad (5.4)$$

To this end he allocates a fraction θ^* of his initial nominal wealth W_t^* to the domestic security DB, and a fraction $(1-\theta^*)$ to the foreign security FB:

$$\theta_t^* W_t^* = \frac{DB_t^*}{S_t} \qquad (5.5)$$

$$(1-\theta_t^*) W_t^* = FB_t^*.$$

Next period real wealth for foreign investors can thus be written as:

$$w_{t+1}^* = \frac{(1+rr_t)\theta_t^* W_t^* S_t}{S_{t+1}} + (1+rr_t^*)(1-\theta_t^*) W_t^*. \qquad (5.6)$$

The exchange rate in the next period is assumed to be determined by:

$$\frac{1}{S_{t+1}} = \frac{1 + \epsilon_{t+1}}{S_t}, \qquad (5.7)$$

where ϵ is a stochastic variable distributed with expected value $E_t[\epsilon_{t+1}]$ and variance $Var_t[\epsilon_{t+1}]$. If ϵ is positive, the domestic currency appreciates in value, whereas a negative value of ϵ_{t+1} points to a depreciation.

Combining equations (5.1), (5.3), and (5.7), it can readily be shown that the optimal share of initial wealth placed in domestic securities by domestic investors is given by (see appendix A):

$$\theta_t = \frac{rr_t - rr_t^* + (1+rr_t)E_t[\epsilon_{t+1}]}{\phi(1+rr_t)^2 Var_t[\epsilon_{t+1}]}, \qquad (5.8)$$

where $\phi = -2(W/S)U_2/U_1 > 0$ denotes the coefficient of relative risk aversion for domestic investors which is assumed to be constant. Similarly, foreign investors find it optimal to invest a share θ^* of initial wealth in the domestic security, which can be expressed as:

$$\theta_t^* = \frac{rr_t - rr_t^* + (1+rr_t)E_t[\epsilon_{t+1}]}{\phi^*(1+rr_t)^2 Var_t[\epsilon_{t+1}]}, \tag{5.9}$$

where the coefficient of relative risk aversion for foreign investors is represented by $\phi^* = -2W^*U_2^*/U_1^* > 0$, which is also assumed to be constant. The equilibrium condition for the domestic securities market can now be expressed by:

$$SB = \frac{rr_t - rr_t^* + (1+rr_t)E_t[\epsilon_{t+1}]}{(1+rr_t)^2 Var_t[\epsilon_{t+1}]}\left(\frac{W_t}{\phi} + \frac{S_t W_t^*}{\phi^*}\right), \qquad SB > 0, \tag{5.10}$$

where SB denotes the supply of domestic securities assumed to be constant, and the right-hand side of (5.10) represents the total demand for the domestic security, $DB+DB^*$. Solving for a stable equilibrium (stable in the sense that $\delta(DB+DB^*)/\delta rr > 0$) yields:

$$rr_t - rr_t^* = -(1+rr_t)E_t[\epsilon_{t+1}] + \frac{SB(1+rr_t)^2 Var_t[\epsilon_{t+1}]}{W_t/\phi + S_t W_t^*/\phi^*},$$

$$for \quad 1+rr_t < \frac{2(1+rr_t^*)}{1+E_t[\epsilon_{t+1}]}. \tag{5.11}$$

From equation (5.11) we can deduce that in addition to the uncovered interest parity condition $rr_t + (1+rr_t)E_t[\epsilon_{t+1}] = rr_t^*$ there exists a (country-specific) risk premium, which is non-linear in the nominal rate of return, and further depends on the supply of domestic securities relative to the total amount of domestic as well as foreign wealth, the uncertainty concerning the expected exchange rate movement $Var_t[\epsilon_{t+1}]$, and the degree of risk aversion of market participants. Risk-averse investors require a higher premium to invest in a security with uncertain real return, that is the domestic security.

Furthermore, in case of a bilateral exchange rate with a target zone and an explicitly-pronounced central parity, the expected exchange rate change can be split into two parts: the expected realignment, that is a jump in the central parity, and the expected exchange rate movement within the band. To fix such notions, we define the exchange rate within the band x_t as the log (percentage) deviation from bilateral central parity (Svensson, 1993):

$$x_t = s_t - c_t \equiv \ln S_t - \ln C_t, \qquad (5.12)$$

where C_t denotes the central parity. Then, applying the familiar approximation of the natural logarithm to equation (5.7):

$$\epsilon_{t+1} = s_t - s_{t+1} = c_t - c_{t+1} + x_t - x_{t+1}. \qquad (5.13)$$

Thus far, we have only considered a maturity of one period, without further specification. For a period (maturity) of τ years equations (5.11) to (5.13) may be combined as follows:

$$i_t^\tau - i_t^{\tau,*} = (1+\tau i_t^\tau)\frac{E_t[\Delta c_{t+\tau}]}{\tau} + (1+\tau i_t^\tau)\frac{E_t[\Delta x_{t+\tau}]}{\tau} + \psi_t, \quad where$$

$$\psi_t = \frac{SB(1+\tau i_t^\tau)^2 \, Var_t[\epsilon_{t+1}]}{\tau\,(W_t/\phi + S_t W_t^*/\phi^*)}, \quad \Delta c_{t+\tau} = c_{t+\tau} - c_t, \quad \Delta x_{t+\tau} = x_{t+\tau} - x_t,$$

$$(5.14)$$

and $i_t^\tau \equiv rr_t/\tau$ is the annualised net rate of return (nominal interest rate) for the maturity τ. From equation (5.14) we can see that the nominal interest rate differential roughly consists of three explanatory components: the expected rate of devaluation, the expected exchange rate movement within the band, and a country-specific risk premium. However, Svensson (1992a) argues that the incidence of the latter is likely to be negligible in a target zone system, even when there is devaluation risk.[7] Hence, by far the largest part of interest rate differentials remains to be explained by the other two components, on which we will therefore mainly concentrate in this chapter.

II.2 The target zone model of exchange rate determination
We use the basic log-linear model of exchange rate determination in a small open economy. Following Krugman (1991) and others, it is assumed that the exchange rate satisfies an asset-pricing relationship:

$$s_t = f_t + \alpha\,\frac{E_t[ds_t]}{dt}, \qquad (5.15)$$

where $E_t[\cdot]$ denotes the expectation taken conditionally on the information available at time t. Equation (5.15) postulates that the log of the actual exchange rate is equal to a scalar indicator of underlying economic factors, the 'fundamental' exchange rate f_t, plus a speculative term proportional to the expected rate of depreciation of the actual exchange rate. The indicator f_t is assumed to follow an exogenously given Markov process, to be defined later.

It is controlled by the monetary authorities so as to keep the exchange rate within a pre-specified fluctuation band $[s^l, s^u]$ by reflecting the fundamental at appropriately specified boundaries, unless a realignment occurs (Bertola and Svensson, 1993). When a realignment occurs, the upper and lower boundaries of the target zone are re-specified and the central parity, the actual exchange rate and the fundamental exchange rate all jump to their new levels, without changing their relative positions.

Analoguously to equation (5.12) we can also split the expected rate of change of the actual exchange rate into the expected movement of the exchange rate within the band and the expected rate of devaluation:

$$\frac{E_t[ds_t]}{dt} = \frac{E_t[dx_t]}{dt} + \frac{E_t[dc_t]}{dt}. \tag{5.16}$$

Market expectations of realignments can be modelled as the product of the time-varying probability of a realignment p_t and the per unit time expected conditional realignment size $E_t[dc_t|Realignment]/dt$. If in one of these terms an (exogenous) stochastic element is present, $E_t[dc_t]/dt$ will also fluctuate stochastically over time. Moreover, we assume that part of the expected rate of devaluation is endogenous and depends in a linear way on the position of the exchange rate within the band.[8] We therefore model the expected rate of devaluation as a hybrid:

$$\frac{E_t[dc_t]}{dt} = \frac{p_t E_t[dc_t|R]}{dt} \equiv g_t + \gamma x_t, \tag{5.17}$$

where g_t is also a diffusion process, to be defined later. If we assume that the vector process $[f_t, g_t]$ is Markov in levels, it is reasonable to postulate that both the exchange rate and the expected rate of total depreciation can be written, for given target zone boundaries, as functions of the two state variables. If we subsequently define a new composite state variable:

$$h_t \equiv f_t - c_t + \alpha g_t, \tag{5.18}$$

it can easily be seen by combining equations (5.15) to (5.18) that the exchange rate determination can now be reduced to a single state-variable problem, in which one must solve the stochastic differential equation:

$$x_t(h_t) = \frac{1}{\alpha \mu} h_t + \frac{1}{\mu} \frac{E_t[dx_t]}{dt}, \qquad with \ \mu \equiv \frac{1 - \alpha \gamma}{\alpha}, \tag{5.19}$$

and newly defined boundary conditions:

$$x(h^l) = s^l - c, \quad x(h^u) = s^u - c, \quad x'(h^l) = x'(h^u) = 0, \quad (5.20)$$

where the last equality represents the smooth-pasting conditions that the exchange rate must obey.

From the boundary conditions of equation (5.20) we can see that the authorities' concern for nominal exchange rate movements must take the form of a fluctuation band $[h^l,h^u]$ for the composite fundamental process h_t; it is allowed to fluctuate but it is also subject to infrequent regulation, which can take various forms. In reality central banks mainly defend exchange rate bands by intramarginal 'leaning-against-the-wind' interventions, so as to keep the exchange rate well away from the edges.[9] In the presence of such mean-reverting intramarginal interventions in f, h has a variable drift which becomes negative when h exceeds its central value (where $x(h_0)=0$), and vice versa (Lindberg and Söderlind, 1993). Allowing for correlation ρ in the increments to f and g, we can model the process for h as regulated Ornstein–Uhlenbeck:

$$
\begin{aligned}
df_t &= -\lambda(h_t-h_0)dt+\sigma_f dW_{f,t}+dc_t+dL_t-dU_t, \quad \begin{cases} dL>0 \ \text{only if } h=h^l \\ dU>0 \ \text{only if } h=h^u \end{cases} \\
dg_t &= \sigma_g dW_{g,t}, \quad dW_{g,t}dW_{f,t}=\rho\,dt \\
dh_t &= -\lambda(h_t-h_0)dt + \sigma dW_t+dL_t-dU_t, \quad \sigma \equiv \sqrt{\sigma_f^2+\alpha^2\sigma_g^2+2\alpha\rho\sigma_f\sigma_g}.
\end{aligned}
\qquad (5.21)
$$

in which λ is a constant positive policy parameter; the σ's denote constant instantaneous standard deviations; dW_t stands for an increment to a standard Wiener process; L_t and U_t are lower and upper regulators which represent the cumulated infinitesimal interventions at the margins. As noted by Tristani (1994), formulating the model in this way also provides a stronger economic rationale for modelling devaluation expectations depending on the position of the exchange rate within the band (equation 5.17). If the monetary authorities prefer intramarginal interventions, the exchange rate should rarely approach the edges of the band. If this does happen nevertheless, it could be interpreted as a sign that the monetary authorities start to lose control over the exchange rate process, thereby offering a justification for increased realignment expectations. In turn, endogenous devaluation expectations seriously limit Svensson's (1994) case for intramarginal 'leaning-with-the-wind' interventions in reaction to possible shocks in foreign interest rates, exogenous devaluation expectations, and/or foreign exchange risk premia, since the trade-off between exchange rate and interest rate variability all but vanishes. In appendix B it is shown that the solution to the model (5.19)–(5.21) is isomorph to the one obtained by Delgado and Dumas (1991), Froot and Obstfeld (1991a), and Lindberg and Söderlind (1993):

$$x_t(h_t) = \frac{\mu h_t + \lambda h_0}{\alpha \mu (\mu + \lambda)} + A_1 M\left[\frac{\mu}{2\lambda}; \frac{1}{2}; \frac{\lambda (h_t - h_0)^2}{\sigma^2}\right]$$

$$+ A_2 M\left[\frac{\mu + \lambda}{2\lambda}; \frac{3}{2}; \frac{\lambda (h_t - h_0)^2}{\sigma^2}\right] \frac{\sqrt{\lambda}(h_t - h_0)}{\sigma},$$

(5.22)

where $M[\cdot;\cdot;\cdot]$ is Kummer's (confluent hypergeometric) function; $A_{1,2}$ denote constants of integration to be determined by the boundary conditions of equation (5.20). The last two components of this solution capture the effect of the infinitesimal regulators at the margins. As in Lindberg and Söderlind (1993), the first component can be interpreted as a managed floating exchange rate, where intramarginal interventions take place, albeit in the absence of reflecting barriers to the exchange rate. This solution takes the form of what Tristani (1994) has dubbed 'the steeper S'. In contrast to the managed float solution of Lindberg and Söderlind (1993), which has a slope equal to $1/[1+\alpha\lambda]<1$, the one obtained here has a slope equal to $1/[1+\alpha(\lambda-\gamma)]$; this slope is smaller than one only if $\lambda>\gamma$. But a low-speed mean-reverting process of the fundamental, and/or a high sensitivity of devaluation expectations with respect to the position of the exchange rate within the band may lead to a situation where $\partial x/\partial h>1$ and $x(h)>h$, even for a region where x and h are positive, a feature that will also apply to the target zone solution.

II.3   The term structure of interest differentials in a target zone

As section II.1 has already demonstrated, in a small open economy the interest rate differential vis-à-vis the rest of the world can roughly be decomposed into three explanatory parts: the expected exchange rate movement within the band, the expected rate of devaluation, and a country-specific risk premium ψ_t (equation 5.14). Hence, the instantaneous interest differential (that is for $\tau\to 0$) δ can be written as a function of g, h, and ψ:

$$\delta_t(g_t, h_t; \psi_t) = \delta_{x,t}(h_t) + \delta_{c,t}(g_t, h_t) + \psi_t$$

$$= \frac{x_t(h_t) - h_t}{\alpha} + g_t + \psi_t, \quad \text{for } h^l \le h_t \le h^u,$$

(5.23)

where $\delta_x \equiv E[dx]/dt$, $\delta_c \equiv E[dc]/dt$, and the last equality follows from substitution of (5.17) and (5.19). The expected instantaneous depreciation within the exchange rate band for a zero expected rate of devaluation ($g, \gamma=0$) only depends on h with $\delta_x'(h)<0$ (Svensson, 1991a). Since the relation between h and the exchange rate is positive and monotonic, $\delta_x'(x)$ is also negative: the higher the value of the exchange rate within the band, the greater the probability of a (mean-reverting) intervention to appreciate the exchange rate within the band.

With non-zero devaluation risk, however, the observable negative relation between exchange rates and (instantaneous) interest differentials may break down due to two (closely related) mechanisms. First, for given f an increase in g directly raises δ as well as h, and the exchange rate depreciates within the band as investors, fearing imminent devaluation, shy away from domestic currency positions. Second, the expected rate of devaluation may be very sensitive to the position of the exchange rate within the band, leading to the before-mentioned 'steeper S' solution, where $x(h)>h$ and $\partial[(x-h)/\alpha]/\partial x>0$: the expected rate of depreciation within the band may also be dominated by the effect of an expected instantaneous realignment, which more than offsets the mean-reverting effect of future (intramarginal) interventions.

Thus far, we have concentrated on instantaneous interest differentials. For short maturities the finite-maturity τ interest differential (5.14) is often approximated by:[10]

$$\delta_t^\tau(g_t,h_t;\psi_t) = \delta_{x,t}^\tau(h_t) + \delta_{c,t}^\tau(g_t,h_t) + \psi_t^\tau$$

$$= \frac{E_t[x_{t+\tau}]-x_t}{\tau} + \frac{E_t\left[\int_t^{t+\tau}\{g_u+\gamma x_u\}\,du\right]}{\tau} + \psi_t^\tau, \tag{5.24}$$

where $\delta_j^\tau \equiv E[\Delta j_{t+\tau}]/\tau$, $j=x,c$. The first term on the right-hand side of equation (5.24) is the interest differential resulting solely from exchange rate movements within the band absent any devaluation. This term is extensively examined in Svensson (1991b). For each maturity, it is decreasing in the exchange rate, although less so for longer maturities. When the maturity approaches infinity, this differential becomes zero, since the movement within the band itself is bounded but subsequently divided by an unbounded maturity. For finite maturities the effect of dividing by τ can be shown to dominate also, so that the differential will be less responsive to the exchange rate the longer the maturity is.

The second term of (5.24) is the expected cumulative devaluation per unit maturity. It depends on the stochastic process followed by the expected rate of devaluation as well as on what is assumed to occur to that process at devaluation times, as one or more devaluations may occur between t and $t+\tau$.[11] Here we assume that the expected rate of devaluation always follows the process in (5.24), with no changes in parameters and no discrete jumps across devaluations. The expected devaluation per unit maturity then equals:

$$\delta^{\tau}_{c,t}(g_t, h_t) = g_t + \frac{E_t \left[\int_t^{t+\tau} \gamma x_u(h_u) \, du \right]}{\tau}, \qquad (5.25)$$

from which we can infer that the expected rate of devaluation over the time interval $[t, t+\tau]$ is determined by the expected instantaneous rate of devaluation g_t and the sequence of expected future realisations of the exchange rate within the band during that interval. Even in the absence of devaluation risk, the latter would be positively (serially) correlated with the actual exchange rate, as they are expected to remain at the same edge of the band (Svensson, 1991b). Besides, unless f and g are strongly negatively correlated, x and g will also be positively correlated, so that the differential $\delta^{\tau}_c{}'(x)$ will undoubtedly be positive.[12] Moreover, unlike the declining sensitivity of the differential $\delta^{\tau}_x(h)$ with respect to both h and x as the maturity τ increases, the differential $\delta^{\tau}_c(g,h)$ is equally responsive to g for each maturity. For longer maturities the effect of expected devaluation on the total interest differential will therefore outweigh the mean-reverting effect of the exchange rate within the band, leading to a positive correlation between exchange rates and interest differentials. Clearly, the resulting dependence can take a variety of shapes, making it also possible to be negative for small maturities and positive for large maturities. This result contrasts with Svensson's (1991b) model without a time-varying devaluation risk, which predicts that interest differentials are always negatively correlated with the exchange rate.

III   Empirical testing

This section presents estimates of the relationship between interest rate structure differentials vis-à-vis Germany and the position of the exchange rate within the band for the various currencies participating in the ERM. Given the relatively short period of participation, Spain, Portugal, and the United Kingdom will not be included in our empirical analysis. Although Austria has not been a formal member of the ERM until January 1995, it was often regarded as a 'shadow member' since it already pegged its currency to the Deutschemark. So the countries included in our analysis are: Austria, Belgium, Denmark, France, Ireland, Italy and The Netherlands. We differentiate between stable and unstable periods for the various currencies taken into account. In his analysis of the Swedish term structure of interest differentials, Svensson (1991b) focused upon a rather stable period for the Swedish target zone, so that devaluation risk was negligible. We will analyse the period 1983–93, so that realignment expectations need no longer be moderate and devaluation risk cannot be neglected. Figures 5.1–5.7 show the development of the various exchange rates (left-hand scale) and interest differentials (right-hand scale) for the terms under consideration vis-à-vis Germany.

Figure 5.1: Interest differentials and exchange rates: Austria

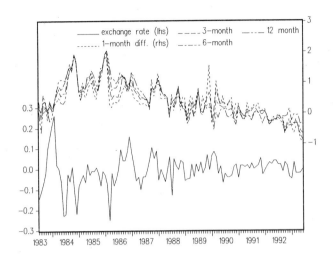

Figure 5.2: Interest differentials and exchange rates: Belgium

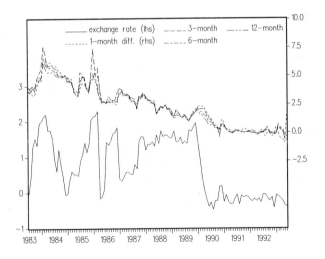

Figure 5.3: Interest differentials and exchange rates: Denmark

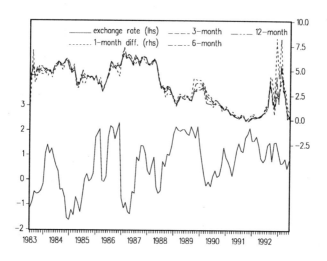

Figure 5.4: Interest differentials and exchange rates: France

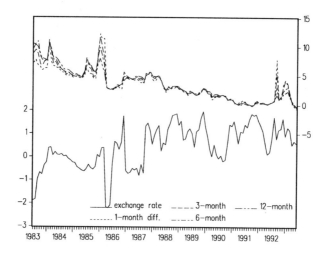

Figure 5.5: Interest differentials and exchange rates: Ireland

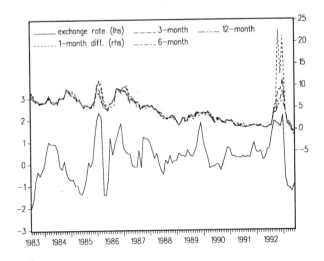

Figure 5.6: Interest differentials and exchange rates: Italy

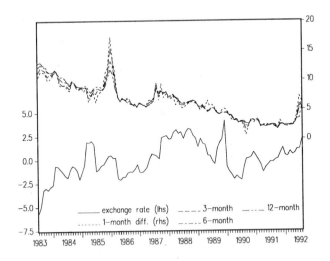

Figure 5.7: Interest differentials and exchange rates: The Netherlands

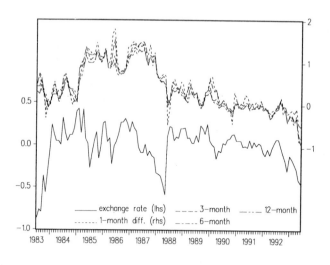

Monthly data (last day of month quotations) of the exchange rates vis-à-vis the Deutschemark, and interest rates for terms 1, 3, 6, and 12 months have been kindly provided by De Nederlandsche Bank.[13] Following Svensson (1991b), we have estimated the following linear approximation of the relationship between interest rate differentials and the exchange rate, for given terms τ:

$$\delta_t^\tau = \beta_0(\tau) + \beta_1(\tau)x_t + \eta_t^\tau. \tag{5.26}$$

The coefficients $\beta_1(\tau)$ should be negative and decreasing (in absolute terms), according to Svensson's (1991b) theory. In the absence of systematic fundamental drift, the constants $\beta_0(\tau)$ are zero if there is no significant risk premium. Tables 5.1–5.7 present our empirical estimates. Like Svensson (1991b), we have estimated equation (5.26) with the two-step two-stage least squares method as described in Cumby, Huizinga, and Obstfeld (1983) with Newey and West's (1987) modification of the variance-covariance matrix. Since the residual pattern clearly exposed an $AR(1)$-structure, this method was combined with a correction for first-order autocorrelation of the error terms using Hildreth–Lu; the estimated $AR(1)$ coefficient of the residuals is shown in the fourth column.[14]

Table 5.1: Interest rate differentials and the exchange rate: Austria

Variable	Mean	Standard Deviation	Minimum	Maximum	Correlation with x
Summary Statistics, 1983.07–93.06					
δ^1	0.42	0.57	−0.91	1.94	−0.24
δ^3	0.44	0.56	−0.86	1.96	−0.24
δ^6	0.41	0.59	−0.66	2.06	−0.23
δ^{12}	0.40	0.60	−0.63	2.06	−0.22
x	−0.01	0.07	−0.25	0.26	1.00

	Dependent Variable	Constant	Coefficient of x	AR(1)	R^2	DW
Two-Step Two-Stage Least Squares Regressions, N=120						
(5.1.1a)	δ^1	0.37	−5.24	0.64	0.56	2.07
		(7.7)	(4.5)	(5.3)		
(5.1.1b)	δ^3	0.34	−2.68	0.84	0.81	1.97
		(6.7)	(9.6)	(31.9)		
(5.1.1c)	δ^6	0.30	−2.45	0.86	0.81	2.10
		(6.3)	(9.4)	(55.2)		
(5.1.1d)	δ^{12}	0.35	−1.19	0.87	0.84	2.14
		(8.4)	(5.9)	(89.8)		

Notes: t-statistics in parentheses. The number of off-diagonal elements of the residual covariance matrix has been set to $\tau-1$, being the number of MA-terms of the residual process under the null hypothesis (which equals 0, 2, 5, and 11, respectively). Two lags of the exchange rate and the interest differential in question have been used as instruments. The t-values are not very sensitive to either the number of off-diagonal elements, or choices of different combinations of instruments available. N: # Observations; DW: Durbin Watson statistic; AR(1): First-order serial correlation coefficient.

Rows 1a–1d of each table present the estimation results for the period July 1983 until June 1993, except for Italy, where our sample period ends in August 1992. The tables also show some summary statistics and partial correlation coefficients. According to Svensson's (1991b) theory, the mean of the interest rate differentials is zero, absent any systematic (roughly constant) devaluation risk, while the interest rate differentials will be negatively correlated with the exchange rate. Furthermore, the band for each interest differential should be decreasing in term.

The first thing to note when contemplating the results in Tables 5.1 to 5.7 is that in most cases the constant terms are significantly different from zero, indicating the presence of some kind of risk premium.[15] (An exception here is France, where the constant terms do not differ significantly from zero.) The

Table 5.2: Interest rate differentials and the exchange rate: Belgium

Variable	Mean	Standard Deviation	Minimum	Maximum	Correlation with x
		Summary Statistics, 1983.07–93.06			
δ^1	2.38	1.89	−0.94	6.62	0.58
δ^3	2.45	2.00	−0.72	7.59	0.62
δ^6	2.30	1.86	−0.75	6.50	0.60
δ^{12}	2.26	1.81	−0.39	6.12	0.59
x	0.74	0.84	−0.49	2.29	1.00

	Dependent Variable	Constant	Coefficient of x	AR(1)	R^2	DW
	Two-Step Two-Stage Least Squares Regressions, N=120					
(5.2.1a)	δ^1	1.92	−0.88	0.95	0.95	1.78
		(1.1)	(0.8)	(29.1)		
(5.2.1b)	δ^3	−1.10	4.62	0.83	0.72	1.97
		(0.4)	(1.3)	(8.7)		
(5.2.1c)	δ^6	−0.17	2.67	0.86	0.89	2.04
		(0.2)	(2.7)	(15.7)		
(5.2.1d)	δ^{12}	−1.37	−0.36	0.99	0.98	2.09
		(1.2)	(4.0)	(158.1)		

Variable	Mean	Standard Deviation	Minimum	Maximum	Correlation with x
		Summary Statistics, 1990.03–92.08			
δ^1	0.48	0.71	−0.51	2.30	0.26
δ^3	0.39	0.62	−0.21	2.09	0.31
δ^6	0.32	0.53	−0.25	1.81	0.34
δ^{12}	0.28	0.41	−0.13	1.50	0.38
x	−0.16	0.18	−0.49	0.40	1.00

	Dependent Variable	Constant	Coefficient of x	AR(1)	R^2	DW
	Two-Step Two-Stage Least Squares Regressions, N=30					
(5.2.2a)	δ^1	−0.19	0.15	0.81	0.75	2.68
		(1.7)	(0.7)	(21.5)		
(5.2.2b)	δ^3	−0.11	−0.80	0.72	0.88	2.10
		(3.4)	(9.7)	(47.2)		
(5.2.2c)	δ^6	−0.16	−0.95	0.76	0.89	2.23
		(6.4)	(22.2)	(60.9)		
(5.2.2d)	δ^{12}	−0.11	−0.91	0.72	0.86	2.00
		(9.5)	(33.2)	(37.3)		

Table 5.3: Interest rate differentials and the exchange rate: Denmark

Variable	Mean	Standard Deviation	Minimum	Maximum	Correlation with x
		Summary Statistics, 1983.07–93.06			
δ^1	3.59	2.03	−0.13	8.45	−0.36
δ^3	3.49	2.02	−0.12	7.31	−0.41
δ^6	3.42	2.03	0.00	6.75	−0.41
δ^{12}	3.42	2.01	0.00	6.63	−0.40
x	0.63	1.03	−1.62	2.30	1.00

	Dependent Variable	Constant	Coefficient of x	$AR(1)$	R^2	DW
		Two-Step Two-Stage Least Squares Regressions, N=120				
(5.3.1a)	δ^1	2.85	0.62	0.92	0.89	2.91
		(1.4)	(0.5)	(17.2)		
(5.3.1b)	δ^3	2.90	−0.12	0.96	0.95	2.72
		(2.1)	(0.4)	(35.7)		
(5.3.1c)	δ^6	2.41	−0.11	0.97	0.97	2.23
		(2.2)	(0.7)	(57.3)		
(5.3.1d)	δ^{12}	3.01	−0.07	0.97	0.98	1.85
		(2.9)	(0.7)	(73.8)		

Variable	Mean	Standard Deviation	Minimum	Maximum	Correlation with x
		Summary Statistics, 1987.11–92.08			
δ^1	2.32	1.75	−0.13	6.13	−0.22
δ^3	2.24	1.79	−0.12	6.45	−0.26
δ^6	2.17	1.78	0.00	6.38	−0.25
δ^{12}	2.17	1.78	0.00	6.32	−0.23
x	1.03	0.76	−0.55	2.15	1.00

	Dependent Variable	Constant	Coefficient of x	$AR(1)$	R^2	DW
		Two-Step Two-Stage Least Squares Regressions, N=58				
(5.3.2a)	δ^1	0.75	−0.15	0.93	0.97	2.05
		(1.9)	(0.9)	(35.8)		
(5.3.2b)	δ^3	2.30	−0.58	0.93	0.97	1.66
		(3.6)	(3.0)	(32.5)		
(5.3.2c)	δ^6	1.79	−0.43	0.93	0.98	1.68
		(4.5)	(4.3)	(59.9)		
(5.3.2d)	δ^{12}	1.63	−0.30	0.93	0.98	1.72
		(5.6)	(3.9)	(68.7)		

Table 5.4: Interest rate differentials and the exchange rate: France

Variable	Mean	Standard Deviation	Minimum	Maximum	Correlation with x
		Summary Statistics, 1983.07–93.06			
δ^1	3.49	2.56	−0.72	12.25	−0.41
δ^3	3.67	2.67	−0.47	11.69	−0.46
δ^6	3.60	2.75	−0.50	11.00	−0.51
δ^{12}	3.58	2.73	−0.33	10.56	−0.53
x	0.43	0.93	−2.21	1.96	1.00

	Dependent Variable	Constant	Coefficient of x	AR(1)	R^2	DW
		Two-Step Two-Stage Least Squares Regressions, N=120				
(5.4.1a)	δ^1	0.79	1.20	0.93	0.89	2.53
		(0.4)	(1.4)	(13.3)		
(5.4.1b)	δ^3	0.83	1.15	0.93	0.93	2.29
		(0.6)	(2.0)	(26.3)		
(5.4.1c)	δ^6	0.83	0.81	0.94	0.97	1.99
		(1.0)	(3.1)	(62.4)		
(5.4.1d)	δ^{12}	0.48	0.59	0.95	0.98	1.78
		(0.9)	(4.7)	(125.5)		

Variable	Mean	Standard Deviation	Minimum	Maximum	Correlation with x
		Summary Statistics, 1987.11–92.08			
δ^1	1.92	1.41	−0.06	5.38	0.02
δ^3	1.96	1.51	−0.25	5.69	0.04
δ^6	1.85	1.53	−0.25	5.62	0.05
δ^{12}	1.84	1.54	−0.19	5.57	0.05
x	1.01	0.58	−0.18	1.96	1.00

	Dependent Variable	Constant	Coefficient of x	AR(1)	R^2	DW
		Two-Step Two-Stage Least Squares Regressions, N=58				
(5.4.2a)	δ^1	0.52	0.22	0.94	0.97	2.15
		(1.7)	(1.8)	(83.9)		
(5.4.2b)	δ^3	−0.29	0.38	0.96	0.98	2.01
		(0.7)	(4.2)	(74.4)		
(5.4.2c)	δ^6	−0.06	0.27	0.95	0.98	1.80
		(0.3)	(3.8)	(90.9)		
(5.4.2d)	δ^{12}	−0.11	0.34	0.95	0.98	2.02
		(0.5)	(8.4)	(134.1)		

Table 5.5: Interest rate differentials and the exchange rate: Ireland

		Summary Statistics, 1983.07–93.06			
Variable	Mean	Standard Deviation	Minimum	Maximum	Correlation with x
δ^1	4.86	3.75	−1.04	23.00	0.21
δ^3	4.63	2.99	−1.35	11.62	0.15
δ^6	4.49	2.77	−1.06	9.63	0.10
δ^{12}	4.38	2.62	−0.51	9.57	0.06
x	0.28	0.86	−1.99	2.33	1.00

		Two-Step Two-Stage Least Squares Regressions, $N=120$			
	Dependent Variable	Constant	Coefficient of x	$AR(1)$	R^2	DW
(5.5.1a)	δ^1	2.94 (1.9)	2.68 (0.9)	0.75 (3.3)	0.85	2.37
(5.5.1b)	δ^3	3.05 (1.5)	−0.19 (0.2)	0.91 (18.5)	0.95	1.57
(5.5.1c)	δ^6	2.93 (1.4)	0.01 (0.0)	0.96 (32.7)	0.97	1.65
(5.5.1d)	δ^{12}	2.71 (2.3)	−0.03 (0.2)	0.96 (59.3)	0.98	1.55

		Summary Statistics, 1987.11–92.08			
Variable	Mean	Standard Deviation	Minimum	Maximum	Correlation with x
δ^1	2.31	1.35	0.37	5.32	0.15
δ^3	2.35	1.43	0.31	5.44	0.19
δ^6	2.37	1.51	0.25	5.68	0.19
δ^{12}	2.36	1.48	0.38	5.57	0.21
x	0.41	0.44	−0.49	1.86	1.00

		Two-Step Two-Stage Least Squares Regressions, $N=58$			
	Dependent Variable	Constant	Coefficient of x	$AR(1)$	R^2	DW
(5.5.2a)	δ^1	1.76 (5.1)	−0.33 (1.4)	0.90 (29.4)	0.96	2.14
(5.5.2b)	δ^3	1.69 (4.6)	−0.58 (3.4)	0.91 (24.3)	0.97	1.70
(5.5.2c)	δ^6	1.38 (3.9)	−0.35 (2.5)	0.91 (29.5)	0.97	1.89
(5.5.2d)	δ^{12}	1.52 (4.8)	−0.23 (1.8)	0.92 (41.8)	0.97	2.02

Table 5.6: Interest rate differentials and the exchange rate: Italy

Variable	Mean	Standard Deviation	Minimum	Maximum	Correlation with x
		*Summary Statistics, 1983.07–92.08*			
δ^1	6.31	3.07	0.62	17.50	−0.21
δ^3	6.34	3.06	1.50	15.44	−0.24
δ^6	6.36	3.07	1.63	13.32	−0.27
δ^{12}	6.44	3.04	1.75	13.12	−0.28
x	0.01	1.79	−5.65	4.12	1.00

	Dependent Variable	Constant	Coefficient of x	$AR(1)$	R^2	DW
		*Two-Step Two-Stage Least Squares Regressions, N=110*				
(5.6.1a)	δ^1	5.31 (1.6)	0.48 (0.3)	0.91 (10.7)	0.97	2.26
(5.6.1b)	δ^3	4.93 (3.8)	0.35 (1.1)	0.94 (29.4)	0.98	1.83
(5.6.1c)	δ^6	4.22 (4.3)	0.18 (1.1)	0.96 (72.4)	0.99	1.53
(5.6.1d)	δ^{12}	4.28 (7.2)	0.17 (2.0)	0.96 (118.1)	0.99	1.59

Variable	Mean	Standard Deviation	Minimum	Maximum	Correlation with x
		*Summary Statistics, 1990.02–92.08*			
δ^1	2.88	1.27	0.62	7.32	0.28
δ^3	2.80	1.04	1.50	6.00	0.19
δ^6	2.73	0.78	1.63	5.56	0.13
δ^{12}	2.86	0.88	1.75	5.82	0.18
x	−0.15	1.08	−2.15	2.14	1.00

	Dependent Variable	Constant	Coefficient of x	$AR(1)$	R^2	DW
		*Two-Step Two-Stage Least Squares Regressions, N=31*				
(5.6.2a)	δ^1	3.07 (8.5)	0.32 (1.1)	0.65 (6.3)	0.92	1.72
(5.6.2b)	δ^3	2.67 (9.6)	0.11 (0.7)	0.81 (16.1)	0.95	1.52
(5.6.2c)	δ^6	2.74 (20.5)	0.08 (1.6)	0.79 (10.2)	0.95	1.57
(5.6.2d)	δ^{12}	2.62 (19.5)	0.18 (2.2)	0.84 (22.9)	0.97	1.40

Table 5.7: Interest rate differentials and the exchange rate: The Netherlands

Summary Statistics, 1983.07–93.06

Variable	Mean	Standard Deviation	Minimum	Maximum	Correlation with x
δ^1	0.47	0.59	−0.91	1.81	0.18
δ^3	0.44	0.55	−0.91	1.56	0.17
δ^6	0.40	0.52	−0.82	1.44	0.16
δ^{12}	0.38	0.47	−0.51	1.32	0.16
x	−0.01	0.23	−0.86	0.42	1.00

Two-Step Two-Stage Least Squares Regressions, N=120

	Dependent Variable	Constant	Coefficient of x	AR(1)	R^2	DW
(5.7.1a)	δ^1	0.51	−0.60	0.92	0.86	2.21
		(5.7)	(3.0)	(61.6)		
(5.7.1b)	δ^3	0.32	−1.26	0.93	0.85	2.12
		(3.3)	(7.0)	(60.9)		
(5.7.1c)	δ^6	0.26	−1.72	0.93	0.80	2.11
		(2.7)	(7.5)	(54.4)		
(5.7.1d)	δ^{12}	0.25	−2.29	0.90	0.65	2.20
		(0.8)	(1.9)	(10.5)		

Summary Statistics, 1984.03–92.08

Variable	Mean	Standard Deviation	Minimum	Maximum	Correlation with x
δ^1	0.56	0.55	−0.50	1.81	−0.02
δ^3	0.53	0.53	−0.31	1.56	−0.00
δ^6	0.48	0.50	−0.31	1.44	−0.01
δ^{12}	0.44	0.47	−0.19	1.32	0.00
x	0.04	0.17	−0.59	0.42	1.00

Two-Step Two-Stage Least Squares Regressions, N=102

	Dependent Variable	Constant	Coefficient of x	AR(1)	R^2	DW
(5.7.2a)	δ^1	0.57	−1.23	0.92	0.87	2.26
		(5.5)	(8.0)	(51.4)		
(5.7.2b)	δ^3	0.51	−1.01	0.91	0.90	2.07
		(8.2)	(10.3)	(72.0)		
(5.7.2c)	δ^6	0.45	−0.64	0.94	0.93	2.13
		(8.1)	(9.6)	(135.5)		
(5.7.2d)	δ^{12}	0.22	−0.32	0.98	0.93	2.42
		(2.4)	(7.9)	(227.9)		

mean of the interest differentials is also clearly not zero for all countries, including France. Svensson has reported similar results for Sweden. However, the other implications of his model were supported by the Swedish experience. So, we will now examine whether this also holds for the countries in our sample, focusing first on the total period considered here.

Various conclusions can be drawn. First, the interest differentials are generally not decreasing in term. Second, only in the case of Austria the estimated $\beta_1(\tau)$ coefficients are negative, significant and decreasing in absolute terms as implied by Svensson's (1991b) theory. For Austria the partial correlation coefficients are also negative. For the Netherlands we find significant and negative coefficients, which are, however, not decreasing in term. The correlation coefficients are positive. In Belgium, Denmark, and Ireland some of the estimated coefficients are negative, but generally not significantly different from zero.[16] For Ireland the partial correlation coefficients are also not negative. In the context of the model presented in the previous section, zero coefficients on the exchange rate would point at the emergence of devaluation expectations, cancelling out the negative impact of the exchange rate on interest differentials arising from the mean-reversion component within the band. For France and Italy we even find consistently positive coefficients, which are most significant for France, especially for longer maturities. Apparently, devaluation risk in those countries cannot be neglected. Presumably, the stop-go economic policy of the French government especially in the first half of the 1980s may have had something to do with this result; for Italy the almost continuous *real* appreciation of the lira must have raised some anxiety at financial markets (see also Chapter 6). So in general, for the total sample period, the results for most countries are not in accordance with the Svensson (1991b) model, but do not contradict the model outlined in the previous section.

This conclusion is, however, not entirely fair for the Svensson model, as our estimation period also includes years with substantial turbulence in the ERM. Following Svensson (1991b) we have therefore re-estimated the models (except for Austria), now choosing periods which could be characterised as relatively stable, not only for the currency itself (see Figures 5.1–5.7), but in most cases also for the ERM as a whole. The differences with our previous findings are striking. In general, the estimated coefficients are now significantly different from zero. For Belgium, Denmark, Ireland and the Netherlands we find significantly negative coefficients, which are generally also decreasing in the term. Except for Belgium and Ireland, the partial correlation coefficients are also negative. So these results are broadly in line with the Svensson (1991b) model. For Belgium most estimated coefficients are negative, but not decreasing in term. For France and Italy the results are still more in accordance with our model with a time-varying devaluation risk, even for the relatively stable periods.[17]

IV Conclusion

In this chapter we have investigated interest rate differentials vis-à-vis Germany for most member countries of the EMS. It followed from our theoretical model that these differentials predominantly consist of three components: expectations about realignments of central parities, expected exchange rate movements within the band, and country-specific risk premia. We have extended Svensson's (1991b) analysis of the term structure of interest rate differentials in a target zone in several directions. We first included a time-varying devaluation risk as well as (mean-reverting) intramarginal interventions in the model. Furthermore, we analysed the term structure of interest differentials in seven countries: Austria, Belgium, Denmark, France, Ireland, Italy and the Netherlands for the period 1983–93. In our analysis we explicitly differentiated between stable and unstable periods for the various currencies taken into account.

The findings for Austria and for Belgium, Denmark, Ireland, and the Netherlands in the relatively stable period are broadly in line with Svensson's theory, whereas the other results are more in accordance with the model that also allows for a time-varying devaluation risk. In the next chapter devaluation expectations in these countries will be investigated in greater detail. After having employed a number of methods to determine the approximate size of the devaluation expectations that have prevailed, we will try to come up with an explanation by linking such expectations to a broad set of so-called 'economic fundamentals'. As a consequence, budget deficits will also make their re-entrance in the analysis.

Appendix A: Derivation portfolio compositions (5.8) and (5.9)

Next period real wealth of domestic investors can be written as:

$$w_{t+1} = \frac{(1+rr_t)\theta_t W_t}{S_{t+1}} + \frac{(1+rr_t^*)(1-\theta_t)W_t}{S_t}, \tag{A1}$$

so that

$$E_t[w_{t+1}] = (1+rr_t)\theta_t W_t E_t[S_{t+1}^{-1}] + (1+rr_t^*)\frac{(1-\theta_t)W_t}{S_t}, \tag{A2}$$

which, by means of equation (5.7), can be rewritten as:

$$E_t[w_{t+1}] = (1+rr_t)(1+E_t[\epsilon_{t+1}])\frac{\theta_t W_t}{S_t} + (1+rr_t^*)\frac{(1-\theta_t)W_t}{S_t}. \tag{A3}$$

Furthermore:

$$(A4)$$

$$Var_t[w_{t+1}] = E_t[w_{t+1} - E_t[w_{t+1}]]^2$$

$$= E_t\left[(1+rr_t)\frac{\theta_t W_t}{S_{t+1}} - (1+rr_t)(1+E_t[\epsilon_{t+1}])\frac{\theta_t W_t}{S_t}\right]^2$$

$$= (1+rr_t)^2\theta_t^2 W_t^2\left\{E_t[S_{t+1}^{-2}] - \frac{2(1+E_t[\epsilon_{t+1}])}{S_t}E_t[S_{t+1}^{-1}] + \frac{(1+E_t[\epsilon_{t+1}])^2}{S_t^2}\right\}$$

$$= \frac{(1+rr_t)^2\theta_t^2 W_t^2}{S_t^2}\{E_t[\epsilon_{t+1}^2] - E_t^2[\epsilon_{t+1}]\}$$

$$= \frac{(1+rr_t)^2\theta_t^2 W_t^2}{S_t^2} Var_t[\epsilon_{t+1}].$$

Utility maximisation implies $\partial U/\partial\theta = 0$:

$$U_1\frac{\partial E_t[w_{t+1}]}{\partial\theta} + U_2\frac{\partial Var_t[w_{t+1}]}{\partial\theta} =$$

$$(A5)$$

$$U_1\frac{W_t}{S_t}\{rr_t - rr_t^* + (1+rr_t)E_t[\epsilon_{t+1}]\} + U_2 2\theta(1+rr_t)^2\frac{W_t^2}{S_t^2}Var_t[\epsilon_{t+1}] = 0,$$

from which it can easily be seen that:

$$\theta_t = \frac{rr_t - rr_t^* + (1+rr_t)E_t[\epsilon_{t+1}]}{\phi(1+rr_t)^2 Var_t[\epsilon_{t+1}]}, \quad where \ \phi = -2\frac{W_t}{S_t}\frac{U_2}{U_1}. \quad (A6)$$

Likewise:

$$E_t[w_{t+1}^*] = (1+rr_t)\theta_t^* W_t^*(1+E_t[\epsilon_{t+1}]) + (1+rr_t^*)(1-\theta_t^*)W_t^*, \quad (A7)$$

$$Var_t[w_{t+1}^*] = (1+rr_t)^2\theta_t^{*2} W_t^{*2} Var_t[\epsilon_{t+1}], \quad (A8)$$

$$\theta_t^* = \frac{rr_t - rr_t^* + (1+rr_t)E_t[\epsilon_{t+1}]}{\phi^*(1+rr_t)^2 Var_t[\epsilon_{t+1}]}, \quad \text{where } \phi^* = -2W_t^* \frac{U_2^*}{U_1^*}. \quad (A9)$$

Appendix B: Derivation of the exchange rate solution (5.22)

The differential equation (5.19) can be integrated forward to yield the solution:

$$x_t = \frac{1}{\alpha}\int_t^\infty \{E_t[h_v]\}\, e^{-\mu(v-t)}\, dv. \quad (B1)$$

assuming that explosive solutions are irrelevant. This representation is valid under any policy regime. If we ignore the infinitesimal regulators at the boundaries and take:

$$dh_t = -\lambda(h_t - h_0)dt + \sigma dW_t \quad \therefore \quad E_t[h_v] = h_0 + (h_t - h_0)e^{-\lambda(v-t)}, \quad (B2)$$

then a particular solution of (5.19) is given by:

$$x_t(h_t) = \frac{\mu h_t + \lambda h_0}{\alpha\mu(\mu+\lambda)}, \quad \text{with } \mu = \frac{1-\alpha\gamma}{\alpha}. \quad (B3)$$

As in Lindberg and Söderlind (1993), this solution can be interpreted as a managed floating exchange rate, where intramarginal interventions do take place, albeit in the absence of reflecting barriers (boundaries) to the exchange rate. If we also abstain from intramarginal interventions (implying no target parity either), equation (B3) simply resorts to the free float solution $x(h)=h$ ($\lambda=\gamma=0$).

In order to find the complete solution to the model we first apply Itô's lemma to $x(h)$:

$$\begin{aligned} dx_t(h_t) &= x_t'(h_t)dh_t + \frac{1}{2}x_t''(h_t)\{dh_t\}^2 \\ &= \{-x_t'(h_t)\lambda(h_t-h_0) + \frac{1}{2}x_t''(h_t)\sigma^2\}dt + x_t'(h_t)\sigma dW_t. \end{aligned} \quad (B4)$$

Taking (time-t) expectations on (B4), equation (5.19) can be rewritten as:

$$x_t(h_t) = \frac{1}{\alpha\mu}h_t - \frac{\lambda}{\mu}(h_t - h_0)\frac{dx_t}{dh_t} + \frac{\sigma^2}{2\mu}\frac{d^2x_t}{dh^2}. \tag{B5}$$

A change of variable:

$$z_t \equiv \frac{\lambda(h_t - h_0)^2}{\sigma^2}, \tag{B6}$$

turns equation (B5) into:

$$z_t\frac{d^2x_t}{dz_t^2} + (\frac{1}{2} - z_t)\frac{dx_t}{dz_t} - \frac{\mu}{2\lambda}x_t = -\frac{h_t}{2\lambda\alpha}, \tag{B7}$$

which can easily be recognised as Kummer's equation with $a=\mu/2\lambda$, $b=\frac{1}{2}$, and $z_t=\lambda(h_t-h_0)^2/\sigma^2$ (Abramowitz and Stegun, 1972, p.504).

The general solution to the model (5.19)–(5.21) can therefore be written as the sum of the particular solution obtained above (B3) and the general solution to the homogeneous equation:

$$x_t(z_t(h_t)) = \frac{\mu h_t + \lambda h_0}{\alpha\mu(\mu + \lambda)} + A_1 M\left[\frac{\mu}{2\lambda}; \frac{1}{2}; \frac{\lambda(h_t - h_0)^2}{\sigma^2}\right]$$

$$+ A_2 M\left[\frac{\mu+\lambda}{2\lambda}; \frac{3}{2}; \frac{\lambda(h_t - h_0)^2}{\sigma^2}\right]\frac{\sqrt{\lambda}(h_t - h_0)}{\sigma}, \tag{B8}$$

where $M[\cdot;\cdot;\cdot]$ represents Kummer's (confluent hypergeometric) function; A_1 and A_2 are constants of integration to be determined by the boundary behaviour (including the smooth-pasting conditions of 5.20). In case of a symmetric target zone $(x''=-x')$ A_1 must be zero, since it is the coefficient of the only non-symmetric term (Delgado and Dumas, 1991).

Notes

1. See for example De Cecco and Giavazzi (1994), Genberg (1990), Giavazzi and Spaventa (1990), Giovannini (1990), De Grauwe and Vanhaverbeke (1990), Icard (1994), and Wellink (1989).
2. Bakker (1994) and Gruijters (1995) both offer an extensive overview of the various capital restrictions that have been in vogue in the EMS area since the demise of the Bretton–Woods system. One should draw a distinction, nevertheless, between *formal* and *effective* capital regulations. Take for instance Belgium, that until March 1990 had witnessed a two-tier exchange rate system, which is economically equivalent to capital controls (Gros, 1988). As De Grauwe and Vanhaverbeke (1990, p.152) note with respect to its efficiency, however, *'capital flows were mostly free'* in Belgium during the 1980s. Estimated offset coefficients

suggest that the Austrian Central Bank also enjoyed rather limited autonomy with respect to setting interest rates in the 1980s, indicating that capital controls in Austria have not been very effective either (Eglin, 1989, for example reports an offset coefficient of –0.79 over the period 1980–88).

3. For example, according to research by the National Bank of Belgium, the withholding tax change introduced in March 1990 (reduction from 25% to 10%) has led to a substantial reduction in long-term interest differentials vis-à-vis Germany (National Bank of Belgium, 1992). See, however, also Koen (1991), p.6.

4. There is a fifth possible explanation for interest rate differentials vis-à-vis Germany: trade in bonds denominated in currencies of the small countries is considerably less than that of DM-bonds. In other words, a liquidity premium may explain the interest differentials. See for example Cooper (1990). To our knowledge this explanation has never been tested. However, this elucidation can also not explain why interest differentials have fluctuated that much, since the *relative* size of the domestic bonds markets as against Germany has hardly changed during the period under consideration.

5. The so-called 'drift-adjustment' procedure will be illuminated in Chapter 6.

6. Unless nominal rigidities exist somewhere in the economy, this property prevails rather generally in open economy macro models (for example Marston, 1985). In the remainder of this chapter it can also be interpreted as an assumption that expectations are formed likewise.

7. Svensson (1992a) shows that risk premia for an imperfectly credible band consist of two elements: the first originating from uncertainty due to exchange rate movements within the band, and the second arising from uncertainty due to realignments of the band itself. The former element is presumably rather unimportant, since exchange rate variability within a band is smaller than variability in a free float, and since empirical estimates of risk premia in a free float appear to be fairly small (Froot and Thaler, 1990). The latter element is likely to be more important than the former, but still of moderate size in proportion to the total interest differential. Even with a coefficient of relative risk aversion of 8 and an expected conditional devaluation size of 10%, the foreign exchange risk premium is no more than 1/5 of the total interest differential (Svensson, 1992a, pp.33–34).

8. The structure of realignment expectations postulated here is analogous to the one of Bertola and Caballero (1992) with one important difference: they allow realignments to be feasible at the edges of the band only, whereas we allow them to take place from any point in the band.

9. The fundamental f is assumed to consist of two components: one component, 'velocity', is assumed to be exogenous to the central bank and stochastic; the other component, 'money supply', is controlled by the central bank and changed by 'interventions'. It does not matter precisely how the central bank implements its monetary policy, for instance, whether it affects domestic credit and money supply indirectly by manipulating the interest rate or whether it directly influences money supply and the fundamental by foreign exchange market interventions (compare Bertola, 1993, and Svensson, 1992b).

10. For example Svensson (1991b) and Appendix to Bertola and Svensson (1993), as kindly provided by Svensson. Note that this approximation is only valid for small τ, otherwise the first two elements of (5.23) and (5.24) should be multiplicated by $(1+\tau i^{\tau}_{t})$ as in (5.14).

11. For a non-zero drift in the expected rate of devaluation, Bertola and Svensson (1993) consider three assumptions for what happens to g_t at devaluation times: no resetting, resetting of devaluation size and of its drift, and resetting of the probability intensity of devaluation (Appendix to Bertola and Svensson, 1993).

12. Direct estimation of γ in (5.17) would therefore result in an identification problem since in that case all of the covariation between the exchange rate and the expected rate of devaluation is attributed to γ (Svensson, 1994).

13. Central parities for the Schilling/Deutschemark rate are 'Jahresmittelkurse' and have been taken from Österreichische Nationalbank (1991).

14. We scanned the autocorrelation- and partial autocorrelation-functions in order to find possible deviations from white noise in the residuals. In most cases the $AR(1)$-specification was so evident that formal testing was superfluous. In the remaining cases $AR(1)$-specifications were found to be valid also, using descriptive as well as predictive criteria, such as Akaike's Information Criterion and the Bayesian Information Criterion (Brockwell and Davis, 1987). Two other (minor) modifications of the estimation procedure as compared to Svensson's method can be found in the instruments used and the number of non-zero autocorrelations (see Table 5.1).

15. We also tried to account for the different regimes between the various realignments in our analysis of the complete sample by allowing the intercepts to vary. However, the resulting changes in the estimates of $\beta_1(\tau)$ were neither significant nor noteworthy.

16. The results for Belgium have to be interpreted with care as Belgium until February 1990 witnessed a dual exchange rate system. The financial exchange rate was not explicitly targeted by the monetary authorities; the official BF/DM exchange rate only covered current account transactions so that financial arbitrage cannot have taken place at this rate. See Chapter 6 and Knot and de Haan (1995b) for a more extensive treatment of this issue.

17. The positive coefficients reported for France and Italy for both sample periods are in line with the results of Caramazza (1993), Chen and Giovannini (1993), and Thomas (1994). They all find that among a set of potential macroeconomic determinants of French and Italian devaluation expectations during their membership of the EMS, the exchange rate within the band is by far the most important one.

6 Fundamental determinants of interest rate differentials in the EMS

A greater danger is that these governments will try to solve their budgetary problems by combining growth with a lax monetary policy, thereby stoking inflation and risking a currency devaluation . . . investors are now quick to punish any government that pursues such a strategy by demanding sharply higher long-term interest rates.

The Economist, 19 November 1994, p.92

I   Introduction

The previous chapter has made it plausible, that for economies participating in the Exchange Rate Mechanism (ERM) of the European Monetary System (EMS), interest differentials vis-à-vis Germany mainly reflect exchange rate expectations. In economic theory, it has become common practice to think of exchange rates, like any other asset price, as being determined by fundamentals and expectations. It is well-known, however, that available models are inconclusive as to what constitutes this somewhat vague notion of 'fundamentals'. The terminology used in the target zone literature leads to even further confusion, because of availing itself synonymously and interchangeably of the concepts of 'interventions', 'adjustment of the money stock', and 'change of fundamentals'. Krugman (1991), for example, assumes that the fundamentals are adequately described by money supply and velocity, thus implying that monetary policy can largely control these fundamentals. This chapter offers a much more basic ('fundamental') interpretation of the concept of fundamentals, in the sense that this concept may capture a broad spectrum of underlying macroeconomic variables, not always under direct control of whatever economic authority.

Under a pure floating exchange rate regime, the exchange rate will adjust to its fundamental determinants (provided no bubbles emerge), whereas under a fixed exchange rate regime the fundamentals must adjust given the exchange rate. Krugman (1991) has shown that a target zone is a nonlinear compromise between both polar cases, which, under the crucial assumption of perfect credibility, is self-stabilising. As a consequence of the overwhelmingly large number of studies rejecting virtually all of its empirical implications, the

Krugman model has later on been modified and improved to accommodate intramarginal interventions and, above all, by assuming that the credibility of the pronounced central parity may be challenged, as the likelihood of a realignment increases (see Chapter 5). Sutherland (1994) has stressed the generality of this modified (flex-price) model by demonstrating that it is observationally equivalent to a sticky-price target zone model.

This chapter empirically explores the credibility of proclaimed exchange rate policies of various ERM member countries, each examined individually. After a straightforward test of this credibility inspired by previous work of Svensson (1991c, 1993), we extract measures of devaluation expectations from (raw) data on interest differentials, employing the so-called 'drift-adjustment' method (Bertola and Svensson, 1993). Subsequently, we aim to estimate the link between such expectations and a broad set of fundamental determinants which allows for a very general model of exchange rate determination in a target zone. Earlier attempts in this direction for a number of different European currencies include Koen (1991), Lindberg, Svensson, and Söderlind (1991), Bartolini (1993), Edin and Vredin (1993), Chen and Giovannini (1993), Caramazza (1993), Thomas (1994), Eichengreen, Rose, and Wyplosz (1994), and Hochreiter and Winckler (1995). Contrary to all such (mainly single-equation) studies, we will employ a vector autoregressive (VAR) methodology, thereby also incorporating potential feedback mechanisms from interest differentials on fundamentals. Here, we will present new evidence on this issue for seven economies that have more or less pursued a similar monetary policy aimed at exchange rate stability vis-à-vis the Deutschemark. For Austria, Belgium, Denmark, France, Ireland, Italy, and the Netherlands we will try to quantify the relation between a broad set of country-specific fundamentals and devaluation expectations. For the latter we will employ three different measures: unadjusted short-term interest differentials, filtered short-term interest differentials, and (unadjusted) long-term interest differentials. In this way, it will also be able to assess the impact of the fundamentals on the term structure of devaluation expectations and target zone credibility.

The remainder of this chapter is organised as follows. Section II examines the credibility of proclaimed hard-currency options in the ERM member countries in the short-run as well as in the long-run. Short-term (total) devaluation expectations are distilled from corresponding interest differentials by the so-called 'drift-adjustment' method (section III). Section IV investigates whether all three types of interest differentials can accurately be explained by our set of fundamental determinants, employing a vector autoregressive methodology. Finally, section V presents some concluding remarks.

II   Credibility of the exchange rate policies

In Chapter 5 we have demonstrated that interest rate differentials vis-à-vis Germany are predominantly explained by two factors: expected rates of realignment and expected exchange rate movements within the band. This section investigates empirically whether during the EMS era for the countries under consideration non-zero expectations about realignments of central parities against the Deutschemark have existed. Ever since the foundation of the EMS in 1979, its prominent goal has been to bring about greater exchange rate stability among its members. Nevertheless, market participants may have perceived a devaluation risk at some points in time. In such cases the credibility of the proclaimed exchange rate policy will have been challenged, for example due to persistent imbalances in economic fundamentals.[1]

In order to determine whether the exchange rate policy in the countries concerned has been fully credible over the last decade, that is whether expected rates of realignment $E_t[\Delta c_{t+\tau}]/\tau$ have been zero or not, a simple test is developed and applied, similar in spirit to the one proposed by Svensson (1991c). In a fully credible target zone the expected depreciation within the band $E_t[\Delta x_{t+\tau}]$ must be bounded by the maximum and minimum depreciation that are possible within the band, that is:

$$x_t - x^u \leq E_t[\Delta x_{t+\tau}] \leq x_t - x^l, \tag{6.1}$$

where upper and lower limits of the exchange rate band are denoted by x^u and x^l. In case of the functioning of the ERM before 2 August 1993, those limits were ±0.0225 for most currencies, and $E_t[\Delta c_{t+\tau}] = 0$, provided that the target zone was credible.[2] Hence, given foreign interest rates, these restrictions imply limits on domestic currency rates of return to foreign investment as well as on domestic interest rates, by virtue of equation (5.14). In turn, in the absence of a country-specific risk premium, those limits define a rate-of-return band around the foreign interest rate, with upper and lower bounds:

$$
\begin{aligned}
i_t^{\tau,u} &= i_t^{\tau,*} + (1 + \tau i_t^{\tau}) \frac{[x^u - x_t]}{\tau} \\
i_t^{\tau,l} &= i_t^{\tau,*} - (1 + \tau i_t^{\tau}) \frac{[x_t - x^l]}{\tau}.
\end{aligned}
\tag{6.2}
$$

We assume that for the countries under consideration capital mobility is sufficiently free, so that no international arbitrage possibilities remain.[3] Then it follows that, in the absence of a country-specific risk premium, the exchange rate regime can only be completely credible for the horizon implied by the term of the investment, if the domestic interest rate for that term is inside the rate-of-return band (6.2). If it is outside that band, investors must either perceive a devaluation risk (shift of the central parity and thereby of the band) before maturity, or the required risk premia are non-zero. In the first case it follows that the target zone is not credible.

It should be noted from the outset that this test is asymmetrical: if the interest rate falls within the rate-of-return corridor, it does *not necessarily* follow that the target zone is credible. A target zone is *perfectly* credible if and only if the probability that condition (6.1) will be fulfilled equals unity for *all* τ. Since it is not possible to observe the entire probability distribution of $\Delta x_{t+\tau}$ for any arbitrary value of τ, only the weaker condition (6.1) for a pair of specific maturities as such will be examined. Additionally, the expectation of a small shift in the exchange rate band that would not imply a discrete jump of the exchange rate out of the existing band is compatible with this pattern. Furthermore, capital market imperfections, intercountry differences in tax treatment of capital income, and country-specific risk premia all imply that interest rates wandering outside the corridor may not unambiguously reflect a credibility gap (see for instance Koen, 1991, and Halikias, 1994).[4]

Figures 6.1A1 to 6.1G1 and 6.1A2 to 6.1G2 show the rate-of-return bands around the German interest rate in combination with various domestic interest rates for a time to maturity of one month (τ=1/12) and approximately ten years (τ=10), respectively, for Austria (as in Chapter 5, considered here to be a shadow member of the ERM), Belgium, Denmark, France, Ireland, Italy, and the Netherlands.[5] The short-term interest rates used here are annualised monthly averages of working days for Euromarket bills, originating from the Bank of International Settlements; long-term interest rate and exchange rate data also consist of monthly averages, and originate from the International Monetary Fund.[6] The period covered is 1979.04 to 1992.12, except for Austria (starting date 1980.01, that is after sufficient hardening of the hard-currency strategy), Ireland (lack of Euromarket rates until 1981.11), and Italy (sample ending 1992.08 and 1992.06, due to suspension of its ERM membership and lack of long-term interest data, respectively).

Based on the Figures 6.1A1–6.1G2 our sample of countries can roughly be subdivided in three distinct groups: Austria and the Netherlands, Italy (a class in its own), and Belgium, Denmark, France and Ireland. For Austria and the Netherlands (Figures 6.1A and 6.1G), the hard-currency option generally has been credible in the short run as short-term interest rates have stayed well within the corridors during the period under investigation. Long-term interest rates have hovered slightly above the upper edge of the corresponding corridor until about 1986 for the Dutch guilder and 1988 for the Austrian schilling. Towards the end of the decade, the tight link with the Deutschemark in Austria and the Netherlands seems to have also achieved long-run credibility. The experience of both economies suggests that credibility apparently does not come overnight when a country commits itself to a stable exchange rate. Take for example the Netherlands, where it took around three years after the last devaluation (March 1983) before full credibility had been restored.

On the other hand, the Belgian, Danish, French, and Irish target zones have definitely lacked credibility even within a one-month horizon at several points in time, especially at times right before actual devaluations of the various currencies (Figures 6.1B1 to 6.1E2). Long-run credibility has continuously been lacking. Still, credibility has improved towards the end of

Figure 6.1A1: Austria; short-run credibility

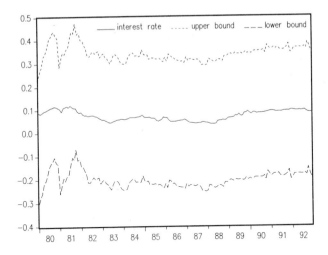

Figure 6.1A2: Austria; long-run credibility

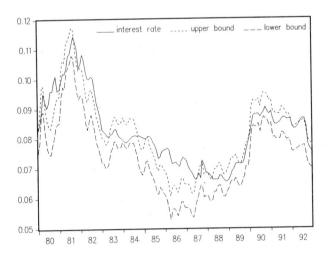

Figure 6.1B1: Belgium; short-run credibility

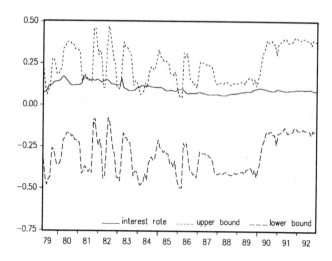

Figure 6.1B2: Belgium; long-run credibility

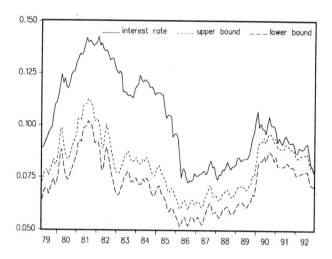

Figure 6.1C1: Denmark; short-run credibility

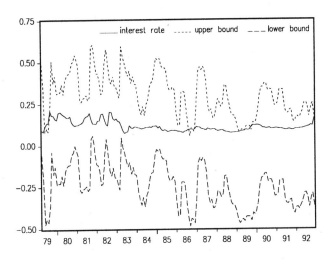

Figure 6.1C2: Denmark; long-run credibility

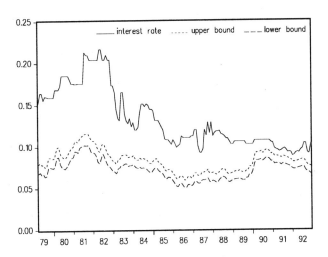

Figure 6.1D1: France; short-run credibility

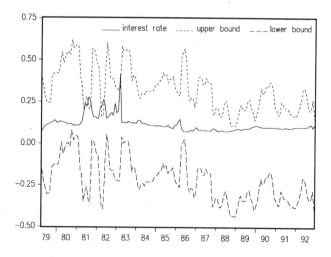

Figure 6.1D2: France; long-run credibility

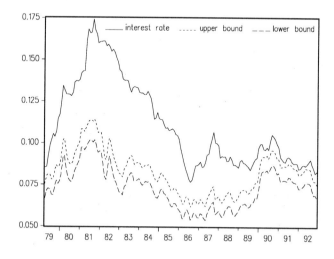

Figure 6.1E1: Ireland; short-run credibility

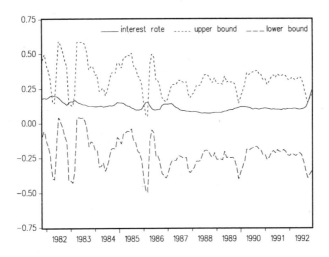

Figure 6.1E2: Ireland; long-run credibility

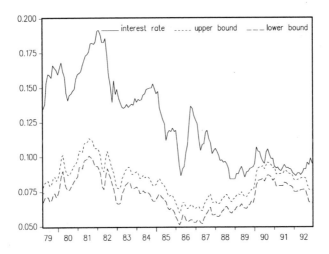

Figure 6.1F1: Italy; short-run credibility

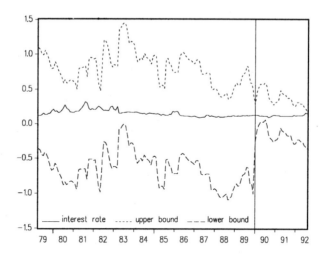

Figure 6.1F2: Italy; long-run credibility

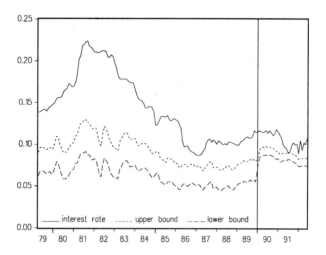

Figure 6.1G1: The Netherlands; short-run credibility

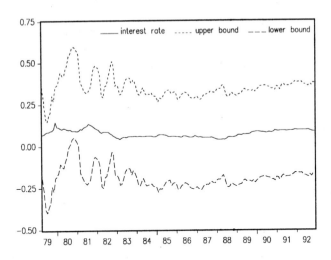

Figure 6.1G2: The Netherlands; long-run credibility

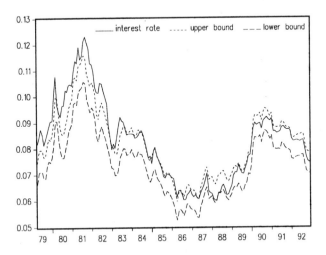

the 1980s, probably due to the combined effect of a more favourable development of some economic fundamentals and the Basle–Nyborg agreement of September 1987. At that time, the Committee of Central Bank Governors decided to strengthen the Exchange Rate Mechanism of the EMS by adopting a number of policy actions, including in particular an extension of the facilities to finance intra-marginal interventions.[7] All EMS member countries were encouraged to commit themselves more firmly to the hard-currency option, and the more or less frequent devaluations against the Deutschemark came to a halt. Figures 6.1B2 and 6.1D2 clearly demonstrate the impact of the 'franc-fort' policies in Belgium and France that became effective somewhere around 1990. Credibility of the Irish target zone seems to have profited substantially from the entrance in the ERM of the British pound (which is of key importance to Ireland due to the close trade relations between Ireland and the UK) in October 1990; as soon as pound sterling left the ERM again (September 1992), renewed pressure emerged on the Irish punt (Figure 6.1E2).[8]

Finally, at first sight Italy seems to take a middle position, with perfect credibility in the short-run together with imperfect credibility in the long-run (Figure 6.1F). It should be noted, however, that for the period until January 1990 Italy had obtained a (wider) exchange rate band of plus/minus 6 percent, implying that even an annualised interest rate (or expected depreciation rate) of 144 (= $2x^u/\tau$) percent could be compatible with perfect credibility in the short-run (in case the lira would be at the strong edge of the 'band'). Nevertheless, from January 1990 onwards Italian monetary authorities also succeeded in achieving credibility for the smaller margin, albeit this gain in credibility vanished steadily towards the fall of 1992.

There is a rather disturbing problem, however, with the empirical treatment of the Belgian franc, that is usually neglected in the literature. As already mentioned in Chapter 5, Belgium has experienced a dual exchange rate system for most of the period under analysis. Underlying Figure 6.1B are data on the commercial exchange rate, since that rate has been targeted by Belgian monetary authorities within the ERM. This official rate, however, only covers current account transactions, so that financial arbitrage cannot have taken place at this rate. If instead we would employ the financial exchange rate, we would introduce an apparent contradiction in the analysis as this rate has not been explicitly targeted. As Knot and De Haan (1995b) demonstrate, however, the basic conclusion with respect to the credibility of the Belgian exchange rate policy is quite similar for both exchange rates. Therefore, the commercial exchange rate is usually employed in the literature, even in combination with interest rates and other financial variables.[9] Nevertheless, we do think that this common practice in the literature to employ the official rate for Belgium is a serious imperfection in this context, especially if we keep in mind that the time-series properties of both exchange rates are fundamentally different (Knot and De Haan, 1995b, p.11).

III   Drift-adjustment

Chapter 5 already demonstrated that interest differentials are endogenous and jointly determined by exogenous fundamentals and devaluation risks, summarised in the composite fundamental h_t. Before proceeding by estimating the parameters of this relationship, we can go one step further by noting that devaluation expectations $\delta_{c,t}$ can also be inferred from the model laid out above, employing the so-called 'drift-adjustment' method (Bertola and Svensson, 1993). The starting point for this procedure is the notion that the exchange rate band has a stabilising or mean-reverting effect on x_t. In the target zone literature, this point of view has been advanced on both theoretical as well as on empirical grounds.

From equation (5.24) the (total) expected rate of devaluation over the time interval $[t,t+\tau]$ can be measured as the corresponding (τ-term) interest differential adjusted for the expected exchange rate movement within the band during the same interval:[10]

$$\delta_{c,t}^{\tau} = \frac{E_t[\Delta c_{t+\tau}]}{\tau} = \delta_t^{\tau} - \delta_{x,t}^{\tau} = i_t^{\tau} - i_t^{\tau,*} - \frac{E_t[\Delta x_{t+\tau}]}{\tau}. \tag{6.3}$$

For sufficiently long maturities the expected rate of depreciation within the band will be approximately zero, since the maximum amount is bounded by the width of the band and then divided by a high term to maturity ($\tau \to \infty$). For short maturities, on the other hand, expected rates of depreciation within the band may be in the same order of magnitude as interest rate differentials, so that adjustment is essential.

Modelling the process for the exchange rate within the band is complicated by the fact that the exchange rate within the band usually takes a jump at realignments. This introduces a so-called 'Peso problem', since the sample distribution of realignments may not be representative of the underlying distribution of the error term, unless the sample includes a large number of realignments (Froot and Thaler, 1991, Svensson, 1993). Therefore, the expected rates of depreciation within the band will be estimated conditional upon no realignment. In order to do so, we first recall that market expectations of realignments were modelled in the following way (compare equation 5.17):

$$E_t[\Delta c_{t+\tau}] = p_t^{\tau} E_t[\Delta c_{t+\tau} \mid Realignment] + (1 - p_t^{\tau})0, \tag{6.4}$$

where p_t^{τ} is the time-varying probability of a realignment of independent random size during the time to maturity and $E_t[\Delta c_{t+\tau} | Realignment]$ denotes the expected conditional size of the realignment. Likewise, the expected rate of depreciation within the band can be subdivided into two components:

$$E_t[\Delta x_{t+\tau}] = p_t^\tau E_t[\Delta x_{t+\tau} | R] + (1 - p_t^\tau) E_t[\Delta x_{t+\tau} | NR]$$
$$= E_t[\Delta x_{t+\tau} | NR] + p_t^\tau \{ E_t[x_{t+\tau} | R] - E_t[x_{t+\tau} | NR] \}, \tag{6.5}$$

where $(N)R$ denotes (no) realignment. Combining equations (6.3), (6.4), and (6.5), and rearranging yields:

$$\delta_{c',t}^\tau \equiv \frac{E_t[\Delta c_{t+\tau}]}{\tau} + \frac{p_t^\tau \{ E_t[x_{t+\tau} | R] - E_t[x_{t+\tau} | NR] \}}{\tau}$$

$$= \delta_t^\tau - \frac{E_t[\Delta x_{t+\tau} | NR]}{\tau}. \tag{6.6}$$

We shall use equation (6.6) as our operational definition of the expected rate of devaluation. The right-hand side of equation (6.6) demonstrates that expected devaluation may be captured by corresponding interest differentials after the expected exchange rate movement within the band (conditional upon no realignment) has been filtered out. The expected rate of devaluation differs from the expected rate of realignment $E_t[\Delta c_{t+\tau}]/\tau$ by the per unit time difference between the expected exchange rate at maturity conditional upon a realignment and the expected exchange rate at maturity conditional upon no realignment. Longer maturities allow for more mean reversion of $x_{t+\tau}$, regardless of whether a realignment occurs during the remaining time to maturity. So, in this case the expected rate of devaluation all but coincides with the expected rate of realignment. If τ approaches zero, the expected rate of devaluation is the per unit time expected jump in the actual exchange rate at a realignment, which differs from the jump in central parity by the expected movement of the exchange rate within the band. For short maturities the latter effect may be sizable. Hence, for sufficiently long maturities the normal differential will apply as an adequate measure of the expected rate of devaluation, whereas for shorter maturities it makes sense to adjust the differential according to equation (6.6).

Ball and Roma (1994) found that for the various ERM-currencies the process for the exchange rate within the band can be modelled most appropriately as a mean-reverting Ornstein–Uhlenbeck process. Moreover, Svensson (1991b) has shown that the relationship between the expected rate of depreciation over a finite horizon equal to a month or longer, and the position of the exchange rate within the band can be approximated by a linear function for fairly reasonable parameter values. In addition, in a model of optimal intervention policy in a managed-float regime like in Delgado and Dumas (1991) and Lindberg and Söderlind (1993), the expected rate of depreciation within the band is generally not only a function of the current exchange rate; at least domestic and foreign interest rates should be taken into consideration (Svensson, 1994, p.190). Hence, $E_t[\Delta x_{t+\tau}|NR]/\tau$ can be estimated using the fitted values of a regression of the actual rate of depreciation within the band on these observable variables:

$$\frac{\Delta x_{t+\tau}}{\tau\,dt} = \sum_j \beta_{0j}d_j + \beta_1 x_t + \beta_2 i_t^\tau + \beta_3 i_t^{\tau,*} + \eta_{t+\tau}, \qquad (6.7)$$

where the variable d_j is a dummy for each period between two realignments, in order to allow the intercepts to vary. The error term $\eta_{t+\tau}$ is uncorrelated with the regressors, heteroskedastic, and serially correlated for overlapping time-intervals ($\tau > dt$). Ordinary least squares will give consistent estimates of the coefficients, but their standard errors may be inappropriate.[11]

Equation (6.7) is estimated separately for the cross-Deutschemark exchange rates of Austria (ÖS/DM), Belgium (BF/DM), Denmark (DK/DM), France (FF/DM), Ireland (IP/DM), Italy (IL/DM), and the Netherlands (NG/DM), for a time to maturity of one month ($\tau = dt = 1/12$ year). The data used have been described in detail in the previous section. The period covered starts at the beginning of the EMS in March 1979 except for Austria (January 1980), and ends in December 1992, except for Italy (August 1992). Months before a realignment occurred are excluded from the sample in order not to include potential jumps.[12] So the estimation results presented in Table 6.1 must be interpreted as conditional upon no realignment. As heteroskedasticity in the error terms $\eta_{t+\tau}$ of all regressions is likely, White's (1980) covariance matrix has been used to calculate standard errors.

The first column of Table 6.1 reports our estimates of the expected rate of depreciation within the band of the ÖS/DM exchange rate. Although the Austrian monetary authorities have never announced an official target zone for the schilling, the exchange rate has continually been firmly pegged, without a single realignment during the period under consideration. The intercept is slightly positive, but insignificant at conventional levels. The degree of mean reversion in the ÖS/DM exchange rate is very strong and highly significant even at the 1%-level, as can be inferred from the coefficient on x_t and its corresponding t-statistic. These results indicate that the Austrian monetary authorities have implicitly defended a very narrow target zone. The sign pattern on the interest rate coefficients is also consistent with a purposive intervention strategy under such a managed-float regime (Lindberg and Söderlind, 1993).[13]

It follows from the second column of Table 6.1 that the Belgian franc has witnessed 7 realignments since the beginning of the EMS: the intercepts vary between 0.122 and 0.302 and they are all significant. Similar results are found for the Danish krona, the Irish punt, and the Dutch guilder. This could point at a systematic (positive) drift in the exchange rates vis-à-vis the Deutschemark, albeit this magnitude of the drift varies substantially over the

Table 6.1: Exchange rate depreciation within the band: 1 month

	ÖS/DM	BF/DM	DK/DM	FF/DM	IP/DM	IL/DM	NG/DM
β_{0j}: 79.03 (*intercepts*)	--	0.157 (4.4)	0.165 (3.0)	0.018 (0.7)	--	-0.043 (0.6)	0.090 (5.7)
79.09	--	0.226 (4.7)	0.300 (6.3)	0.014 (0.4)	--	0.011 (0.1)	0.020 (1.5)
79.11	--	|	0.152 (3.3)	|	--	|	|
80.01	0.007 (1.3)	|	|	|	--	|	|
81.03	|	|	|	|	--	-0.010 (0.1)	|
81.10	|	0.240 (4.5)	0.132 (3.1)	0.037 (0.7)	0.099 (2.2)	0.033 (0.3)	|
82.02	|	0.302 (4.9)	0.195 (4.1)	|	|	|	|
82.06	|	0.234 (4.5)	0.180 (4.3)	0.024 (0.6)	0.085 (2.3)	0.021 (0.2)	|
83.03	|	0.179 (5.0)	0.101 (3.7)	0.000 (0.0)	0.049 (1.8)	0.006 (0.1)	0.023 (2.6)
85.07	|	|	|	|	|	0.023 (0.4)	|
86.04	|	0.153 (5.5)	0.134 (4.5)	0.024 (0.9)	0.060 (1.6)	-0.013 (0.2)	|
86.08	|	|	|	|	0.087 (2.6)	|	|
87.01	|	0.122 (5.1)	0.105 (3.9)	0.004 (0.2)	0.029 (1.2)	0.017 (0.4)	|
90.01 -92.12	|	|	|	|	|	-0.039 (0.5)	|
β_1 (x_t):	-4.070 (5.3)	-1.384 (3.4)	-1.764 (3.9)	-1.500 (2.7)	-1.106 (2.0)	-0.965 (2.2)	-1.865 (3.8)
β_2 (i_t^{τ}):	-0.301 (1.6)	-1.908 (4.0)	-1.125 (4.2)	-0.164 (0.6)	-0.451 (2.1)	-0.236 (0.7)	-1.498 (5.3)
β_3 ($i_t^{\tau*}$):	0.200 (1.3)	0.650 (2.2)	0.351 (1.5)	0.383 (1.5)	0.333 (1.3)	0.781 (1.0)	1.251 (4.9)
R^2	0.22	0.31	0.29	0.13	0.16	0.10	0.24
σ	0.016	0.039	0.049	0.049	0.049	0.070	0.028
N	156	157	156	158	127	150	164

Notes: t-statistics in parentheses. OLS with White's (1980) heteroskedasticity-consistent covariance matrix. A vertical bar indicates no change in intercept. N: # Observations. R^2: Adjusted R-squared. σ: Standard Error of Regression.

various regimes. The same holds for the relative magnitude of the intercepts if a comparison is made between the various currencies. For France and Italy, on the other hand, such a systematic drift in the cross-DM exchange rate cannot be discerned. Significant mean reversion can be asserted in all currencies, although in a much weaker form than in the case of Austria.[14]

For France, Ireland, and Italy it seems that the coefficient β_1 hardly indicates a mean-reverting process in x_t. It is well known, however, that if the true coefficient β_1 is zero, there is a downward bias in the estimate of the coefficient and the usual t-distribution does not apply. The critical level for a standard Dickey–Fuller test on a 5% significance level is –2.88 for this sample size (MacKinnon, 1991, p.275), so that our test cannot reject the hypothesis of a unit root in x_t for France, Ireland, and Italy.[15] As we saw in the previous section, the exchange rate policies pursued in these countries have lacked credibility within the one-month horizon at several points in time during the 1980s. Consequently, the position of the exchange rate within the band may have fuelled devaluation expectations in light of the model presented in Chapter 5, thereby limiting the degree of mean reversion (recall equation 5.17, together with Tables 5.1.4 and 5.1.6). Besides, accompanying estimates of β_2 and β_3 suggest that monetary policy has been least effective in France and Italy, compared to the other EMS countries. France and Italy constitute the larger countries in the EMS, in which the willingness to follow the German interest rate 'dictation' has presumably been more limited than in smaller member countries that depend more on Germany as a partner in foreign trade. Consequently, the vigour with which the exchange rate policy is being pursued might well have been somewhat more restricted by conflicting interests in those countries.[16]

With the estimates of Table 6.1, we can adjust short-term interest differentials according to equation (6.6), and end up with an operational measure of (total) devaluation expectations. Figures 6.2A–G show the (quarterly averages of) one-month adjusted and non-adjusted interest differentials, as well as the long-term interest differentials vis-à-vis Germany for Austria, Belgium, Denmark, France, Ireland, Italy, and the Netherlands.[17] It can readily be seen that on average these differentials were much more moderate in Austria and the Netherlands than in the other EMS countries. Towards the end of our sample, exchange rate volatility diminished, and interest rate differentials narrowed in all countries. For short maturities the discrepancies between (unfiltered) interest differentials and devaluation expectations appear to be substantial, both in magnitude and in sign. In general, filtering out the movements of the exchange rate within the band increases the volatility of interest differentials. (Compare the standard deviations of the differentials reported in Table 6A1 of Appendix A to this chapter.) Apparently, monetary authorities have utilised the exchange rate within the band as a buffer for (possibly undesirable) interest rate adjustments.

Figure 6.2A: Interest differentials with Germany: Austria

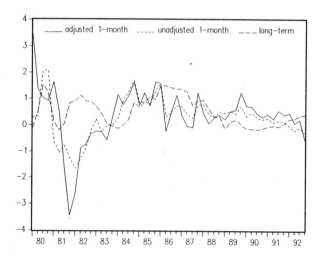

Figure 6.2B: Interest differentials with Germany: Belgium

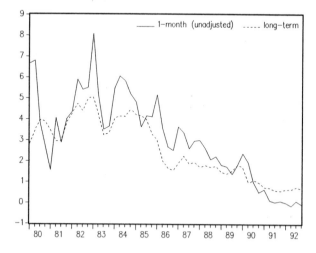

Figure 6.2C: Interest differentials with Germany: Denmark

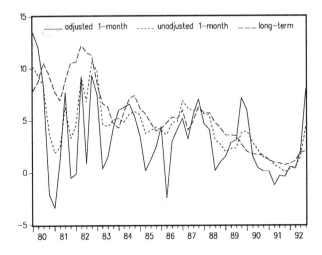

Figure 6.2D: Interest differentials with Germany: France

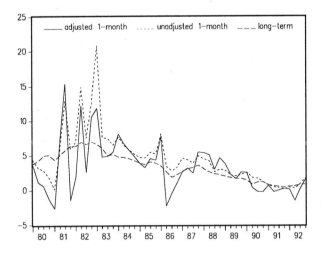

Figure 6.2E: Interest differentials with Germany: Ireland

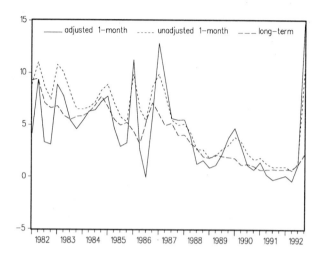

Figure 6.2F: Interest differentials with Germany: Italy

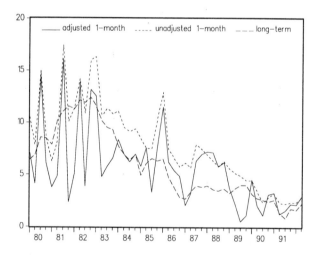

Figure 6.2G: Interest differentials with Germany: The Netherlands

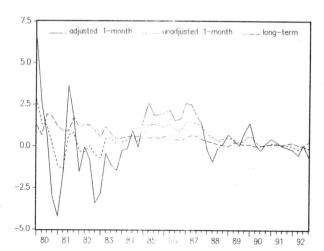

IV   Fundamental determinants

IV.1   Theoretical background: Review of the literature

In the previous section interest differentials have been empirically subdivided into devaluation expectations and movements of the exchange rate within the band. From the target zone model presented in Chapter 5 it can be inferred that both components must ultimately be determined by the expected trend in the composite fundamental h during the time to maturity $[t, t+\tau]$ (combine for example equations 5.22 to 5.25 from section 5.II.3). Due to the assumption reflected in the driving process (5.21) that h is strong Markov in levels, expectations of h are uniquely determined by the current level of the composite fundamental. Consequently, the sample paths of the expected rate of depreciation within the band, the expected rate of devaluation, and hence the fixed-term τ interest differential are all fully determined by fluctuations in exogenous fundamentals and devaluation risks, as summarised in the current level of our composite fundamental h_t.

The interpretation of h, and hence of f, will thus be crucial for most of what follows, and will depend on the specific model of exchange rate determination one has in mind. It is well known, however, that available theoretical models are inconclusive as to what these fundamentals are, so they can be suggestive at best (compare Clark et al., 1994). In case of the monetary approach, for example, the fundamental mainly consists of variables appearing in excess money demand functions, such as liquidity and activity levels. But in an 'escape-clause' model like that of Giovannini (1990), or in a 'projection-equation' approach as in Chen and Giovannini (1993), any variable will do, provided only that it appears in the central bank's reaction function or in the market participants' information set, respectively. Instead of resorting to a particular model, we take an eclectic (and pragmatic) attitude towards the selection of potential determinants of interest differentials. The objective then is to find proxies that cover a broad spectrum of fundamentals and that capture the essence of expected exchange rate changes, within the band or of the band itself. Chapter 5 made it clear that, in addition to 'pure' fundamentals, the set of possible determinants should also include certain policy variables that aim to measure intervention activities from the part of the monetary authorities, like reserve positions and money supply, the latter merely in case of unsterilised intervention.[18]

In order to select additional explanatory variables we consider various models of speculative attacks and subsequent balance-of-payments crises.[19] Krugman's (1979) model, for example, assumes that an exogenous government budget deficit lays at the root of the crisis. Expansionary fiscal policy is financed by domestic credit. According to this model the monetary authorities are prepared to defend the exchange rate peg until reserves reach a pre-specified lower bound. As investors permanently rebalance their portfolios, some of the additional domestic assets will be exchanged for foreign exchange reserves of the central bank.[20] So it becomes inevitable that eventually reserves will approach their lower limit. It is straightforward to extend the model to a (semi) small country setting by relaxing the assumption of purchasing power parity (Goldberg, 1991, 1994). In that case a shift to more expansionary fiscal policies increases the demand for domestic goods, which drives up the price level and leads to a real exchange rate appreciation, and a decline in national competitiveness. The empirical implication of these first generation speculative attack models, then, is that one should look for expansionary fiscal and monetary policies, and/or real exchange rate appreciation prior to a switch in regime, which may in turn consist of a simple devaluation or of a change to a floating exchange rates system.

The second generation of speculative attack models has different empirical implications. Flood and Garber (1984b) and Obstfeld (1986) formalise the idea that a pegged exchange rate can be successfully attacked even without any apparent problem with its sustainability due to insufficient reserves. Multiple equilibria may exist in the foreign exchange market because of the contingent nature of the authorities' policy rule. In the absence of an attack, monetary and fiscal policies are in balance, and nothing prevents the maintenance of the currently prevailing peg. An attack may occur, however, if investors rationally anticipate that, if and only if attacked, policy will become more expansionary, which is only consistent with a lower level for the exchange rate.

Internal and external macroeconomic balance are two (medium-term) objectives that must be reconciled with 'fundamental equilibrium exchange rates' (Williamson, 1991, 1994), and are likely to dominate the authorities' (contingent) policy rule. Internal equilibrium is normally defined as achieving the underlying level of potential output; information on internal balance may be gathered from domestic inflation and unemployment (Clark et al., 1994). Ozkun and Sutherland (1994) postulate a trade-off in the authorities' policy rule between the level of the domestic interest rate and the rate of unemployment. They show that high and rising unemployment might lead the government to abandon the peg. Anticipations of such a policy change could lead to an immediate attack on the national currency. Under the Drazen and Masson (1994) notion of the policymaker's credibility, the unemployment rate signals the stance of government policy and the costs of maintaining a particular stance. Therefore, expectations of a realignment also reflect pressures to stimulate employment and growth after a period of restrictive policies. Similarly, De Grauwe (1994) stresses the role of different preferences regarding the weights to be attached to inflation and unemployment in the interpretation of internal balance in the various EMS countries. This asymmetry in preferences produces conflicts of policies concerning the appropriate stance of monetary policy for the system as a whole, thereby increasing doubts about the commitment towards fixed exchange rates.

External balance may be defined as achieving an equilibrium position in the current and capital accounts (Clark et al., 1994). As such it would imply a value of the current account that is consistent with investment and demographic needs of the country in question, which is also influenced by the level of competitiveness. Seen in this light, the equilibrium current account represents the desired intertemporal reallocation of resources between countries; identifying the preferred path for the current account now means identifying the preferred path for international debt. A related issue in this respect is the impact of government balance on the current account. As has already been spelled out in Chapters 1–3, Ricardian Equivalence predicts that changes in taxation will be associated with offsetting changes in private saving; hence there will be no net impact on the current account. Alternatively, if private sector savings behaviour is unaffected by such actions of the government, changes in the government budget would feed into the external accounts on a one-for-one basis. Chapter 3 demonstrated that available empirical evidence for the European Union points somewhere between these extremes, showing the private sector partially offsetting changes in government debt.

On the basis of the previous review of the literature we have included in our set of fundamentals the domestic rate of consumer price inflation (π); export price competitiveness relative to Germany (*EPC*); the liquidity ratio (*M/Y*); the stock of foreign exchange reserves (*F*); the government budget deficit (*D*); the current account (*CA*); and the rate of unemployment (*U*):[21]

$$h = h(\pi, EPC, M/Y, F/Y, D/Y, CA/Y, U, \ldots). \tag{6.8}$$

Thus, we aim to detect a causal relationship between these fundamentals and devaluation expectations, whichever measure is used to trace such expectations. An interesting issue here is, whether we can find support for the observation of Svensson (1993) that the adjustment of interest differentials as suggested in section III represents a step forward in the measurement of realignment expectations. Therefore, section IV.2 will present estimates of empirical models encompassing (6.8) in order to reveal any potential form of causality between country-specific fundamentals and expected rates of devaluation for the countries under consideration.

IV.2   Empirical results

We have used quarterly data regarding our fundamental variables, mainly from the *IFS*-database of the IMF. Data on government budget deficits, foreign exchange reserves and current account positions are measured as ratios to (quarterly) GNP.[22] The estimation period is 1981.Q1 to 1992.Q4, except for Ireland (1982.Q1–92.Q4; due to lack of interest rate data) and Italy (1981.Q1–92.Q2; end of ERM participation). Before estimating the model, each variable is converted into a stationary process using the proper degree of differencing implied by the augmented Dickey–Fuller test. In Table 6A1 of Appendix A to this chapter it is shown that in general for all countries the three types of interest differentials are (trend-) stationary, whereas the first-difference operator is needed to induce stationarity for the fundamental variables in the analysis.[23] A clear exception from that regularity is the case of Ireland, where both measures of short-term devaluation expectations seem to be non-stationary at first sight. However, further investigation has shown that this result is caused by a single observation, being the fourth quarter of 1992 (see also Figure 6.2E). After the British pound sterling was forced to leave the ERM in September 1992, pressure on the Irish punt mounted, and short-term interest rates had to be raised to unprecedented levels.[24] For the sake of mutual comparison we decided to include all interest differentials in levels, while all fundamentals were inserted in first differences, denoted by D^1 ($=1-L$).

To allow for possible feedback mechanisms among the variables considered, a 8×8 vector autoregressive (VAR) system has been specified and estimated. As has already been elucidated in Chapter 1, this VAR modelling technique has been recommended by Sims (1980a, 1982) among others, because the procedure takes into account the potential endogeneity of explanatory variables, thereby imposing no restrictions on the dynamic linkages among variables in the model. Although it may be difficult to interpret individual coefficient estimates due to the reduced-form nature of VAR models, more general Granger-causality inferences may be derived from the joint significance of a group of coefficients in the system. The general form of our vector autoregressive model can be represented by the following reduced-form system:

$$Z_t = I + \Delta(L)Z_t + \eta_t, \tag{6.9}$$

where I is a 8×1 vector of intercepts, η_t is a 8×1 vector of white-noise disturbance terms, and $\Delta(L)$ is a 8×8 matrix of lagged polynomial coefficients. Each (i,j)th element of $\Delta(L)$ is defined in terms of the lag operator L, as in equation (1.2). Finally, Z_t is a 8×1 column vector of the endogenous variables, in which we can substitute interest differentials as well as (adjusted) devaluation expectations according to equation (6.6):

$$Z \equiv [\delta, D^1(\pi), D^1(EPC), D^1(M/Y),$$
$$D^1(F/Y), D^1(D/Y), D^1(CA/Y), D^1(U)]^T. \tag{6.10}$$

The number of lags on each variable in each equation is determined by Akaike's Final Prediction Error criterion (*FPE*) whilst the maximum number of lags is set at four. The variables are ranked for inclusion in each equation by the 'specific gravity' criterion of Caines, Keng, and Sethi (1981). The use of such an *FPE* criterion prevents the rather arbitrary restrictions of any pre-imposed lag structure, as in Caramazza (1993) and Lindberg, Svensson, and Söderlind (1991). Moreover, the *FPE* criterion can also take into account the cumulative effects of certain fundamentals, albeit to a limited extent. Under fairly general conditions, Hsiao (1981) has shown that the inclusion of a variable based on the *FPE* criterion is evidence for a weak Granger-causal ordering. If the included variable further exerts a statistically significant effect, the Granger-causal impact can be identified as strong form (Kawai, 1980).

  Once the lag structure has been specified, the system is estimated by means of full information maximum likelihood (FIML), an iterative procedure that takes into account the cross-equation correlations between the various residuals. The model specifications based on the *FPE* criterion as described above are reported in Appendix B for Austria, Belgium, Denmark, France, Ireland, Italy, and the Netherlands, respectively. Tables 6.2A to 6.2G present system Likelihood Ratio (χ^2) tests of multivariate strong Granger-causality hypotheses on the lagged polynomial coefficients of the fundamentals in the equations for the interest differentials. We test for long-run and short-run restrictions, the former implying that the sum of the coefficients is zero, while the latter also require that all individual coefficients are zero.

  It follows from Table 6.2A that from our collection of fundamentals, foreign exchange reserves and current account positions both have weakly Granger-caused Austrian interest differentials vis-à-vis Germany, regardless of the term under investigation; unemployment only appears to have affected short-term credibility. Measuring devaluation expectations within the one-month horizon by adjusting corresponding differentials for the expected movement of the exchange rate within the band, makes the set of fundamentals of interest expand: it now also includes policy variables like money supply and the budget deficit. It is conceivable that those fundamentals

Table 6.2A: Strong Granger-causality tests: Austria

For Z including one-month (unadjusted) interest differentials:

		long-run restrictions		short-run restrictions	
Hypothesis	Z_j	LR-statistic	p-value	LR-statistic	p-value
$d_{15}(L) = 0$	F/Y	$\chi^2(1) = 28.00**$	0.000	$\chi^2(4) = 33.14**$	0.000
$d_{17}(L) = 0$	CA/Y	$\chi^2(1) = 2.01$	0.156	$\chi^2(3) = 7.10$	0.069
$d_{18}(L) = 0$	U	$\chi^2(1) = 5.34*$	0.021	idem	

For Z including one-month devaluation expectations (adjusted differentials):

		long-run restrictions		short-run restrictions	
Hypothesis	Z_j	LR-statistic	p-value	LR-statistic	p-value
$d_{14}(L) = 0$	M/Y	$\chi^2(1) = 11.40**$	0.001	idem	
$d_{15}(L) = 0$	F/Y	$\chi^2(1) = 28.34**$	0.000	$\chi^2(4) = 45.20**$	0.000
$d_{16}(L) = 0$	D/Y	$\chi^2(1) = 0.70$	0.403	$\chi^2(3) = 24.00**$	0.000
$d_{17}(L) = 0$	CA/Y	$\chi^2(1) = 13.97**$	0.000	$\chi^2(4) = 23.94**$	0.000
$d_{18}(L) = 0$	U	$\chi^2(1) = 41.27**$	0.000	$\chi^2(2) = 42.91**$	0.000

For Z including long-term devaluation expectations (unadjusted differentials):

		long-run restrictions		short-run restrictions	
Hypothesis	Z_j	LR-statistic	p-value	LR-statistic	p-value
$d_{15}(L) = 0$	F/Y	$\chi^2(1) = 20.61**$	0.000	$\chi^2(2) = 20.70**$	0.000
$d_{17}(L) = 0$	CA/Y	$\chi^2(1) = 3.48$	0.062	$\chi^2(4) = 21.09**$	0.000

Notes: The vector Z of the dependent variables is defined in equation (6.10). LR-statistic is Likelihood Ratio test-statistic: $N[log|U_r'U_r| - log|U_u'U_u|]$, where $U_{u,r}$ represent the residual covariance matrices of the unrestricted and restricted models, respectively. p-value denotes the marginal significance level. $d_{ij}=0$ means that the hypothesis is tested whether it is allowed to restrict (that is to eliminate) the lags on variable j included in the specification of variable i if inclusion has been decided upon in Appendix B according to the FPE criterion. Significance at the 5%- (*) and 1%-level (**) is indicated. Definitions and sources of the variables are in Appendix A.

have given rise to inflationary expectations, thereby challenging the preservation of the 'hard-currency' option. On the other hand, it is remarkable that in case of the Austrian schilling neither the inflation rate nor the index of export price competitiveness relative to Germany show up as underlying determinants of devaluation expectations. Hochreiter and Winckler (1995) argue that the development of these variables should be regarded as the biggest threat to the Austrian 'hard-currency' strategy. The policy of fixing the schilling to the Deutschemark explains the convergence of the Austrian inflation rate towards the German rate during most of the decade. However, since convergence has been less than perfect, the schilling has appreciated slightly in real terms vis-à-vis the Deutschemark (Genberg, 1990, p.204).

Table 6.2B: Strong Granger-causality tests: Belgium

For Z including one-month (unadjusted) interest differentials:

		long-run restrictions		short-run restrictions	
Hypothesis	Z_j	*LR-statistic*	*p-value*	*LR-statistic*	*p-value*
$d_{14}(L) = 0$	*M/Y*	$\chi^2(1) = 3.48$	0.062	idem	
$d_{17}(L) = 0$	*CA/Y*	$\chi^2(1) = 2.65$	0.103	$\chi^2(3) = 11.15^*$	0.011
$d_{18}(L) = 0$	*U*	$\chi^2(1) = 15.63^{**}$	0.000	idem	

For Z including long-term devaluation expectations (unadjusted differentials):

		long-run restrictions		short-run restrictions	
Hypothesis	Z_j	*LR-statistic*	*p-value*	*LR-statistic*	*p-value*
$d_{13}(L) = 0$	*EPC*	$\chi^2(1) = 7.05^{**}$	0.008	idem	
$d_{15}(L) = 0$	*F/Y*	$\chi^2(1) = 1.24$	0.266	idem	
$d_{16}(L) = 0$	*D/Y*	$\chi^2(1) = 6.51^*$	0.010	idem	
$d_{17}(L) = 0$	*CA/Y*	$\chi^2(1) = 0.51$	0.476	$\chi^2(2) = 16.91^{**}$	0.000
$d_{18}(L) = 0$	*U*	$\chi^2(1) = 6.84^{**}$	0.009	idem	

Notes: See Table 6.2A.

Apparently, the impact of this appreciation has not been so devastating as to be observable over and above its impact on the current account balance.

Furthermore, Table 6.2A also demonstrates that in most cases the Granger-causal impact of the Austrian fundamentals mentioned above on devaluation expectations can also be identified as strong form. The only exception here is the influence of the current account on one-month (raw) interest differentials, while a strong Granger-causal ordering between that fundamental and long-term differentials only exists in the short run; the same goes for budget deficits and adjusted short-term differentials.

In case of the Belgian one-month interest differential only money supply, current account positions, and the unemployment rate have survived the *FPE*-selection process (Table 6.2B). The current account turned from deficit into surplus towards the end of the 1980s. This surplus is often regarded as one of the building blocks of the franc-fort policy pursued by the Belgian authorities ever since. Long-term interest differentials have also been weakly Granger-caused by (improvements in) export price competitiveness, foreign exchange reserves, and the deteriorating state of the Belgian public finances.[25] At first sight it appears that these fundamentals have merely affected the credibility of the Belgian exchange rate policy in the long run. One has to keep in mind, however, the potential discrepancy between short-term interest differentials and devaluation expectations, which, unfortunately, we cannot further analyse in the Belgian case. Finally, Table 6.2B also reveals that the Granger-causal impact of export price competitiveness, budget deficits, the current account, and unemployment can additionally be characterised as strong form, albeit that the influence of the current account remains restricted to the short run.

Table 6.2C: Strong Granger-causality tests: Denmark

For Z including one-month (unadjusted) interest differentials:

		long-run restriction		short-run restrictions	
Hypothesis	Z_j	*LR-statistic*	*p-value*	*LR-statistic*	*p-value*
$d_{12}(L) = 0$	π	$\chi^2(1) = 9.91**$	0.002	$\chi^2(4) = 16.65**$	0.002
$d_{18}(L) = 0$	U	$\chi^2(1) = 5.66*$	0.017	idem	

For Z including one-month devaluation expectations (adjusted differentials):

		long-run restrictions		short-run restrictions	
Hypothesis	Z_j	*LR-statistic*	*p-value*	*LR-statistic*	*p-value*
$d_{16}(L) = 0$	D/Y	$\chi^2(1) = 2.54$	0.111	idem	
$d_{18}(L) = 0$	U	$\chi^2(1) = 0.19$	0.662	$\chi^2(4) = 18.95**$	0.001

For Z including long-term devaluation expectations (unadjusted differentials):

		long-run restrictions		short-run restrictions	
Hypothesis	Z_j	*LR-statistic*	*p-value*	*LR-statistic*	*p-value*
$d_{12}(L) = 0$	π	$\chi^2(1) = 5.62*$	0.017	$\chi^2(3) = 17.48**$	0.001
$d_{14}(L) = 0$	M/Y	$\chi^2(1) = 19.99**$	0.000	idem	
$d_{15}(L) = 0$	F/Y	$\chi^2(1) = 2.27$	0.132	idem	
$d_{16}(L) = 0$	D/Y	$\chi^2(1) = 6.69**$	0.010	$\chi^2(4) = 11.01*$	0.026
$d_{18}(L) = 0$	U	$\chi^2(1) = 2.26$	0.133	$\chi^2(4) = 14.37**$	0.006

Notes: See Table 6.2A.

For Denmark (Table 6.2C) we can discern a Granger-causal relationship between all three types of interest differentials and the unemployment rate. Inflation seems to have affected short-term and long-term interest differentials, but this does not show up in the equation for one-month filtered differentials. The budget deficit variable, on the other hand, does show up in short-term adjusted and long-term interest differentials, but has not been included in the specification for short-term unadjusted differentials. Additionally, long-term credibility also seems to have been affected by the 'intervention variables' money supply and foreign exchange reserves.

From the subset of Danish fundamentals mentioned above, inflation and unemployment explain a significant part of the development of long-term as well as short-term differentials in a strong Granger-causal sense, this in contrast to the government budget deficit (Table 6.2C).The deficit only seems to have significantly affected long-term interest differentials, together with money supply. As might have been expected beforehand, the variables that are mostly associated with the Danish stabilisation program of 1982, also show up as determinants of interest rate movements. The stabilisation program consisted of three elements (De Grauwe and Vanhaverbeke, 1990). First, a decision was made to stop the policy of creeping devaluations and to peg the krona to the Deutschemark. Second, a dramatic change in fiscal policies was

Table 6.2D: Strong Granger-causality tests: France

For Z including one-month (unadjusted) interest differentials:

		long-run restrictions		short-run restrictions	
Hypothesis	Z_j	LR-statistic	p-value	LR-statistic	p-value
$d_{12}(L) = 0$	π	$\chi^2(1) = 6.47*$	0.011	$\chi^2(4) = 43.47**$	0.000
$d_{14}(L) = 0$	M/Y	$\chi^2(1) = 9.63**$	0.002	$\chi^2(2) = 12.31**$	0.002
$d_{16}(L) = 0$	D/Y	$\chi^2(1) = 10.48**$	0.001	$\chi^2(2) = 17.81**$	0.000
$d_{17}(L) = 0$	CA/Y	$\chi^2(1) = 6.14*$	0.013	$\chi^2(2) = 17.34**$	0.000
$d_{18}(L) = 0$	U	$\chi^2(1) = 4.05*$	0.044	idem	

For Z including one-month devaluation expectations (adjusted differentials):

		long-run restrictions		short-run restrictions	
Hypothesis	Z_j	LR-statistic	p-value	LR-statistic	p-value
$d_{12}(L) = 0$	π	$\chi^2(1) = 6.75**$	0.009	$\chi^2(4) = 18.10**$	0.001
$d_{14}(L) = 0$	M/Y	$\chi^2(1) = 4.78*$	0.029	idem	
$d_{17}(L) = 0$	CA/Y	$\chi^2(1) = 4.52*$	0.033	idem	

For Z including long-term devaluation expectations (unadjusted differentials):

		long-run restrictions		short-run restrictions	
Hypothesis	Z_j	LR-statistic	p-value	LR-statistic	p-value
$d_{12}(L) = 0$	π	$\chi^2(1) = 8.39**$	0.004	$\chi^2(3) = 21.80**$	0.000
$d_{13}(L) = 0$	EPC	$\chi^2(1) = 0.85$	0.358	$\chi^2(4) = 11.54*$	0.021
$d_{14}(L) = 0$	M/Y	$\chi^2(1) = 13.24**$	0.000	$\chi^2(3) = 16.90**$	0.001
$d_{15}(L) = 0$	F/Y	$\chi^2(1) = 0.46$	0.500	$\chi^2(3) = 36.66**$	0.000
$d_{16}(L) = 0$	D/Y	$\chi^2(1) = 5.10*$	0.024	idem	
$d_{17}(L) = 0$	CA/Y	$\chi^2(1) = 20.04**$	0.000	$\chi^2(4) = 28.28**$	0.000
$d_{18}(L) = 0$	U	$\chi^2(1) = 24.16**$	0.000	idem	

Notes: See Table 6.2A.

instituted with spending cuts and tax increases. Last, but certainly not least, capital movements were liberalised. Because of the once-and-for-all stock adjustment effect brought about by the large capital inflows that occurred and the upward revision of private future incomes arising from permanently lower government spending and taxation (Giavazzi and Pagano, 1990), the economy witnessed an investment and consumption boom, leading to a strong increase in employment and a gradual decrease in inflation. As a side effect, the krona started to appreciate in real terms, while relatively large current account deficits persisted. Our results do not indicate, however, that either the loss in competitiveness or the persistent deficits on the current account have markedly challenged the credibility of the Danish hard-currency option. On the contrary, interest rates (and corresponding differentials) declined swiftly.

Table 6.2D demonstrates that equation (6.8) is, especially in the case of France, broadly supported by the data.[26] One-month unadjusted interest

Table 6.2E: Strong Granger-causality tests: Ireland

For Z including one-month (unadjusted) interest differentials:

		long-run restrictions		short-run restrictions	
Hypothesis	Z_j	*LR-statistic*	*p-value*	*LR-statistic*	*p-value*
$d_{12}(L) = 0$	π	$\chi^2(1) = 26.89**$	0.000	$\chi^2(2) = 27.91**$	0.000
$d_{13}(L) = 0$	*EPC*	$\chi^2(1) = 0.23$	0.629	$\chi^2(3) = 16.82**$	0.001
$d_{14}(L) = 0$	*M/Y*	$\chi^2(1) = 0.24$	0.623	$\chi^2(4) = 11.27*$	0.024
$d_{15}(L) = 0$	*F/Y*	$\chi^2(1) = 10.37**$	0.001	idem	
$d_{17}(L) = 0$	*CA/Y*	$\chi^2(1) = 7.39**$	0.007	idem	
$d_{18}(L) = 0$	*U*	$\chi^2(1) = 6.56*$	0.010	$\chi^2(4) = 35.86**$	0.000

For Z including one-month devaluation expectations (adjusted differentials):

		long-run restrictions		short-run restrictions	
Hypothesis	Z_j	*LR-statistic*	*p-value*	*LR-statistic*	*p-value*
$d_{12}(L) = 0$	π	$\chi^2(1) = 12.68**$	0.000	idem	
$d_{13}(L) = 0$	*EPC*	$\chi^2(1) = 6.07*$	0.014	idem	
$d_{17}(L) = 0$	*CA/Y*	$\chi^2(1) = 4.11*$	0.043	idem	
$d_{18}(L) = 0$	*U*	$\chi^2(1) = 5.51*$	0.019	$\chi^2(4) = 30.90**$	0.000

For Z including long-term devaluation expectations (unadjusted differentials):

		long-run restrictions		short-run restrictions	
Hypothesis	Z_j	*LR-statistic*	*p-value*	*LR-statistic*	*p-value*
$d_{12}(L) = 0$	π	$\chi^2(1) = 6.04*$	0.014	idem	
$d_{13}(L) = 0$	*EPC*	$\chi^2(1) = 1.26$	0.262	idem	
$d_{14}(L) = 0$	*M/Y*	$\chi^2(1) = 3.27$	0.071	$\chi^2(3) = 9.28*$	0.026
$d_{18}(L) = 0$	*U*	$\chi^2(1) = 3.15$	0.076	idem	

Notes: See Table 6.2A. Sample 1983.Q1–92.Q4 (#Obs.=40).

differentials have been strongly Granger-caused by inflation, money supply, budget deficits, current account positions, and unemployment. Once these differentials are corrected for expected exchange rate movements within the band, budget deficits and unemployment drop out of the equation. Apparently, these variables have mainly affected the movement of the franc within the band that is excluded from the adjusted differential. Presumably, this component was welcomed by the French monetary authorities, because it enabled them to avoid undesirable interest adjustments. Long-term interest differentials have been strongly Granger-caused by all fundamentals, albeit the impact of competitiveness and foreign exchange reserves remained restricted to the short run.[27] As might be expected, the stop–go fiscal policy pursued by the French government in the first half of the 1980s has also influenced market perceptions of devaluation expectations.

Table 6.2E reports on Ireland. Short-term devaluation expectations have been affected predominantly by inflation, competitiveness, current account,

Table 6.2F: Strong Granger-causality tests: Italy

For Z including one-month (unadjusted) interest differentials:

		long-run restrictions		short-run restrictions	
Hypothesis	Z_j	*LR-statistic*	*p-value*	*LR-statistic*	*p-value*
$d_{12}(L) = 0$	π	$\chi^2(1) = 3.92^*$	0.048	$\chi^2(4) = 26.57^{**}$	0.000
$d_{16}(L) = 0$	D/Y	$\chi^2(1) = 10.79^{**}$	0.0041	$\chi^2(4) = 12.44^*$	0.014
$d_{18}(L) = 0$	U	$\chi^2(1) = 14.40^{**}$	0.000	idem	

For Z including one-month devaluation expectations (adjusted differentials):

		long-run restrictions		short-run restrictions	
Hypothesis	Z_j	*LR-statistic*	*p-value*	*LR-statistic*	*p-value*
$d_{12}(L) = 0$	π	$\chi^2(1) = 3.82$	0.051	idem	
$d_{15}(L) = 0$	F/Y	$\chi^2(1) = 3.55$	0.060	idem	
$d_{18}(L) = 0$	U	$\chi^2(1) = 5.75^*$	0.016	$\chi^2(4) = 11.34^*$	0.023

For Z including long-term devaluation expectations (unadjusted differentials):

		long-run restrictions		short-run restrictions	
Hypothesis	Z_j	*LR-statistic*	*p-value*	*LR-statistic*	*p-value*
$d_{13}(L) = 0$	EPC	$\chi^2(1) = 11.50^{**}$	0.001	idem	
$d_{16}(L) = 0$	D/Y	$\chi^2(1) = 6.20^*$	0.013	idem	
$d_{17}(L) = 0$	CA/Y	$\chi^2(1) = 11.22^{**}$	0.001	$\chi^2(4) = 17.76^{**}$	0.001

Notes: See Table 6.2A. Sample 1981.Q1–92.Q2 (#Obs.=46).

and unemployment. The results for long-term interest differentials are somewhat disappointing.[28] Only the liquidity ratio (in the short run) and inflation have strongly Granger-caused interest differentials vis-à-vis Germany. It might be that long-term differentials vis-à-vis the United Kingdom are more relevant from an Irish perspective, given the importance of the UK as a partner in foreign trade and investment.[29] This factor might be less important for short-term differentials, as their development is more directly constrained by the exchange rate target vis-à-vis the Deutschemark.

For Italy Table 6.2F shows that inflation, unemployment, foreign exchange reserves, and budget deficits have all weakly Granger-caused short-term interest differentials and devaluation expectations vis-à-vis Germany. Moreover, unemployment, and inflation and budget deficits in case of unadjusted differentials have also exerted a statistically significant effect on interest differentials. The results obtained with the VAR methodology thus seem to be a clear improvement upon Chen and Giovannini (1993) and Thomas (1994), who barely found any evidence of economic fundamentals having affected short-term devaluation expectations in Italy.

Long-term credibility of the Italian target zone is affected (in a strong Granger-causal sense) by export price competitiveness, and the twin deficits on the government budget and the current account. Presumably, the fiscal

Table 6.2G: Strong Granger-causality tests: The Netherlands

For Z including one-month (unadjusted) interest differentials:

		long-run restrictions		short-run restrictions	
Hypothesis	Z_j	LR-statistic	p-value	LR-statistic	p-value
$d_{12}(L) = 0$	π	$\chi^2(1) = 3.13$	0.077	$\chi^2(2) = 5.69$	0.058
$d_{15}(L) = 0$	F/Y	$\chi^2(1) = 11.00**$	0.001	idem	
$d_{16}(L) = 0$	D/Y	$\chi^2(1) = 4.05*$	0.044	$\chi^2(3) = 9.18*$	0.027
$d_{18}(L) = 0$	U	$\chi^2(1) = 6.40*$	0.011	idem	

For Z including one-month devaluation expectations (adjusted differentials):

		long-run restrictions		short-run restrictions	
Hypothesis	Z_j	LR-statistic	p-value	LR-statistic	p-value
$d_{13}(L) = 0$	EPC	$\chi^2(1) = 2.10$	0.148	idem	
$d_{14}(L) = 0$	M/Y	$\chi^2(1) = 5.39*$	0.020	$\chi^2(2) = 6.90*$	0.032
$d_{15}(L) = 0$	F/Y	$\chi^2(1) = 9.61**$	0.002	idem	
$d_{18}(L) = 0$	U	$\chi^2(1) = 6.39*$	0.011	idem	

For Z including long-term devaluation expectations (unadjusted differentials):

		long-run restrictions		short-run restrictions	
Hypothesis	Z_j	LR-statistic	p-value	LR-statistic	p-value
$d_{12}(L) = 0$	π	$\chi^2(1) = 8.75**$	0.003	$\chi^2(3) = 21.02**$	0.000
$d_{14}(L) = 0$	M/Y	$\chi^2(1) = 20.70**$	0.000	idem	
$d_{16}(L) = 0$	D/Y	$\chi^2(1) = 7.55**$	0.006	$\chi^2(4) = 14.78**$	0.005
$d_{18}(L) = 0$	U	$\chi^2(1) = 2.46$	0.116	$\chi^2(3) = 8.75*$	0.033

Notes: See Table 6.2A.

stance in Italy has been a continuous source of devaluation fears, while the loss in export price competitiveness must have become apparent especially after the monetary authorities narrowed the band-width and wanted to stop the policy of more or less frequent devaluations from January 1990 onwards. However, due to the continuous real appreciation of the lira, this strategy was bound to fail. After two years of relative tranquility, it was corrected by financial markets in September 1992, and the lira immediately fell by about 30 percent.

Finally, Table 6.2G reveals that the main determinants of short-term devaluation expectations for the Netherlands consist of foreign exchange reserves and unemployment, together with money supply (adjusted differentials) or budget deficits (unadjusted differentials), while a minor effect is reported for inflation and export price competitiveness. Despite the policy of fiscal retrenchment that prevailed since 1983, long-term credibility of the Dutch hard-currency option has at certain points in time been endangered by inflation, money supply, government budget deficits, and unemployment, albeit that the fairly favourable development of most of these variables (for example the low inflation record of the Netherlands) contributed to the decline in devaluation expectations over the period considered (see also Figure 6.1G2).

In general, it is interesting to note that in virtually all systems considered (one of the) variables included to capture intervention activities (foreign exchange reserves and the liquidity ratio) indeed affect interest differentials, thereby confirming once more the importance of intramarginal guidance of exchange rate developments. In line with results reported by Rose and Svensson (1994) and De Grauwe (1994), inflation and unemployment also played a significant role in the determination of devaluation expectations for all ERM currencies. This would tend to lend empirical support to models stressing the *internal* balance objective of an exchange rate policy and to studies which postulate an explicit link between (policy) credibility and political pressures arising from the employment situation, as assumed by Drazen and Masson (1994), and Ozkun and Sutherland (1994). On the other hand, our results do not indicate that fundamentals appear more relevant for drift-adjusted devaluation risk than for raw interest differentials, with the single exception of Austria. So, netting out the movement of the exchange rate relative to its central parity does not automatically remove the 'noise' in the relationship between fundamentals and devaluation risk. Based on this, we cannot confirm the claim of Svensson (1993) that adjusting interest differentials as reported in section III represents a step forward in the measurement of devaluation expectations.

With respect to the role of fiscal policy we conclude that in 5 out of the 7 countries (Belgium, Denmark, France, Italy, and the Netherlands) a direct Granger-causal ordering between government budget deficits and long-term interest rates (that is differentials) is found. This result is consistent with the evidence obtained in a loanable funds setting reported in Chapter 3. Different from results reported in Chapter 3, the impact of fiscal policy on interest rates through devaluation expectations does not remain confined to long maturities, but is also present for the one-month horizon. Taken more generally, it seems difficult to subdivide our collection of fundamentals based on the evidence presented here into a group that has mainly affected short-run credibility and a group that has affected long-run credibility. Apparently, with credibility defined as the mirror image of devaluation fears, one might also speak of a 'term structure' of (target zone) credibility that has important intertemporal interdependencies which cannot be neglected.

V   Conclusion

In this chapter we have analysed interest differentials and devaluation expectations vis-à-vis Germany for Austria, Belgium, Denmark, France, Ireland, Italy, and the Netherlands during the (narrow-margin) EMS era. As part of the analysis, expected exchange rate movements were subdivided into realignment expectations and expected exchange rate movements within the band. Since the minimum and maximum amount of depreciation within the band is limited by the band-width of the target zone, we were able to perform a simple test of target zone credibility. According to this test Austrian and Dutch exchange rate policies were fairly credible over the period under consideration, while the other exchange rate policies definitely lacked credibility at several points in time.

Subsequently, we have calculated time-varying devaluation expectations by adjusting corresponding interest differentials for the movement of the exchange rate within the band. Based on the *FPE* criterion we specified a number of vector autoregressive systems to perform Granger-causality tests between the various measures of devaluation expectations and a broad set of country-specific fundamentals. We found no evidence that the fundamentals are more relevant for drift-adjusted devaluation risk than for unadjusted interest differentials. It proved difficult to detect systematic patterns by comparing the various currencies under investigation. However, a significant impact of intervention variables, unemployment, inflation, and fiscal policy on devaluation expectations and interest differentials became evident for almost all ERM participants.

The analysis performed in this chapter can easily be extended. It would be worthwhile, for example, not to confine the concept of credibility to individual member countries of the EMS, but to apply it also to the system as a whole, that is in the aggregate (compare De Grauwe, 1994, and Rose and Svensson, 1994). Furthermore, direct inferences on the time series characteristics and the driving process of the (unobservable) fundamental exchange rates f and h could be made, using approximations of the latter based on data on (observable) exchange rates and interest rates (Flood, Rose, and Mathieson, 1991, Rose and Svensson, 1991). Subsequently, the impact of our set of fundamentals on the fundamental exchange rate could directly be estimated. Finally, more attention could be paid to the separate impact of the risk premium, by subdividing the international investor's risk into several components like foreign exchange rate risk and sovereign credit risk, with the latter potentially affected separately by domestic fiscal policy (Halikias, 1994).

Appendix A: Definitions and sources of the variables used

δ^1 Differential vis-à-vis Germany of 1-month Euromarket interest rates, being period averages of working days, from the Bank of International Settlements (BIS), kindly provided by De Nederlandsche Bank.

δ^l Long-term interest rate differential against Germany, measured as government bond yields, *International Financial Statistics (IFS)* line 61.

S   Spot exchange rate against the Deutschemark, period averages, computed from *IFS* line rf.

C   Central parities against the Deutschemark. For Belgium, Denmark, France, Ireland, Italy, and the Netherlands this series was taken from De Nederlandsche Bank, *Kwartaalbericht*, various editions. For Austria these are proxied by 'Jahresmittelkurse' taken from Österreichische Nationalbank (1991).

π CPI-inflation quarter to quarter, computed from *IFS* line 64.

EPC   Export price competitiveness relative to Germany, measured as the real exchange rate in terms of export prices (index, 1980=100). Export prices were taken from *IFS* line 74.

M   Money supply, *IFS* lines 34+35. For Belgium it was taken from *Tijdschrift van de Nationale Bank van België*, Table XV (M3).

Y   Gross National Product, *IFS*, line 99a for Austria and Denmark. This series has been used as a scaling variable and is not available on a quarterly base for Denmark before 1987 and for Belgium, France, Ireland, and Italy over the whole sample. We therefore interpolated the annual series, using quarterly index numbers on total industrial production for each year from OECD, *Main Economic Indicators (MEI)* or *IFS* line 66. For the Netherlands we used data from the Centraal Bureau voor de Statistiek (CBS), *Kwartaalrekeningen*.

F   Foreign exchange reserves, *IFS* line 11.d (Total Reserves minus Gold).

D   Government budget deficit, *IFS* line 80. For Belgium these data were kindly provided by Mrs. Frieda de Wit from De Nationale Bank van België. For Denmark this series was constructed from data on Governments Bonds Outstanding, kindly provided by Sören Carlsen from Danmark Statistik.

CA   Current account balance, *IFS* line 77ad.

U   Standardised unemployment rate (percentage of labour force), OECD *Main Economic Indicators*.

Unit Root tests for the various variables and their first differences are reported in Table 6A1.

Table 6A1: Unit root tests of the variables used

Series	Mean	Std. Dev.	ADF	I,T,#	ADF(Δ)	I,#(Δ)
Austria:						
δ^1	0.304	0.772	−2.975**	1		
δ^1_{c}	0.380	1.056	−3.266**	0		
δ^l	0.514	0.548	−3.063*	I,1		
π	0.915	3.220	−0.605	3	−12.056**	2
EPC	102.6	5.639	−1.043	2	−7.130**	1
M/Y	3.285	0.224	−1.920	I,4	−2.721**	3
F/Y	25.21	2.908	−2.796	I,T,1	−9.807**	I,0
D/Y	−4.271	3.617	−1.524	I,3	−28.330**	2
CA/Y	−0.291	2.131	−2.982	I,T,1	−33.041**	I,0
U	4.610	1.597	−1.976	I,3	−13.795**	2
Belgium:						
δ^1	3.139	2.054	−4.039*	I,T,0		
δ^l	2.566	1.407	−3.801*	I,T,1		
π	1.072	0.746	−1.777	I,T,3	−7.587**	I,2
EPC	107.6	6.579	−2.366	I,T,1	−5.523**	I,0
M/Y	2.991	0.250	−1.995	I,T,2	−4.143**	I,1
F/Y	22.81	3.244	−3.514*	I,1		
D/Y	−8.917	8.190	−3.124	I,T,3	−33.651**	I,2
CA/Y	0.428	3.115	−1.684	I,T,3	−8.764**	I,2
U	9.967	1.953	−2.729	I,T,1	−4.352**	I,0
Denmark:						
δ^1	4.432	2.600	−4.586**	I,T,3		
δ^1_{c}	3.355	3.713	−4.934**	I,T,2		
δ^l	5.381	3.119	−3.870*	I,T,1		
π	1.340	0.981	−2.339	I,T,3	−10.137**	I,2
EPC	95.03	3.132	−2.118	I,2	−6.222**	1
M/Y	2.093	0.284	−0.099	I,T,3	−12.712**	I,2
F/Y	25.48	7.478	−1.942	I,0	−6.523**	0
D/Y	−6.191	6.889	−0.637	3	−9.262**	2
CA/Y	−1.999	2.717	−2.188	I,T,1	−11.509**	I,0
U	9.215	1.271	−3.005*	I,1		
France:						
δ^1	4.596	3.982	−4.293**	I,T,0		
δ^1_{c}	3.281	3.772	−5.554**	I,T,0		
δ^l	3.340	1.980	−3.811*	I,T,1		
π	1.471	1.048	−1.586	1	−9.847**	0
EPC	102.0	4.754	−2.105	I,T,0	−6.471**	I,0
M/Y	2.665	0.151	−1.217	I,T,4	−3.804**	I,3

Series	Mean	Std. Dev.	ADF	I,T,#	ADF(Δ)	I,#(Δ)
France (continued):						
F/Y	13.70	3.217	−2.553	I,T,0	−7.396**	I,0
D/Y	−2.255	4.731	−1.798	I,3	−27.483**	2
CA/Y	−0.580	0.952	−2.665	I,1	−13.822**	0
U	9.140	1.279	−1.895	I,1	−2.447*	0
Ireland:						
δ^l	5.443	3.217	−2.613	I,T,1	−5.259**	1
$\delta^l_{c'}$	4.311	3.621	−2.090	I,2	−6.570**	1
δ^l	4.049	2.561	−3.756*	I,T,1		
π	1.253	1.022	−4.383**	I,2		
EPC	98.58	9.944	−2.338	I,T,1	−5.052**	I,0
M/Y	1.777	0.148	−2.289	I,T,2	−7.346**	I,1
F/Y	57.93	11.09	−2.352	I	−6.709**	0
D/Y	−8.085	7.308	−1.948	3	−12.648**	2
CA/Y	−2.168	6.624	−2.161	I,T,3	−13.945**	I,2
U	15.114	1.728	−3.189*	I,1		
Italy:						
δ^l	7.837	3.923	−5.603**	I,T,0		
$\delta^l_{c'}$	5.635	3.635	−7.812**	I,T,0		
δ^l	5.872	3.362	−2.536	I,T,0	−6.222**	I,0
π	2.371	1.368	−1.954	I,T,2	−10.559**	I,1
EPC	85.92	7.781	−2.232	I,2	−3.669**	1
M/Y	2.406	0.187	−3.090	I,T,4	−3.369**	3
F/Y	17.20	3.635	−1.822	I,2	−7.327**	1
D/Y	−12.09	3.833	−1.898	I,3	−14.327**	2
CA/Y	−1.031	1.557	−2.582	I,3	−9.728**	2
U	9.588	1.171	−1.836	I,0	−8.375**	0
The Netherlands:						
δ^l	0.464	0.725	−3.365**	2		
$\delta^l_{c'}$	0.384	1.808	−6.113**	1		
δ^l	0.543	0.482	−5.380**	I,T,0		
π	0.718	0.718	−2.273	I,1	−15.950**	0
EPC	103.5	11.08	−2.776	I,T,1	−4.529**	I,0
M/Y	3.104	0.222	−2.870	I,T,4	−4.316**	I,3
F/Y	27.00	3.230	−2.777	I,3	−5.401**	2
D/Y	−4.920	3.728	−2.051	I,T,3	−14.497**	I,2
CA/Y	2.531	2.084	−2.195	I,3	−9.044**	2
U	9.208	1.890	−2.418	I,2	−2.679**	1

Notes: Sample 1980.Q1–92.Q4 except Ireland (1982.Q1–92.Q4, see section IV) and Italy (1980.Q1–92.Q2). ADF: Augmented Dickey–Fuller, I: Intercept, T: Trend, #: Number of lags included. Δ: First difference operator.

Significance at the 5%- (*) and 1%-level (**) is indicated. In order to compute the augmented Dickey–Fuller (ADF) test statistics the following procedure was persevered: 1) We started with the most general model including a trend, a constant, and 4 lags; 2) We first tested for the significance of a trend and a constant term; 3) Starting from the maximum of 4, the number of lags was subsequently diminished until the coefficient of the last lag showed significance at the 10%-level at least, thereby also incorporating its effect on the serial correlation in the residuals.

Appendix B: System specifications based on FPE

$Z = [\delta \quad D^1\pi, \quad D^1EPC, \quad D^1M/Y, \quad D^1F/Y, \quad D^1D/Y, \quad D^1CA/Y, \quad D^1U]^T$

Austria: $\Delta(L)$ for Z including one-month (unadjusted) interest differentials

$d^3_{11}(L)$	0	0	0	$d^4_{15}(L)$	0	$d^3_{17}(L)$	$d^1_{18}(L)$
0	$d^3_{22}(L)$	$d^1_{23}(L)$	$d^4_{24}(L)$	0	0	0	0
0	$d^1_{32}(L)$	$d^2_{33}(L)$	0	0	0	0	$d^1_{38}(L)$
0	$d^3_{42}(L)$	0	$d^4_{44}(L)$	$d^3_{45}(L)$	$d^2_{46}(L)$	0	$d^1_{48}(L)$
0	0	0	$d^4_{54}(L)$	$d^4_{55}(L)$	$d^2_{56}(L)$	$d^2_{57}(L)$	0
0	$d^2_{62}(L)$	0	0	$d^2_{65}(L)$	$d^3_{66}(L)$	0	$d^4_{68}(L)$
$d^2_{71}(L)$	$d^3_{72}(L)$	$d^1_{73}(L)$	0	0	$d^4_{76}(L)$	$d^3_{77}(L)$	$d^4_{78}(L)$
$d^1_{81}(L)$	$d^3_{82}(L)$	$d^2_{83}(L)$	$d^2_{84}(L)$	0	$d^2_{86}(L)$	0	$d^4_{88}(L)$

Z including one-month devaluation expectations (adjusted differentials)

$d^2_{11}(L)$	0	0	$d^1_{14}(L)$	$d^4_{15}(L)$	$d^3_{16}(L)$	$d^4_{17}(L)$	$d^2_{18}(L)$
0	$d^3_{22}(L)$	$d^1_{23}(L)$	$d^4_{24}(L)$	0	0	0	0
0	$d^1_{32}(L)$	$d^2_{33}(L)$	0	0	0	0	$d^1_{38}(L)$
0	$d^3_{42}(L)$	0	$d^4_{44}(L)$	$d^3_{45}(L)$	$d^2_{46}(L)$	0	$d^2_{48}(L)$
0	0	0	$d^4_{54}(L)$	$d^4_{55}(L)$	$d^2_{56}(L)$	$d^2_{57}(L)$	0
0	$d^2_{62}(L)$	0	0	$d^2_{65}(L)$	$d^3_{66}(L)$	0	$d^4_{68}(L)$
$d^2_{71}(L)$	$d^3_{72}(L)$	$d^1_{73}(L)$	0	0	$d^3_{76}(L)$	$d^3_{77}(L)$	$d^4_{78}(L)$
$d^2_{81}(L)$	$d^3_{82}(L)$	$d^1_{83}(L)$	$d^2_{84}(L)$	$d^3_{85}(L)$	0	$d^3_{87}(L)$	$d^4_{88}(L)$

Z including long-term devaluation expectations (unadjusted differentials)

$d^2_{11}(L)$	0	0	0	$d^2_{15}(L)$	0	$d^4_{17}(L)$	0
$d^4_{21}(L)$	$d^3_{22}(L)$	$d^4_{23}(L)$	$d^4_{24}(L)$	$d^1_{25}(L)$	0	0	0
0	$d^1_{32}(L)$	$d^2_{33}(L)$	0	0	0	0	$d^1_{38}(L)$
$d^1_{41}(L)$	$d^3_{42}(L)$	0	$d^4_{44}(L)$	$d^3_{45}(L)$	$d^3_{46}(L)$	$d^4_{47}(L)$	$d^1_{48}(L)$
$d^2_{51}(L)$	0	0	$d^4_{54}(L)$	$d^4_{55}(L)$	$d^2_{56}(L)$	$d^2_{57}(L)$	0
0	$d^2_{62}(L)$	0	0	$d^2_{65}(L)$	$d^3_{66}(L)$	0	$d^4_{68}(L)$
$d^2_{71}(L)$	$d^3_{72}(L)$	0	0	$d^3_{75}(L)$	0	$d^3_{77}(L)$	$d^4_{78}(L)$
0	$d^3_{82}(L)$	$d^2_{83}(L)$	$d^2_{84}(L)$	0	$d^2_{86}(L)$	0	$d^4_{88}(L)$

$$Z = [\delta \quad D^1\pi, \quad D^1EPC, \quad D^1M/Y, \quad D^1F/Y, \quad D^1D/Y, \quad D^1CA/Y, \ D^1U]^T$$

Belgium: Δ(L) for Z including one-month (unadjusted) interest differentials

δ	$D^1\pi$	D^1EPC	D^1M/Y	D^1F/Y	D^1D/Y	D^1CA/Y	D^1U
$d_{11}^1(L)$	0	0	$d_{14}^1(L)$	0	0	$d_{17}^3(L)$	$d_{18}^1(L)$
0	$d_{22}^3(L)$	0	$d_{24}^3(L)$	0	0	0	0
$d_{31}^3(L)$	0	$d_{33}^1(L)$	0	$d_{35}^1(L)$	$d_{36}^2(L)$	0	$d_{38}^2(L)$
$d_{41}^1(L)$	0	$d_{43}^1(L)$	$d_{44}^4(L)$	0	$d_{46}^1(L)$	0	0
0	0	$d_{53}^3(L)$	0	$d_{55}^1(L)$	$d_{56}^1(L)$	0	0
$d_{61}^1(L)$	0	$d_{63}^3(L)$	$d_{64}^4(L)$	$d_{65}^4(L)$	$d_{66}^3(L)$	$d_{67}^2(L)$	$d_{68}^2(L)$
$d_{71}^1(L)$	$d_{72}^1(L)$	$d_{73}^4(L)$	0	$d_{75}^1(L)$	$d_{76}^4(L)$	$d_{77}^3(L)$	0
$d_{81}^1(L)$	$d_{82}^4(L)$	0	$d_{84}^3(L)$	$d_{85}^4(L)$	0	$d_{87}^3(L)$	$d_{88}^2(L)$

Z including long-term devaluation expectations (unadjusted differentials)

δ	$D^1\pi$	D^1EPC	D^1M/Y	D^1F/Y	D^1D/Y	D^1CA/Y	D^1U
$d_{11}^1(L)$	0	$d_{13}^1(L)$	0	$d_{15}^1(L)$	$d_{16}^1(L)$	$d_{17}^1(L)$	$d_{18}^1(L)$
$d_{21}^1(L)$	$d_{22}^3(L)$	0	$d_{24}^3(L)$	0	0	0	0
$d_{31}^4(L)$	0	$d_{33}^1(L)$	0	$d_{35}^1(L)$	$d_{36}^2(L)$	0	$d_{38}^2(L)$
$d_{41}^1(L)$	0	$d_{43}^1(L)$	$d_{44}^4(L)$	0	$d_{46}^1(L)$	0	0
0	0	$d_{53}^3(L)$	0	$d_{55}^1(L)$	$d_{56}^1(L)$	0	0
$d_{61}^2(L)$	0	$d_{63}^3(L)$	$d_{64}^4(L)$	$d_{65}^2(L)$	$d_{66}^3(L)$	$d_{67}^2(L)$	$d_{68}^2(L)$
$d_{71}^4(L)$	$d_{72}^1(L)$	$d_{73}^3(L)$	$d_{74}^4(L)$	$d_{75}^4(L)$	$d_{76}^4(L)$	$d_{77}^3(L)$	$d_{78}^2(L)$
$d_{81}^2(L)$	$d_{82}^2(L)$	$d_{83}^1(L)$	0	0	0	$d_{87}^3(L)$	$d_{88}^2(L)$

Denmark: Δ(L) for Z including one-month (unadjusted) interest differentials

δ	$D^1\pi$	D^1EPC	D^1M/Y	D^1F/Y	D^1D/Y	D^1CA/Y	D^1U
$d_{11}^1(L)$	$d_{12}^4(L)$	0	0	0	0	0	$d_{18}^1(L)$
$d_{21}^4(L)$	$d_{22}^3(L)$	$d_{23}^2(L)$	$d_{24}^1(L)$	$d_{25}^3(L)$	0	$d_{27}^4(L)$	$d_{28}^2(L)$
$d_{31}^3(L)$	0	$d_{33}^2(L)$	$d_{34}^1(L)$	0	0	0	$d_{38}^3(L)$
$d_{41}^3(L)$	$d_{42}^2(L)$	$d_{43}^1(L)$	$d_{44}^4(L)$	0	0	$d_{47}^1(L)$	0
$d_{51}^1(L)$	$d_{52}^1(L)$	0	0	0	0	$d_{57}^2(L)$	0
0	$d_{62}^1(L)$	0	0	0	$d_{66}^3(L)$	0	$d_{68}^1(L)$
0	$d_{72}^3(L)$	$d_{73}^3(L)$	$d_{74}^1(L)$	$d_{75}^4(L)$	0	$d_{77}^4(L)$	0
0	$d_{82}^3(L)$	$d_{83}^2(L)$	$d_{84}^4(L)$	0	0	$d_{87}^3(L)$	$d_{88}^4(L)$

Z including one-month devaluation expectations (adjusted differentials)

δ	$D^1\pi$	D^1EPC	D^1M/Y	D^1F/Y	D^1D/Y	D^1CA/Y	D^1U
$d_{11}^1(L)$	0	0	0	0	$d_{16}^1(L)$	0	$d_{18}^4(L)$
$d_{21}^4(L)$	$d_{22}^3(L)$	0	0	$d_{25}^3(L)$	0	0	$d_{28}^3(L)$
$d_{31}^3(L)$	0	$d_{33}^2(L)$	$d_{34}^1(L)$	0	0	0	$d_{38}^3(L)$
$d_{41}^3(L)$	$d_{42}^3(L)$	0	$d_{44}^4(L)$	$d_{45}^4(L)$	$d_{46}^1(L)$	$d_{47}^1(L)$	0
$d_{51}^2(L)$	$d_{52}^1(L)$	0	0	0	0	$d_{57}^2(L)$	0
$d_{61}^1(L)$	$d_{62}^1(L)$	0	0	0	$d_{66}^3(L)$	0	$d_{68}^1(L)$
0	$d_{72}^3(L)$	$d_{73}^2(L)$	$d_{74}^1(L)$	$d_{75}^4(L)$	0	$d_{77}^4(L)$	0
0	$d_{82}^3(L)$	$d_{83}^2(L)$	$d_{84}^4(L)$	0	0	$d_{87}^3(L)$	$d_{88}^4(L)$

$$Z = [\delta, \quad D^1\pi, \quad D^1EPC, \quad D^1M/Y, \quad D^1F/Y, \quad D^1D/Y, \quad D^1CA/Y, \quad D^1U]^T$$

Denmark: long-term devaluation expectations (unadjusted differentials)

$d^2_{11}(L)$	$d^3_{12}(L)$	0	$d^1_{14}(L)$	$d^1_{15}(L)$	$d^4_{16}(L)$	0	$d^4_{18}(L)$
0	$d^3_{22}(L)$	0	0	$d^3_{25}(L)$	0	0	$d^3_{28}(L)$
0	0	$d^2_{33}(L)$	$d^1_{34}(L)$	0	0	0	$d^3_{38}(L)$
$d^3_{41}(L)$	0	0	$d^4_{44}(L)$	0	$d^1_{46}(L)$	$d^3_{47}(L)$	0
0	0	0	0	0	0	$d^2_{57}(L)$	0
0	$d^1_{62}(L)$	0	0	0	$d^3_{66}(L)$	0	$d^1_{68}(L)$
0	$d^3_{72}(L)$	$d^2_{73}(L)$	$d^1_{74}(L)$	$d^4_{75}(L)$	0	$d^4_{77}(L)$	0
0	$d^3_{82}(L)$	$d^3_{83}(L)$	$d^4_{84}(L)$	0	0	$d^3_{87}(L)$	$d^4_{88}(L)$

France: $\Delta(L)$ for Z including one-month (unadjusted) interest differentials

$d^4_{11}(L)$	$d^4_{12}(L)$	0	$d^2_{14}(L)$	0	$d^2_{16}(L)$	$d^2_{17}(L)$	$d^1_{18}(L)$
0	$d^3_{22}(L)$	0	0	0	$d^2_{26}(L)$	$d^3_{27}(L)$	$d^3_{28}(L)$
$d^2_{31}(L)$	0	0	0	0	0	0	0
$d^1_{41}(L)$	0	0	$d^4_{44}(L)$	0	$d^3_{46}(L)$	0	$d^2_{48}(L)$
0	$d^4_{52}(L)$	$d^1_{53}(L)$	0	0	0	0	0
0	0	$d^1_{63}(L)$	$d^4_{64}(L)$	0	$d^3_{66}(L)$	0	0
$d^3_{71}(L)$	$d^4_{72}(L)$	0	0	$d^1_{75}(L)$	$d^3_{76}(L)$	$d^4_{77}(L)$	$d^3_{78}(L)$
$d^4_{81}(L)$	0	0	0	0	0	0	$d^1_{88}(L)$

Z including one-month devaluation expectations (adjusted differentials)

$d^3_{11}(L)$	$d^4_{12}(L)$	0	$d^1_{14}(L)$	0	0	$d^1_{17}(L)$	0
0	$d^3_{22}(L)$	0	0	0	$d^3_{26}(L)$	$d^1_{27}(L)$	$d^3_{28}(L)$
0	0	0	$d^1_{34}(L)$	0	0	0	0
$d^4_{41}(L)$	0	0	$d^4_{44}(L)$	$d^2_{45}(L)$	$d^3_{46}(L)$	0	0
$d^1_{51}(L)$	$d^4_{52}(L)$	0	0	0	0	0	0
0	0	$d^1_{63}(L)$	$d^4_{64}(L)$	0	$d^3_{66}(L)$	0	0
$d^3_{71}(L)$	$d^4_{72}(L)$	$d^1_{73}(L)$	$d^1_{74}(L)$	$d^1_{75}(L)$	$d^3_{76}(L)$	$d^4_{77}(L)$	$d^3_{78}(L)$
0	0	0	0	$d^3_{85}(L)$	$d^2_{86}(L)$	0	$d^1_{88}(L)$

Z including long-term devaluation expectations (unadjusted differentials)

$d^2_{11}(L)$	$d^3_{12}(L)$	$d^4_{13}(L)$	$d^3_{14}(L)$	$d^3_{15}(L)$	$d^1_{16}(L)$	$d^4_{17}(L)$	$d^1_{18}(L)$
0	$d^3_{22}(L)$	0	0	0	$d^3_{26}(L)$	$d^1_{27}(L)$	$d^3_{28}(L)$
0	0	0	$d^1_{34}(L)$	0	0	0	0
0	0	0	$d^4_{44}(L)$	0	$d^3_{46}(L)$	0	0
0	$d^4_{52}(L)$	$d^1_{53}(L)$	0	0	0	0	0
$d^1_{61}(L)$	0	$d^1_{63}(L)$	$d^4_{64}(L)$	0	$d^3_{66}(L)$	0	0
0	$d^4_{72}(L)$	$d^1_{73}(L)$	$d^1_{74}(L)$	$d^1_{75}(L)$	$d^3_{76}(L)$	$d^4_{77}(L)$	$d^3_{78}(L)$
0	0	0	0	$d^3_{85}(L)$	$d^2_{86}(L)$	0	$d^1_{88}(L)$

$$Z = [\,\delta \quad D^1\pi, \quad D^1EPC, \quad D^1M/Y, \quad D^1F/Y, \quad D^1D/Y, \quad D^1CA/Y, \quad D^1U\,]^{\mathrm{T}}$$

Ireland: $\Delta(L)$ for Z including one-month (unadjusted) interest differentials

$$
\begin{matrix}
d^3_{11}(L) & d^2_{12}(L) & d^3_{13}(L) & d^4_{14}(L) & d^1_{15}(L) & 0 & d^1_{17}(L) & d^4_{18}(L) \\
0 & d^3_{22}(L) & 0 & 0 & 0 & d^3_{26}(L) & d^1_{27}(L) & 0 \\
0 & d^2_{32}(L) & 0 & d^4_{34}(L) & d^4_{35}(L) & 0 & 0 & 0 \\
d^1_{41}(L) & 0 & 0 & d^3_{44}(L) & 0 & 0 & 0 & 0 \\
d^1_{51}(L) & d^3_{52}(L) & 0 & d^1_{54}(L) & d^2_{55}(L) & d^1_{56}(L) & 0 & d^4_{58}(L) \\
d^2_{61}(L) & d^2_{62}(L) & 0 & 0 & 0 & d^3_{66}(L) & 0 & 0 \\
0 & d^1_{72}(L) & d^3_{73}(L) & d^4_{74}(L) & 0 & d^2_{76}(L) & d^3_{77}(L) & d^2_{78}(L) \\
0 & 0 & 0 & 0 & 0 & 0 & 0 & d^1_{88}(L)
\end{matrix}
$$

Z including one-month devaluation expectations (adjusted differentials)

$$
\begin{matrix}
d^3_{11}(L) & d^1_{12}(L) & d^1_{13}(L) & 0 & 0 & 0 & d^1_{17}(L) & d^4_{18}(L) \\
0 & d^3_{22}(L) & 0 & 0 & 0 & d^3_{26}(L) & d^1_{27}(L) & 0 \\
0 & d^2_{32}(L) & 0 & d^2_{34}(L) & d^4_{35}(L) & 0 & 0 & 0 \\
0 & 0 & 0 & d^3_{44}(L) & 0 & 0 & 0 & 0 \\
d^1_{51}(L) & d^3_{52}(L) & 0 & d^4_{54}(L) & d^2_{55}(L) & d^1_{56}(L) & d^3_{57}(L) & d^4_{58}(L) \\
d^2_{6\,1}(L) & d^2_{62}(L) & 0 & 0 & 0 & d^3_{66}(L) & 0 & 0 \\
d^4_{71}(L) & 0 & 0 & d^4_{74}(L) & d^1_{75}(L) & d^1_{76}(L) & d^3_{77}(L) & d^2_{78}(L) \\
0 & 0 & 0 & 0 & 0 & 0 & 0 & d^1_{88}(L)
\end{matrix}
$$

Z including long-term devaluation expectations (unadjusted differentials)

$$
\begin{matrix}
d^4_{11}(L) & d^1_{12}(L) & d^1_{13}(L) & d^3_{14}(L) & 0 & 0 & 0 & d^1_{18}(L) \\
d^2_{21}(L) & d^3_{22}(L) & 0 & 0 & 0 & d^3_{26}(L) & d^1_{27}(L) & 0 \\
0 & d^2_{32}(L) & 0 & d^2_{34}(L) & d^4_{35}(L) & 0 & 0 & 0 \\
d^2_{41}(L) & 0 & 0 & d^3_{44}(L) & d^1_{45}(L) & 0 & 0 & 0 \\
d^1_{51}(L) & d^3_{52}(L) & 0 & d^1_{54}(L) & d^2_{55}(L) & d^1_{56}(L) & d^3_{57}(L) & d^4_{58}(L) \\
0 & d^2_{62}(L) & 0 & 0 & d^1_{65}(L) & d^3_{66}(L) & 0 & 0 \\
0 & d^1_{72}(L) & d^3_{73}(L) & d^4_{74}(L) & 0 & d^2_{76}(L) & d^3_{77}(L) & d^2_{78}(L) \\
0 & 0 & 0 & 0 & 0 & 0 & 0 & d^1_{88}(L)
\end{matrix}
$$

Italy: $\Delta(L)$ for Z including one-month (unadjusted) interest differentials

$$
\begin{matrix}
d^3_{11}(L) & d^4_{12}(L) & 0 & 0 & 0 & d^1_{16}(L) & 0 & d^1_{18}(L) \\
0 & d^3_{22}(L) & d^3_{23}(L) & d^3_{24}(L) & 0 & 0 & d^1_{27}(L) & d^1_{28}(L) \\
d^2_{31}(L) & 0 & d^2_{33}(L) & d^1_{34}(L) & 0 & 0 & 0 & 0 \\
0 & 0 & 0 & d^4_{44}(L) & 0 & 0 & d^4_{47}(L) & d^2_{48}(L) \\
0 & 0 & 0 & d^3_{54}(L) & d^4_{55}(L) & d^1_{56}(L) & 0 & 0 \\
0 & 0 & d^1_{63}(L) & 0 & 0 & d^3_{66}(L) & d^3_{67}(L) & 0 \\
0 & d^1_{72}(L) & 0 & d^2_{74}(L) & 0 & 0 & d^4_{77}(L) & d^1_{78}(L) \\
d^2_{81}(L) & d^4_{82}(L) & d^1_{83}(L) & d^2_{84}(L) & 0 & d^4_{86}(L) & 0 & 0
\end{matrix}
$$

$$Z = [\delta \quad D^1\pi, \quad D^1EPC, \quad D^1M/Y, \quad D^1F/Y, \quad D^1D/Y, \quad D^1CA/Y, \quad D^1U]^T$$

Italy: Z including one-month devaluation expectations (adjusted differentials)

$d^3_{11}(L)$	$d^1_{12}(L)$	0	0	$d^1_{15}(L)$	0	0	$d^4_{18}(L)$
0	$d^3_{22}(L)$	$d^3_{23}(L)$	$d^3_{24}(L)$	0	0	$d^1_{27}(L)$	$d^1_{28}(L)$
$d^2_{31}(L)$	0	$d^3_{33}(L)$	$d^2_{34}(L)$	$d^3_{35}(L)$	0	0	$d^1_{38}(L)$
0	0	0	$d^4_{44}(L)$	0	0	$d^4_{47}(L)$	$d^2_{48}(L)$
$d^2_{51}(L)$	0	$d^3_{53}(L)$	$d^3_{54}(L)$	$d^4_{55}(L)$	0	0	$d^2_{58}(L)$
0	0	$d^1_{63}(L)$	0	0	$d^3_{66}(L)$	$d^3_{67}(L)$	0
0	$d^1_{72}(L)$	0	$d^2_{74}(L)$	0	0	$d^4_{77}(L)$	$d^1_{78}(L)$
$d^3_{81}(L)$	$d^4_{82}(L)$	$d^1_{83}(L)$	$d^2_{84}(L)$	0	$d^4_{86}(L)$	0	0

Z including long-term devaluation expectations (unadjusted differentials)

$d^1_{11}(L)$	0	$d^1_{13}(L)$	0	0	$d^1_{16}(L)$	$d^4_{17}(L)$	0
$d^4_{21}(L)$	$d^3_{22}(L)$	$d^3_{23}(L)$	$d^3_{24}(L)$	$d^2_{25}(L)$	0	$d^1_{27}(L)$	$d^1_{28}(L)$
0	0	$d^2_{33}(L)$	$d^2_{34}(L)$	$d^3_{35}(L)$	$d^3_{36}(L)$	0	0
0	0	0	$d^4_{44}(L)$	0	0	$d^4_{47}(L)$	$d^2_{48}(L)$
0	0	0	$d^3_{54}(L)$	$d^4_{55}(L)$	$d^1_{56}(L)$	0	0
0	0	$d^1_{63}(L)$	0	0	$d^3_{66}(L)$	$d^3_{67}(L)$	0
$d^1_{71}(L)$	$d^1_{72}(L)$	$d^3_{73}(L)$	$d^2_{74}(L)$	0	0	$d^4_{77}(L)$	$d^3_{78}(L)$
$d^2_{81}(L)$	$d^4_{82}(L)$	0	$d^2_{84}(L)$	0	$d^4_{86}(L)$	0	0

The Netherlands: Z including one-month (unadjusted) interest differentials

$d^4_{11}(L)$	$d^2_{12}(L)$	0	0	$d^1_{15}(L)$	$d^3_{16}(L)$	0	$d^1_{18}(L)$
0	$d^3_{22}(L)$	$d^1_{23}(L)$	$d^2_{24}(L)$	$d^2_{25}(L)$	$d^1_{26}(L)$	0	$d^1_{28}(L)$
0	0	$d^1_{33}(L)$	$d^2_{34}(L)$	$d^3_{35}(L)$	0	0	0
$d^2_{41}(L)$	$d^3_{42}(L)$	0	$d^4_{44}(L)$	0	0	$d^1_{47}(L)$	0
0	0	0	$d^1_{54}(L)$	$d^4_{55}(L)$	0	$d^1_{57}(L)$	$d^4_{58}(L)$
$d^2_{61}(L)$	0	$d^1_{63}(L)$	0	$d^4_{65}(L)$	$d^3_{66}(L)$	$d^1_{67}(L)$	$d^4_{68}(L)$
0	$d^1_{72}(L)$	$d^2_{73}(L)$	0	0	$d^2_{76}(L)$	$d^3_{77}(L)$	0
0	$d^4_{82}(L)$	0	0	0	0	0	$d^4_{88}(L)$

Z including one-month devaluation expectations (adjusted differentials)

$d^4_{11}(L)$	0	$d^1_{13}(L)$	$d^2_{14}(L)$	$d^1_{15}(L)$	0	0	$d^1_{18}(L)$
0	$d^3_{22}(L)$	$d^1_{23}(L)$	$d^1_{24}(L)$	$d^2_{25}(L)$	$d^2_{26}(L)$	0	$d^1_{28}(L)$
0	0	$d^1_{33}(L)$	$d^2_{34}(L)$	$d^3_{35}(L)$	0	0	0
$d^2_{41}(L)$	$d^3_{42}(L)$	0	$d^4_{44}(L)$	$d^1_{45}(L)$	0	0	0
0	0	0	$d^1_{54}(L)$	$d^4_{55}(L)$	0	$d^1_{57}(L)$	$d^4_{58}(L)$
$d^4_{61}(L)$	0	$d^1_{63}(L)$	0	$d^4_{65}(L)$	$d^3_{66}(L)$	$d^1_{67}(L)$	$d^3_{68}(L)$
0	$d^1_{72}(L)$	$d^2_{73}(L)$	0	0	$d^2_{76}(L)$	$d^3_{77}(L)$	0
0	$d^4_{82}(L)$	0	0	0	0	0	$d^4_{88}(L)$

$$Z = [\delta \quad D^1\pi, \quad D^1EPC, \quad D^1M/Y, \quad D^1F/Y, \quad D^1D/Y, \quad D^1CA/Y, \quad D^1U]^T$$

The Netherlands: long-term devaluation expectations (unadjusted differentials)

$d^4_{11}(L)$	$d^3_{12}(L)$	0	$d^1_{14}(L)$	0	$d^4_{16}(L)$	0	$d^3_{18}(L)$
0	$d^3_{22}(L)$	$d^1_{23}(L)$	$d^2_{24}(L)$	$d^2_{25}(L)$	$d^2_{26}(L)$	0	$d^1_{28}(L)$
0	0	$d^1_{33}(L)$	$d^2_{34}(L)$	$d^3_{35}(L)$	0	0	0
$d^3_{41}(L)$	$d^3_{42}(L)$	0	$d^4_{44}(L)$	0	0	0	0
0	0	0	$d^1_{54}(L)$	$d^4_{55}(L)$	0	$d^1_{57}(L)$	$d^4_{58}(L)$
$d^1_{61}(L)$	0	$d^1_{63}(L)$	$d^2_{64}(L)$	0	$d^3_{66}(L)$	0	0
$d^4_{71}(L)$	0	$d^2_{73}(L)$	0	0	$d^2_{76}(L)$	$d^3_{77}(L)$	$d^1_{78}(L)$
$d^1_{81}(L)$	$d^4_{82}(L)$	0	0	0	0	0	$d^4_{88}(L)$

Notes: $\Delta(L)$ is the coefficient matrix of system (6.9). Sample 1981.Q1–92.Q4 (#Obs.=48), except for Ireland (1983.Q1–92.Q4; #Obs.=40) and for Italy (1981.Q1–92.Q2; #Obs.=46). Definitions and sources of the variables are specified in Appendix A.

Notes

1. Note that the inherently somewhat vague notion of 'credibility' is defined here as the mirror image of devaluation risk: a (target zone) exchange rate policy is said to be credible if market participants do not perceive the risk of a devaluation.
2. Since the EMS is not a bilateral exchange rate mechanism, the maximum and minimum expected change in the exchange rate within the band relative to the Deutschemark may temporarily be restricted by the bands relative to the other participating currencies. In practice, the bands relative to the German mark have been the most important ones, since the Deutschemark generally was one of the strongest currencies in the ERM and the only one that never underwent a (bilateral) devaluation.
3. As explained in Chapter 5 there is ample evidence in support of this assumption, even for countries that have witnessed (formal) barriers to international capital movements.
4. Take, for instance, the effect of differential tax treatment of interest income. In case no arbitrage possibilities remain, international capital mobility will tend to equalise *after-tax* interest rates. Intercountry differences in tax treatment of capital income will then lead to *pre-tax* interest rate differentials that do not reflect insufficient credibility of the exchange rate policy.
5. The distinction between both horizons points to a dual interpretation of the term 'credibility'. Short-run credibility of exchange rate policies as defined here can in principle be achieved even if fundamentals are on an unsustainable course which may be incompatible with long-run fixity of the exchange rate. However, the concepts of credibility of a hard-currency policy and of credibility of overall economic management would tend to coincide in the long run.
6. Exact sources and definitions of the variables are in Appendix A to this chapter. Although the interest rates used in the comparisons were selected so as to minimise possible divergence of the instruments' characteristics, cross-country differences in long-term rates seem unavoidable. Potential sources of discrepancies include differences in attached options like redemption and reinvestment facilities, and dissimilar terms to maturity. The latter do matter especially, if yield curves happen to be extraordinarily steep.
7. According to Giavazzi and Spaventa (1990), the Basle–Nyborg agreement marked the beginning of the 'New EMS'.
8. Frankel and Phillips (1992) reach similar conclusions using survey data on exchange rate expectations instead of expectations implied by interest differentials.

9. Compare for example Koen (1991), Frankel and Phillips (1992), Svensson (1993), and Halikias (1994). Only Flood, Rose, and Mathieson claim to have checked their key results for Belgium with financial rate data and, subsequently, have concluded that their main results remained unaffected (Flood et al., 1991, p.17). It may further be noted that the commercial exchange rate has been targeted by Belgian monetary authorities, presumably amongst others by manipulating short-term interest rates. This way, the relation between interest rates and the official exchange rate has not been completely absent under the two-tier exchange rate regime.

10. The 'drift-adjustment' method of estimating expected rates of devaluation applied here relies on the assumption that foreign exchange risk premia can be neglected. Alternatively, if that assumption is not accepted, what is being estimated in the remainder of this section is the sum of the expected rate of devaluation and a country-specific risk premium.

11. Rose and Svensson (1991) and Lindberg et al. (1991) review a variety of different methods to estimate (6.7) like GLS and 2S2SLS. We have also checked our key results using these techniques; typically the outcomes appear insensitive to the exact choice of the estimation method.

12. To be more precisely, if the realignment took place in the first ten days of a month, the previous month has been eliminated. If it took place during the last ten days of a month, then the current month has been excluded. If the realignment took place in between, then both the previous and the current month have been excluded from the sample.

13. A purposive intervention strategy aims at an appreciation of the domestic currency ($\Delta x<0$) as domestic interest rates are raised relative to foreign interest rates. Like in Svensson (1993), however, only about half of the coefficients on domestic and foreign interest rates are significant. Consequently, the degree of mean reversion in most countries included here is also similar to that reported in Knot and De Haan (1995b), where interest rates were not included.

14. With respect to the rather low significance of β_1 for several countries it may be noted that Froot and Obstfeld (1991b) already concluded from a Monte Carlo simulation that '. . . in samples of the size that have been used to study the EMS, say, it may be difficult to detect evidence of covariance stationarity induced by the target zone' (Froot and Obstfeld, 1991b, p.225).

15. Intercepts that are allowed to differ across subperiods give rise to variants of the Dickey–Fuller test that are likely to have critical values which are somewhat larger in magnitude than the standard test (Perron, 1989). Yet, for Austria, Belgium, Denmark, and the Netherlands, the margins of the estimated t-values to their critical value seem large enough so that a unit root can still be soundly rejected at a 5 percent significance level.

16. Despite our use of monthly data instead of data with a daily frequency, the similarity between our results and those obtained by Svensson (1993) for the three-month horizon is striking, especially as far as the relative degrees of mean reversion and the effectiveness of domestic monetary policy are concerned. This would yet confirm another finding of Froot and Obstfeld that '. . . sampling frequency has no effect on the results' (Froot and Obstfeld, 1991b, p.225).

17. Given the aforementioned problems with the dual exchange rate system it does not make sense to calculate adjusted interest differentials for Belgium. In all cases, quarterly data for interest differentials were obtained by taking the average of the available monthly observations. In case a realignment occurred, the number of available observations on the adjusted differential has simply been reduced to two instead of three observations in the relevant quarter.

18. Lindberg and Söderlind (1993) present evidence for Sweden that unsterilised intervention indeed takes place.

19. A more extensive survey of the empirical implications of this literature is provided by Eichengreen, Rose, and Wyplosz (1994).

20. Compare also the studies of Flood and Garber (1984a) and Claessens (1991), which introduce uncertainty about the rate of domestic credit creation, thereby increasing the likelihood of a regime shift, so that reserve losses may even exceed increases in domestic credit.
21. The small open economy assumption made in Chapter 5, which is appropriate for most of the countries in question, makes it possible to consider only variables appearing in *domestic* money demand functions and to abstain from their German counterparts here. We think that this approach is in line with the perception of foreign exchange market participants. Information on German fundamentals is assumed to be contained in German interest rates, which serve as a floor for domestic interest rates. Interest differentials, then, are thought to be affected by domestic fundamentals only, except for an inherently relative concept like competitiveness, which is measured as the real exchange rate in terms of export prices (see Clark et al., 1994, for a comparison and assessment of several measures for competitiveness). An additional advantage of the combination of fundamentals chosen here is the avoidance of multicollineary disturbances between inflation *differentials* and competitiveness, which become especially apparent if nominal exchange rate movements are limited. Studies that may have been vulnerable to such multicollinearity include among others Caramazza (1993), Chen and Giovannini (1993), and Thomas (1994).
22. Ideally, we should have scaled our foreign exchange reserves variable by using a measure of the size of the market for foreign exchange. However, such a measure is not available for the countries in question so we had to resort to GNP. Inserting the variable in levels, as is done in Caramazza (1993), may lead to spurious results, as it appears to be non-stationary.
23. Presumably, domestic interest rates are cointegrated with their German counterparts, resulting in stationary differentials. Empirical support for this hypothesis is provided by Katsimbris and Miller (1993), and De Haan, Pilat, and Zelhorst (1991).
24. Nevertheless, the punt was devalued by 10% in January 1993, to compensate for the loss in competitiveness arising from the depreciation of pound sterling after this currency had left the ERM.
25. See De Grauwe and Vanhaverbeke (1990) for a more extensive treatment of the macroeconomic developments in Belgium during the EMS.
26. Our results for France and Italy are remotely divergent from Caramazza (1993), Chen and Giovannini (1993), and Thomas (1994). In a single equation setting, they all conclude that, among a set of potential determinants of devaluation expectations, the exchange rate within the band is the most important 'fundamental', without which other fundamentals lose significance or become incorrectly signed (Thomas, 1994, pp.282–3). We chose not to include this variable here, as we find it hard to think of the exchange rate itself as a 'fundamental' determinant of exchange rate movements and interest differentials, especially in the longer run. Perhaps a conceivable 'fundamental' interpretation could be assigned to the exchange rate itself insofar as it might trigger a sort of collective, path-dependent psychose and, hence, a speculative bubble. However, this interpretation only seems relevant if a very short horizon is considered, since longer-lasting bubbles within the ERM would either lead to decisive interventions or to a devaluation of the currency involved.
27. Considering the sample 1987–91, Caramazza (1993) only corroborates the significant impact of inflation, competitiveness, and unemployment on long-term interest differentials.
28. Observe, for instance, the absence of fiscal policy as explanatory variable of long-term interest differentials, despite its central role in the Irish stabilisation efforts (Dornbusch, 1989, and Giavazzi and Pagano, 1990).
29. Bartolini (1993) reports strong links between anticipated devaluations and both a (CPI-based) measure of competitiveness and a measure of the expected devaluation of the currencies of Ireland's main trading partners.

7   Summary and conclusion

*But why should we care about the deficit? Does the deficit do
any harm? There are two stock positions on this subject . . .
The deficit is a terrible monster which threatens our whole way
of life . . . Isn't it obvious that we are on a road to disaster?
The deficit is an unimportant byproduct of a hugely successful
policy . . . who cares if some accountant's number has grown?*

Krugman (1994), pp.156–7

I   Summary

In this book we have tried to shed some light on the relationship between
government budget deficits and interest rates, with the emphasis on empirics.
As a starting point we have sketched the development of budget deficits and
interest rates in the European Union since the early 1960s. The development
of budget deficits can best be characterised as following a 'double-dip'
scenario, where the two dips coincided with the oil crises of 1973–1974 and
1979–1980, respectively. In the aftermath of both oil crises, interest rates rose
contemporaneously. The aim of the study has therefore been to investigate
potential channels through which deficits may have pushed up interest rates.
In order to perform various econometric analyses on these issues, a number
of different approaches have been taken.

Before resorting to these approaches we first have contemplated several
theoretical, empirical, and methodological issues concerning the stance of
fiscal policy. From a discussion of the potential sources of budget deficits, it
appeared that deficits may arise due to normative as well as positive
considerations. Normative considerations include the desire to pursue a
demand-oriented stabilisation policy, the distinction that can be made between
various forms of government spending like consumption and investment
outlays, and the tax-smoothing motive of government deficits and debt.
However, available empirical evidence suggests that all these normative
theories of public debt are of limited importance at most nowadays. So-called
positive theories stress the importance of political and institutional factors in
the determination of government debt. From an empirical investigation into
these determinants for the member countries of the European Union it was
found that public debt debt accumulation is positively related to the frequency
of government changes and negatively to sound budgetary procedures.

Subsequently we have addressed the issue concerning the impact of fiscal policy on the economy. In passing, we have discussed the theoretical background of Ricardian equivalence, of the importance of permanent deficits in the Neoclassical framework, and of the resurrection of the Keynesian view regarding real (inflation-adjusted) deficits as proposed by Eisner and Pieper in a series of papers. Finally, we have dealt with a number of measurement problems one encounters if analysing the stance of fiscal policy and its potential consequences for the economy.

In order to shed some light on the potential impact of fiscal policy on interest rates we first have looked at the common elements in the determination of interest rates in the European Union (Chapter 3). We have assumed that capital markets in member states of the Union are integrated, implying that it is appropriate to investigate the development of the average level of interest rates in the European Union. Within this integrated framework, we have also addressed the question of whether budget deficits in these countries have pushed up interest rates, considering long-term as well as short-term interest rates. From our estimates of a reduced-form equation of long-term nominal interest rates in the European Union we have concluded that movements in these rates can be explained by changes in expected inflation, government budget deficits, government debt, capacity utilisation rates, and foreign (that is US) interest rates. We find that the analysis of the linkage between fiscal variables and interest rates at a European level yields more satisfactory (in the sense of stable) results than analyses performed at the national level. Furthermore, persistent deficits have exercised upward pressure on long-term interest rates, which contradicts the Ricardian proposition of the neutrality of deficit-financing. On the other hand, our outcomes also suggested that the private sector partially discounts future tax liabilities. Finally, the effect of world long-term interest rates on corresponding European interest rates was unmistakably confirmed, although our evidence also pointed at substantial impediments to extra-EMS capital mobility.

As opposed to the analysis of long-term interest rates, variables capturing the impact of fiscal policy were found to be of no importance in the determination of short-term interest rates. A European index of (after-tax) expected short-term real interest rates was mainly driven by changes in real stock returns, temporary income, expected inflation, lagged investment, money growth, oil prices, and corresponding US real rates. It would thus seem that government budget deficits matter for the level of those interest rates that – from the part of the private sector – are more relevant for intertemporal decision making. In a growing economy with capital accumulation, for example, increasing budget deficits may create a shortage of funds available for investment in the long run, in anticipation of which long-term interest rates will rise. The main transmission mechanism here is the term structure of interest rates. The effect of the present budget deficit on present short-term interest rates may be small, while long-term interest rates may rise, for example in anticipation of higher future short-term rates.

After having investigated these common elements in the determination of interest rates, we have shifted our attention towards the interest *differentials* among the countries considered, which have not completely ceased to exist. For this purpose we chose Germany as the reference country, because of its anchor function in the European Monetary System (EMS). We have therefore first investigated the link between budget deficits and interest rates in Germany (Chapter 4). To this end, we have applied the so-called 'announcement effect methodology' to the period of German (re-)unification. The idea behind this approach is that in an efficient market, information about any determinant of interest rates will be incorporated immediately into observed interest rates. Using information on deficit projections from the Ministry of Finance, the Bundesbank and the Council of Economic Advisors, we have indeed found a positive association between 'news' about the consolidated government budget deficit and changes in interest rates, as far as the longer end of the term structure is concerned. This association seems, however, subject to a varying degree of credibility of the various sources of the 'news', as it only appears to be significant if information comes from the Bundesbank and the Council of Economic Advisors. Our findings did not enable us to determine whether this positive and significant relationship between budget deficits and interest rates is due to the fear that government debt may crowd out private investment, or that the debt will be monetised in the near future. Other research suggests, however, that the possibility of the latter actually happening must be judged very unlikely.

The second half of the book studied the behaviour of interest rate differentials vis-à-vis Germany in the other countries participating in the Exchange Rate Mechanism (ERM) of the EMS, within the framework of the target zone model. This model, in which exchange rates are determined by fundamentals and expectations, has been described extensively in Chapter 5. In the model, interest differentials predominantly consist of three components: expectations about realignments of central parities, expected exchange rate movements within the band, and country-specific risk premia. We have extended Svensson's (1991b) analysis of the term structure of interest rate differentials in a target zone in several directions. We have included in the model a time-varying devaluation risk, as well as (mean-reverting) intramarginal interventions. Furthermore, we have explicitly differentiated between stable and unstable periods for the various currencies taken into account. We found that the results for Austria and for Belgium, Denmark, Ireland, and the Netherlands in the relatively stable period are broadly in line with Svensson's theory, whereas the results for France and Italy and for Belgium, Denmark, Ireland, and the Netherlands in the relatively unstable period are more in accordance with the model that also allows for a time-varying devaluation risk.

Subsequently, the credibility of the various EMS target zones has been tested empirically, using so-called 'interest corridor' analysis (Chapter 6). Special attention has again been paid to the term structure of interest rates and differentials. According to this test Austrian and Dutch exchange rate policies were fairly credible over the period under consideration, while the other exchange rate policies have definitely lacked credibility at several points in time. We continued the analysis of interest differentials by extracting devaluation expectations from interest differentials by means of the so-called 'drift-adjustment' method. Additionally, we have investigated whether these devaluation expectations can accurately be explained by a collection of fundamental determinants, including government budget deficits. Based on the *FPE* criterion we specified a number of vector autoregressive systems to perform Granger–causality tests between the various measures of devaluation expectations and a broad set of country-specific fundamentals. We found no evidence that fundamentals are more relevant for drift-adjusted devaluation risk than for unadjusted interest differentials. It proved to be difficult to detect a systematic pattern by comparing the various currencies under investigation, in any case. However, a significant impact of intervention variables, unemployment, inflation, and fiscal policy on devaluation expectations and interest differentials became evident for almost all ERM-participants.

With respect to the role of fiscal policy we concluded that in 5 out of the 7 countries (Belgium, Denmark, France, Italy, and the Netherlands) studied a direct Granger–causal ordering between government budget deficits and long-term interest rates (that is differentials) can be discerned. This result is consistent with the evidence obtained in a loanable funds setting reported in Chapter 3. Unlike Chapter 3, however, the impact of fiscal policy on interest rates by way of devaluation expectations was not confined to long maturities, but it was also present for the one-month horizon. More generally, it seemed difficult to subdivide our collection of fundamentals into a group that has mainly affected short-run credibility versus a group that has mainly affected long-run credibility. Apparently, with credibility defined as the mirror image of devaluation fears, one might also speak of a 'term structure' of (target zone) credibility that has important intertemporal interdependencies that cannot be neglected.

II   Conclusion

Obviously, from a normative point of view the implication of the evidence discussed above seems clear: budget deficits do raise interest rates, especially at the longer end of the term structure. Although one might be tempted to derive straight, unidirectional policy implications from a study like this one, nevertheless, one should also keep in mind various other aspects of budget deficits presented in Chapter 2. For the sake of completeness and unbiasedness, these arguments should be weighted against the evidence presented in this book. From the discussion of Chapter 2, it appears that deficits can be useful if they result from automatic (passive) stabilisation policies or (observationally almost equivalent) tax-smoothing arguments. The case for budget deficits seems more weakly founded if they are mainly the result of political and institutional factors as stressed in the 'public choice' literature. So, if one is eager to draw any policy conclusion from our study, the empirical relevance of the arguments in favour of public debt should be assessed and weighted against the costs of public debt and deficits in terms of higher interest rates and their consequences for economic activity. Interestingly, Krugman (1994) provides an illustrative estimate of these costs for the US economy resulting from the Reaganomics heritage. In providing an answer to the question posed in the quote heading this chapter, he concludes that deficits were 'a bad but not a terrible thing' and certainly 'not nearly the monster some people imagine' (Krugman, 1994, pp.161, 169).

In this concluding section we will try to replicate Krugman's calculations for the European Union,[1] using data underlying the analysis of Chapter 3. To a first approximation we will think of the debt run up since the first oil crisis of 1973 as having taken the place of an equivalent amount of productive investment, thus assuming full crowding-out. Suppose that, alternatively, the countries of the European Union had balanced their budgets from 1973 until the present. At the end of 1973, aggregate public debt in the Union amounted to some DM 400 billion, while by the end of 1991, it was approximately DM 3700 billion. So if the EU-budgets had been balanced, the authorities would have borrowed DM 3300 billion less than it did. That 3300 billion, which amounts to some 38% of 1991 nominal EU-GDP, could have been productively invested instead. Following Krugman, we assume that the real rate of return on the funds that had been released, would have been the same as the average rate of return on all private assets, estimated at roughly 6%. Since the total buildup of debt ever since the oil crisis of 1973 was equal to 38% of one year's output, the returns on that debt would have been 6% times 0.38, or 2.3% of EU GDP. If instead one would rather want to compare the actual level of debt buildup with a (perhaps somewhat more realistic) alternative scenario of a continuous stabilisation of the debt-to-GDP ratio at the initial level of 1973 (14.7%), the 'damage' to the European economy would only have been restricted to 1.7% of one year's output.

Taken together the deliberations offered in this book can provide no positive guidelines on the optimal level of government debt and budget deficits. The trade-off sketched in this concluding section should therefore be based on other – more politically oriented and thus intrinsically more normative – considerations.

Note

1. For the sake of correctness it should be recalled from Chapter 3 that the European Union is proxied for by France, Germany, Italy, the Netherlands, and the United Kingdom, which in 1985 constituted over 85% of total EU-GDP.

Bibliography

Abramowitz, M. and I.A. Stegun (1972), *Handbook of Mathematical Functions*, New York: Dover.

Allen, S.D. (1990), 'The Effect of Federal Deficits and Debt on the Tax-Adjusted, Short-Term, Real Interest Rate', *Economic Letters*, **34**, 169–73.

Alesina, A. and A. Drazen (1991), 'Why Are Stabilizations Delayed? A Political Economy Model', *American Economic Review*, **81**, 1170–88.

Alesina, A. and G. Tabellini (1990), 'A Positive Theory of Fiscal Deficits and Government Debt', *Review of Economic Studies*, **57**, 403–14.

Andersen, T.M. and J.R. Sørensen (1991), 'Uncertain Exchange Rate Policies and Interest Rate Determination', *Kredit und Kapital*, **31**, 468–83.

Arnold, I.J.M. (1994), 'The Myth of a Stable European Money Demand', *Open Economies Review*, **5**, 249–59.

Artis, M.J., R.C. Bladen-Hovell, and W. Zhang (1993), 'A European Money Demand Function', in P.R. Masson and M.P. Taylor (eds), *Policy Issues in the Operation of Currency Unions*, Cambridge: Cambridge University Press, 240–63.

Aschauer, D.A. (1988), 'The Equilibrium Approach to Fiscal Policy', *Journal of Money, Credit, and Banking*, **20**, 41–62.

Atkinson, P. and J.C. Chouraqui (1985), 'The Origins of High Real Interest Rates', *OECD Economic Studies* 5, 8–55.

Bakker, A.F.P. (1994), *The Liberalization of Capital Movements in Europe: The Monetary Committee and Financial Integration 1958–1994*, Ph.D. dissertation, University of Amsterdam.

Ball, C.A. and A. Roma (1994), 'A Jump Diffusion Model for the European Monetary System', *Journal of International Money and Finance*, **12**, 475–92.

Barr, D. (1992), 'The Demand for Money in Europe: Comment on Kremers and Lane', *IMF Staff Papers*, **39**, 718–29.

Barro, R.J. (1974), 'Are Government Bonds Net Wealth?', *Journal of Political Economy*, **81**, 1095–117.

Barro, R.J. (1979), 'On the Determination of Public Debt', *Journal of Political Economy*, **87**, 940–71.

Barro, R.J. (1987), 'Government Spending, Interest Rates, Prices, and Budget Deficits in the United Kingdom, 1701–1918', *Journal of Monetary Economics*, **20**, 221–47.

Barro, R.J. and X. Sala-i-Martin (1990), 'World Real Interest Rates', *NBER Working Paper* 3317.

Bartolini, L. (1993), 'Devaluation and Competitiveness in a Small Open Economy: Ireland 1987–1993', *IMF Working Paper* 83, Washington: International Monetary Fund.

Basmann, R.L. (1972a), 'The Brookings Quarterly Econometric Model: Science or Number Mysticism?', in K. Brunner (ed.), *Problems and Issues in Current Econometric Practice*, Columbus, Ohio: College of Administrative Sciences, The Ohio State University, 3–51.

Basmann, R.L. (1972b), 'Argument and Evidence in the Brookings–S.S.R.C. Philosophy of Econometrics', in K. Brunner (ed.), *Problems and Issues in Current Econometric Practice*, Columbus, Ohio: College of Administrative Sciences, The Ohio State University, 63–118.

Bekx, P., A. Bucher, A. Italianer, and M. Mors (1989), *The QUEST Model*, Bruxelles: Commission of the European Communities.

Bernheim, B.D. (1989), 'A Neoclassical Perspective on Budget Deficits', *Journal of Economic Perspectives*, **3**, 55–72.

Bertola, G. (1993), 'Continuous-Time Models of Exchange Rates and Interventions', in F. van der Ploeg (ed.), *The Handbook of International Macroeconomics*, London: Basil Blackwell, 251–98.

Bertola, G. and R.J. Cabbalero (1992), 'Target Zones and Realignments', *American Economic Review*, **82**, 520–36.

Bertola, G. and L.E.O. Svensson (1993), 'Stochastic Devaluation Risk and the Empirical Fit of Target Zone Models', *Review of Economic Studies*, **60**, 689–712.

Beveridge, S. and C.R. Nelson (1981), 'A New Approach to Decomposition of Economic Time Series into Permanent and Transitory Components with Particular Attention to the Measurement of the Business Cycle', *Journal of Monetary Economics* 7, 151–74.

Bhandari, J.S. and T.H. Mayer (1990), 'A Note on Saving-Investment Correlations in the EMS', *IMF Working Paper* 97, Washington: International Monetary Fund.

Bischoff, C. (1971), 'The Effect of Alternative Lag Distribution', in G. Fromm (ed.), *Investment and Tax Incentives*, Washington: The Brookings Institution.

Blanchard, O.J. (1985), 'Debt, Deficits, and Finite Horizons', *Journal of Political Economy*, **93**, 223–47.

Blanchard, O.J. (1993), 'Suggestions for a New Set of Fiscal Indicators', in H.A.A. Verbon and F.A.A.M. van Winden (eds), *The Political Economy of Government Debt*, Amsterdam: North-Holland.

Blanchard, O.J. and S. Fischer (1989), *Lectures on Macroeconomics*, Cambridge (Massachusetts): The MIT Press.

Blanchard, O.J. and L.H. Summers (1984), 'Perspectives on High World Real Interest Rates', *Brookings Papers on Economic Activity*, 273–324.

Bomhoff, E.J. (1994a), 'Het Centraal Planbureau en Lagere Belastingen', *Economisch Statistische Berichten*, **79**, 289–93 (in Dutch).

Bomhoff, E.J. (1994b), 'Lagere Belastingen in de CPB-Modellen: Naschrift', *Economisch Statistische Berichten*, **79**, 465 (in Dutch).

Boskin, M.J., M.S. Robinson, and A.M. Huber (1987), 'Government Saving, Capital Formation, and Wealth in the United States, 1947–1985', *NBER Working Paper* 2352.

Box, G.E.P. and G.C. Tiao (1975), 'Intervention Analysis with Applications to Economic and Environmental Problems', *Journal of the American Statistical Association*, **70**, 70–9.

Brockwell, P.J. and R.A. Davis (1987), *Time Series: Theories and Methods*, New York: Springer-Verlag.

Brunner, K. (1976), 'Inflation, Money, and the Role of Fiscal Arrangements: An Analytic Framework for the Inflation Problem', in M. Monti (ed.), *The 'New Inflation' and Monetary Policy*, London.

Brunner, K. and A.H. Meltzer (1972), 'Money, Debt, and Economic Activity', *Journal of Political Economy*, **80**, 951–77.

Brunner, K. and A.H. Meltzer (1976), 'An Aggregate Theory for a Closed Economy', in J.E. Stein (ed.), *Monetarism*, Amsterdam.

Buiter, W.H. (1984), 'Measuring Aspects of Fiscal and Financial Policy', *NBER Working Paper* 1332.

Buiter, W.H. (1985), 'A Guide to Public Sector Debt and Deficits', *Economic Policy*, **1**, 13–60.

Burdekin, R.C.K. and M.E. Wohar (1990), 'Monetary Institutions, Budget Deficits and Inflation', *Journal of Monetary Economics*, **6**, 531–51.

Cagan, P. (1983), 'The Effects of Government Deficits on Aggregate Demand and Financial Markets: A Wide-Ranging Review of the Literature and Current Policy Issues', in Federal Reserve Bank of San Francisco, *Conference Supplement Economic Review*.

Caines, P.E., C.W. Keng, and S.P. Sethi (1981), 'Causality Analysis and Multivariate Autoregressive Modelling with an Application to Supermarket Sales Analysis', *Journal of Economic Dynamics and Control*, **3**, 267–98.

Cameron, D.R. (1985), 'Does Government Cause Inflation? Taxes, Spending and Deficits', in L. Lindberg and C. Maier (eds), *The Politics of Inflation and Economic Stagnation*, Washington: Brookings Institution, 224–79.

Caramazza, F. (1993), 'French–German Interest Rate Differentials and Time-Varying Realignment Risk', *IMF Staff Papers*, **40**, 567–83.

Catsambras, T. (1988), 'Budget Deficits, Inflation Accounting, and Macroeconomic Policy: A Skeptical Note', *Journal of Public Policy*, **8**, 49–60.

Central Planning Bureau (1992), *FKSEC, A Macro-Econometric Model for the Netherlands*, Leiden/Antwerpen: Stenfert Kroese.

Chan-Lee, J.H. and H. Kato (1984), A Comparison of Simulation Properties of National Econometric Models, *OECD Economic Studies*, 109–50.

Chen, Z. and A. Giovannini (1993), 'The Determinants of Realignments under the EMS: Some Empirical Regularities', *NBER Working Paper* 4291.

Clark, P., L. Bartolini, T. Bayoumi, and S. Symansky (1994), 'Exchange Rates and Economic Fundamentals: A Framework for Analysis', *IMF Occasional Paper* 115, Washington: International Monetary Fund.

Clark, T.A., D.H. Joines, and G.M. Phillips (1988), 'Social Security Payments, Money Supply Announcements, and the Interest Rates', *Journal of Monetary Economics*, **22**, 257–78.

Claessens, S. (1991), 'Balance of Payments Crisis in an Optimal Portfolio Model', *European Economic Review*, **35**, 81–101.

Cooper, R.N. (1990), 'Comments on Giovannini', *Brookings Papers on Economic Activity*, **2**, 275–81.

Cornell, B. (1983a), 'Money Supply Announcements and Interest Rates: Another View', *Journal of Business*, **56**, 1–24.

Cornell, B. (1983b), 'The Money Supply Announcements Puzzle: Review and Interpretation', *American Economic Review*, **73**, 644–57.

Corsetti, G. and N. Roubini (1991), 'Tax Smoothing Discretion versus Balanced Budget Rules in the Presence of Politically Motivated Fiscal Deficits: The Design of Optimal Fiscal Rules for Europe after 1992', *mimeo.*

Cover, J.P. (1992), 'Asymmetric Effects of Positive and Negative Money-Supply Shocks', *Quarterly Journal of Economics*, **107**, 1261–82.

Cuddington, J.T. and L.A. Winters (1987), 'The Beveridge–Nelson Decomposition of Economic Time Series. A Quick Computational Method', *Journal of Monetary Economics*, **19**, 125–27.

Cukierman, A. (1992), *Central Bank Strategy, Credibility, and Independence*, Cambridge (Massachusetts): The MIT Press.

Cukierman, A., M. Kiguel, and L. Leiderman (1993), 'The Choice of Exchange Rate Bands: Balancing Flexibility and Credibility', *unpublished*: University of Tel Aviv.

Cukierman, A. and J. Mortensen (1983), 'Monetary Assets and Inflation Induced Distortions of the National Accounts: Conceptual Issues and Correction of Sectoral Income Flows in 5 EEC Countries', *Economic Papers* 15, Bruxelles: Commision of the European Communities.

Cumby, R.E., J. Huizinga, and M. Obstfeld (1983), 'Two-Step Two-Stage Least Squares with Rational Expectations', *Journal of Econometrics*, **21**, 333–55.

Cumby, R.E. and F.S Mishkin (1986), 'The International Linkage of Real Interest Rates: The European-US Connection', *Journal of International Money and Finance*, **5**, 5–23.

Cumby, R.E. and M. Obstfeld (1984), 'International Interest-Rate and Price-Level Linkages under Flexible Exchange Rates: A Review of Recent Evidence', in J. Bilson and R. Marston (eds), *Exchange Rate Theory and Practice*, Chicago: University Press of Chicago for the NBER, 121–51.

Darrat, A.F. (1988), 'Have Large Budget Deficits Caused Rising Trade Deficits?', *Southern Economic Journal*, **54**, 879–87.

Darrat, A.F. and M.O. Suliman (1992), 'Real Deficits and Real Growth: Some Further Results', *Journal of Post Keynesian Economics*, **15**, 31–41.

Datta, S. and U.S. Dhillon (1993), 'Bond and Stockmarket Response to Unexpected Earnings Announcements', *Journal of Financial and Quantitative Analysis*, **28**, 565–77.

De Cecco, M. and F. Giavazzi (1994), 'Italy's Experience within and without the European Monetary System: A Preliminary Appraisal', in J.O.H. de Beaufort Wijnholds, S.C.W. Eijffinger, and L.H. Hoogduin (eds), *A Framework for Monetary Stability*, Deventer: Kluwer, 221–38.

De Grauwe, P. (1994), 'Towards EMU without the EMS', *Economic Policy*, **18**, 147–85.

De Grauwe, P. and W. Vanhaverbeke (1990), 'Exchange Rate Experiences of the Small EMS Countries: Belgium, Denmark, and the Netherlands', in V. Argy and P. De Grauwe (eds), *Choosing an Exchange Rate Regime*, Washington: International Monetary Fund, 135–62.

De Haan, J. (1989), *Public Debt: Pestiferous or Propitious?* Ph. D. dissertation, University of Groningen.

De Haan, J., K.P. Goudswaard, and D. Zelhorst (1990), 'Real Deficits and Real Growth: Empirical Evidence for 10 countries', *Public Finance and Steady Economic Growth*, Proceedings of the 45th Congress of the International Institute of Public Finance, Buenos Aires 1989, Special issue of *Public Finance*, 221–30.

De Haan, J., D.-J. Pilat, and D. Zelhorst (1991), 'On the Relationship between Dutch and German Interest Rates', *De Economist*, **139**, 550–65.

De Haan, J., C.G.M. Sterks, and C.A. De Kam (1992), 'Towards Budget Discipline: An Economic Assessment of the Possibilities for Reducing National Deficits in the Run-Up to EMU', Commission of the European Communities, *Economic Papers* 99.

De Haan, J. and J.E. Sturm (1992), 'The Case for Central Bank Independence', *Banca Nazionale del Lavoro Quarterly Review*, **182**, 305–27.

De Haan, J. and J.E. Sturm (1994), 'Political and Institutional Determinants of Fiscal Policy in the European Community', *Public Choice*, **80**, 157–72.

De Haan, J. and J.E. Sturm (1995), 'Is It Real? The Relationship between Real Deficits and Real Growth: New Evidence Using Long-Run Data', *Applied Economics Letters*, **2**, 98–102.

De Haan, J., J.E. Sturm, and B.J. Sikken (1996), 'Government Capital Formation: Explaining the Decline', paper presented at *The Changing Role of the Public Sector: Transition in the 1990s*, 51th Congress of the International Institute of Public Finance, Lisbon 1995.

De Haan, J. and D. Zelhorst (1988), 'The Relationship between Real Deficits and Real Growth: A Critique', *Journal of Post Keynesian Economics*, **11**, 148–60.

De Haan, J. and D. Zelhorst (1990a), 'Financial-Market Effects of Federal Government Budget Deficits: Comment', *Weltwirtschaftliches Archiv*, **126**, 388–92.

De Haan, J. and D. Zelhorst (1990b), 'The Impact of Government Deficits on Money Growth in Developing Countries', *Journal of International Money and Finance*, **9**, 455–69.

De Haan, J. and D. Zelhorst (1992), 'The Intertemporal Substitution Effect of Government Purchases on the Interest Rate: Empirical Estimates for the Netherlands', *Empirical Economics*, **17**, 293–302.

De Haan, J. and D. Zelhorst (1993), 'Positive Theories of Public Debt: Some Evidence for Germany', in H.A.A. Verbon and F.A.A.M. van Winden (eds), *The Political Economy of Government Debt*, Amsterdam: North-Holland, 295–306.

Delgado, F. and B. Dumas (1991), 'Target Zones: Broad and Narrow', in P. Krugman and M. Miller (eds), *Exchange Rate Targets and Currency Bands*, Cambridge: Cambridge University Press.

Demopoulos, G.D., G.M. Katsimbris, and S.M. Miller (1987), 'Monetary Policy and Central-Bank Financing of Government Budget Deficits', *European Economic Review*, **31**, 1023–50.

Denslow, D. and M. Rush (1989), 'Supply Shocks and the Interest Rate', *Economic Inquiry*, **27**, 501–10.

Dornbusch, R. (1989), 'Credibility, Debt and Unemployment: Ireland's Failed Stabilization', *Economic Policy*, **8**, 174–209.

Dramais, A. (1986), 'Compact, a Prototype Macroeconomic Model of the EC in the World Economy', *European Economy*, **27**, 111–62.

Drazen, A. and P.R. Masson (1994), 'Credibility of Policies Versus Credibility of Policymakers', *Quarterly Journal of Economics*, **109**, 735–54.

Dwyer, G.P. and R.W. Hafer (1989), 'Interest Rates and Economic Announcements', *Federal Reserve Bank of St. Louis Review*, **71**, 34–46.

Easterly, W. and S. Rebelo (1993), 'Fiscal Policy and Economic Growth, an Empirical Investigation', *NBER Working Paper* 4499.

Ederington, L.H. and J.H. Lee (1993), 'How Markets Process Information: News Releases and Volatility', *Journal of Finance*, **48**, 1161–91.

Edin, P. and H. Ohlsson (1991), 'Political Determinants of Budget Deficits: Coalition Effects versus Minority Effects', *European Economic Review*, **35**, 1597–603.

Edin, P.A. and A. Vredin (1993), 'Devaluation Risk in Target Zones: Evidence from the Nordic Countries', *Economic Journal*, **103**, 161–75.

Eglin, M. (1989), 'Offset Coefficients as an Indicator of the Effectiveness of Domestic Monetary Policies', *Unpublished*, Geneva: The Graduate Institute of International Studies.

Eichengreen, B., A.K. Rose, and C. Wyplosz (1994), 'Speculative Attacks on Pegged Exchange Rates: An Empirical Exploration with Special Reference to the European Monetary System', *NBER Working Paper* 4898.

Eisner, R. (1986), *How Real is the Federal Deficit?*, New York/London: The Free Press.

Eisner, R. (1989a), 'Taxes, Budget Deficits, and Capital Formation', *Public Finance and the Performance of Enterprises*, Paris: Proceedings of the 43th Congress of the International Institute of Public Finance, 1987, 15–30.

Eisner, R. (1989b), 'Budget Deficits: Rhetoric and Reality', *Journal of Economic Perspectives*, **3**, 73–93.

Eisner, R. (1994), *The Misunderstood Economy: What Counts and How to Count It*, Boston: Harvard Business School Press.

Eisner, R. and P.J. Pieper (1984), 'A New View of the Federal Debt and Budget Deficits', *American Economic Review*, **74**, 11–29.

Eisner, R. and P.J. Pieper (1988a), 'Deficits, Monetary Policy, and Real Economic Activity', in K.J. Arrow and M. Boskin (eds), *Economics of Public Debt*, New York: MacMillan.

Eisner, R. and P.J. Pieper (1988b), 'Rejoinder', *Journal of Post Keynesian Economics*, **11**, 161–168.

Eisner, R. and P.J. Pieper (1992), 'Real Deficits and Real Growth: A Further View', *Journal of Post Keynesian Economics*, **15**, 43–9.

Engel, C. and J. Frankel (1984), 'Why Interest Rates React to Money Announcements: An Explanation from the Foreign Exchange Market', *Journal of Monetary Economics*, **13**, 31–9.

Evans, P. (1985), 'Do Large Deficits Produce High Interest Rates?', *American Economic Review*, **75**, 68–87.

Fackler, J.S. (1985), 'An Empirical Analysis of the Market for Goods, Money, and Credit', *Journal of Money, Credit, and Banking*, **17**, 28–42.

Fase, M.M.G., P. Kramer, and W.C. Boeschoten (1990), 'MORKMON-II, Het DNB Kwartaalmodel voor Nederland', in *Monetaire Monografieën* 11, Amsterdam: De Nederlandsche Bank NV (in Dutch).

Fellner, W. (1982), 'The High Employment Budget and Potential Output', *Survey of Current Business*, **62**, November, 26–33.

Fischer, S. (1993), 'The Role of Macroeconomic Factors in Economic Growth', *Journal of Monetary Economics*, **32**, 485–512.

Flood, R.P and P. Garber (1984a), 'Collapsing Exchange-Rate Regimes: Some Linear Examples', *Journal of International Economics*, **17**, 1–13.

Flood, R.P and P. Garber (1984b), 'Gold Monetization and Gold Discipline', *Journal of Political Economy*, **92**, 90–107.

Flood, R.P, A.K. Rose, and D.J. Mathieson (1991), 'An Empirical Exploration of Exchange-Rate Target-Zones', *Carnegie-Rochester Conference Series on Public Policy*, **35**, 7–66.

Frankel, J. and S. Phillips (1992), 'The European Monetary System: Credible at Last?', *Oxford Economic Papers*, **44**, 791–816.

Frey, B.S. and F. Schneider (1978), 'An Empirical Study of Politico-Economic Interaction in the US', *Review of Economics and Statistics*, **60**, 174–83.

Friedman, M. (1969), 'The Role of Monetary Policy', in *The Optimum Quantity of Money and Other Essays*, Chicago.

Friedman, M. (1976), 'Comments on Tobin and Buiter', in J.E. Stein (ed.), *Monetarism*, Amsterdam.

Fromm, G. and L.R. Klein (1972), 'The Brookings Econometric Model: A Rational Perspective', in K. Brunner (ed.), *Problems and Issues in Current Econometric Practice*, Columbus, Ohio: College of Administrative Sciences, The Ohio State University, 52–62.

Froot, K.A. and M. Obstfeld (1991a), 'Stochastic Process Switching: Some Simple Solutions', *Econometrica*, **59**, 241–50.

Froot, K.A. and M. Obstfeld (1991b), 'Exchange Rate Dynamics under Stochastic Regime Shifts: A Unified Approach', *Journal of International Economics*, **31**, 203–29.

Froot, K.A. and R.H. Thaler (1990), 'Anomalies: Foreign Exchange', *Journal of Economic Perspectives*, **4**, 179–92.

Genberg, H. (1990), 'In the Shadow of the Mark: Exchange Rate Policies in Austria and Switzerland', in V. Argy and P. De Grauwe (eds), *Choosing an Exchange Rate Regime*, Washington: International Monetary Fund, 197–223.

Giavazzi, F. and M. Pagano (1990), 'Can Severe Contractions Be Expansionary? Tales of Two Small European Countries', *NBER Working Paper* 3372.

Giavazzi, F. and L. Spaventa (1990), 'The "New" EMS', in P. De Grauwe and L. Papademos (eds), *The European Monetary System in the 1990s*, London: Longman, 65–85.

Giovannini, A. (1990), 'European Monetary Reform: Progress and Prospects', *Brookings Papers on Economic Activity*, 217–74.

Giovannini, A. and P. Jorion (1988), 'The Time-Variation of Risk and Return in the Foreign Exchange and Stock Market', *NBER Working Paper* 2573.

Goldberg, L.S. (1991), 'Collapsing Exchange Rate Regimes: Shocks and Biases', *Journal of International Money and Finance*, **10**, 252–63.

Goldberg, L.S. (1994), 'Predicting Exchange Rate Crises: Mexico Revisited', *Journal of International Economics*, **36**, 413–30.

Granger, C.W.J. (1969), 'Investigating Causal Relations by Econometric Models and Cross-Spectral Methods', *Econometrica*, **37**, 424–38.

Granger, C.W.J. and P. Newbold (1977), *Forecasting Economic Time Series*, New York: Academic Press.

Grilli, V., D. Masciandaro, and G. Tabellini (1991), 'Political and Monetary Institutions and Public Financial Policies in the Industrial Countries', *Economic Policy*, **13**, 341–92.

Gros, D. (1988), 'Dual Exchange Rates in the Presence of Incomplete Market Separation: Long-Run Ineffectiveness and Implications for Monetary Policy', *IMF Staff Papers*, **35**, 437–60.

Grossman, J. (1981), 'The Rationality of Money Supply Expectations and the Short-Run Response of Interest Rates to Monetary Surprises', *Journal of Money, Credit, and Banking*, **13**, 409–24.

Gruijters, A.P.D. (1995), *Financiële Integratie en Monetair Beleid: Een Empirisch Onderzoek naar de Mobiliteit van het Kapitaalverkeer in de Geïndustrialiseerde Wereld sinds het Einde van het Bretton–Woods Stelsel*, Ph. D. dissertation, Tilburg University (in Dutch).

Guilkey, D.K. and M.K. Salemi (1982), 'Small Sample Properties of Three Tests for Granger-Causal Ordering in a Bivariate Stochastic System', *Review of Economics and Statistics*, **64**, 668–80.

Halikias, I. (1994), 'Testing the Credibility of Belgium's Exchange Rate Policy', *IMF Staff Papers*, **41**, 350–66.

Hall, R.E. (1978), 'Stochastic Implications of the Life Cycle–Permanent Income Hypothesis: Theory and Evidence', *Journal of Political Economy*, **86**, 971–87.

Hamilton, J.D. (1983), 'Oil and the Macroeconomy Since World-War II', *Journal of Political Economy*, **91**, 228–48.

Hansen, L.P. (1982), 'Large Sample Properties of Generalized Method of Moments Estimators', *Econometrica*, **50**, 1029–54.

Hayashi, F. (1985), 'Tests for Liquidity Constraints: A Critical Survey', *NBER Working Paper* 1720.

Hibbs, D.A. (1977), 'Political Parties and Macroeconomic Policy', *American Political Science Review*, **23**, 1467–88.

Hills, J. (1984), 'Public Assets and Liabilities and the Presentation of Budgetary Policy', *IFS Report Series* 8 (Public Finances in Perspective), London.

Hochreiter, E. and G. Winckler (1995), 'The Advantages of Tying Austria's Hands: The Succes of the Hard Currency Strategy', forthcoming in *European Journal of Political Economy*, **11**.

Hoelscher, G.P. (1986), 'New Evidence on Deficits and Interest Rates', *Journal of Money, Credit and Banking*, **18**, 1–17.

Hsiao, C. (1981), 'Autoregressive Modelling and Money-Income Causality Detection', *Journal of Monetary Economics*, **7**, 85–106.

Icard, A. (1994), 'Monetary Policy and Exchange Rates: The French Experience', in J.O.H. De Beaufort Wijnholds, S.C.W. Eijffinger, and L.H. Hoogduin (eds), *A Framework for Monetary Stability*, Deventer: Kluwer, 239–56.

International Monetary Fund (1993), *World Economic Outlook*, October, Washington: International Monetary Fund.

Jacobs, J.P.A.M. and E. Sterken (1995), 'The IBS–CCSO Quarterly Model of the Netherlands', *Economic Modelling*, **12**, 111–63.

Jorion, P. and F.S. Mishkin (1991), 'A Multicountry Comparison of Term-Structure Forecasts at Long Horizons', *Journal of Financial Economics*, **29**, 59–80.

Katsimbris, G.M. and S.M. Miller (1993), 'Interest Rate Linkages within the European Monetary System: Further Analysis', *Journal of Money, Credit, and Banking*, **25**, 772–9.

Kawai, M. (1980), 'Exchange Rate-Price Causality in the Recent Floating Period', in C. Bigman and C. Taya (eds), *The Functioning of Floating Exchange Rates: Theory, Evidence, and Policy Implications*, Cambridge: Ballinger, 189–211.

King, M.A. (1983), 'The Economics of Saving', *NBER Working Paper* 1247.

Klein, L.R. (1988), 'Carrying Forward the Tinbergen Initiative in Macroeconometrics', *De Economist*, **136**, 3–21.

Knoester, A. and W. Mak (1994), 'Real Interest Rates in Eight OECD Countries', *International Review of Economics and Business*, **41**, 325–44.

Knot, K.H.W. (1995), 'On the Determination of Real Interest Rates in Europe', *Empirical Economics*, **20**, 479–500.

Knot, K.H.W. and J. De Haan (1995a), 'Fiscal Policy and Interest Rates in the European Community', *European Journal of Political Economy*, **11**, 171–88.

Knot, K.H.W. and J. De Haan (1995b), 'Interest Differentials and Exchange Rate Policies in Austria, the Netherlands, and Belgium', *Journal of Banking and Finance*, **19**, 363–86.

Koen, V.R. (1991), 'Testing the Credibility of the Belgian Hard-Currency Policy', *IMF Working Paper* 79, Washington: International Monetary Fund.

Kremers, J.J.M. and T.D. Lane (1990), 'Economic and Monetary Integration and the Aggregate Demand for Money in the EMS', *IMF Staff Papers*, **37**, 777–805.

Kremers, J.J.M. and T.D. Lane (1992), 'The Demand for Money in Europe: Reply to Barr', *IMF Staff Papers*, **39**, 730–37.

Krugman, P.R. (1979), 'A Model of Balance of Payments Crises', *Journal of Money, Credit, and Banking*, **11**, 311–25.

Krugman, P.R. (1991), 'Target Zones and Exchange Rate Dynamics', *Quarterly Journal of Economics*, **106**, 669–82.

Krugman, P.R. (1994), *Peddling Prosperity. Economic Sense and Nonsense in the Age of Diminished Expectations*, New York: W.W. Norton and Company.

Lemmen, J.J.G. and S.C.W. Eijffinger (1993), 'The Degree of Financial Integration in the European Community', *De Economist*, **141**, 189–213.

Lemmen, J.J.G. and S.C.W. Eijffinger (1995), 'The Quantity Approach to Financial Integration: The Feldstein–Horioka Criterion Revisited', *Open Economies Review*, **6**, 145–65.

Lindberg, H. and P. Söderlind (1993), 'Intervention Policy and Mean Reversion in Exchange Rate Target Zones', *IIES Seminar Paper*, Stockholm: Institute of International Economic Studies.

Lindberg, H., L.E.O. Svensson, and P. Söderlind (1991), 'Devaluation Expectations: The Swedish Krona 1982–1991', *NBER Working Paper* 3918.

Ljung, G.M. and G.E.P. Box (1978), 'On a Measure of Lack of Fit in Time Series Models', *Biometrika*, **67**, 297–303.

Lucas, R.E. (1972), 'Econometric Testing of the Natural Rate Hypothesis', reprinted in *Studies in Business-Cycle Theory*, Oxford, 1981.

MacKinnon, J.G. (1991), 'Critical Values for Cointegration Tests', in R.F. Engle and C.W.J. Granger (eds), *Long-Term Economic Relationships. Readings in Cointegration*, Oxford: Oxford University Press, 267–76.

Mark, N.C. (1985), 'Some Evidence on the International Equality of Real Interest Rates', *Journal of International Money and Finance*, **4**, 189–208.

Marston, R.C. (1985), 'Stabilisation Policies in Open Economies', in R.W. Jones and P.B. Kenen (eds), *Handbook of International Economics* II, Amsterdam: North-Holland, 859–914.

Ministry of Finance (1996), *Miljoenennota* (Budget Memorandum), The Hague: Ministry of Finance.

Miller, S.M. (1988), 'The Beveridge–Nelson Decomposition of Economic Time Series; Another Economical Computational Method', *Journal of Monetary Economics*, **21**, 141–42.

Mishkin, F.S. (1984a), 'The Real Interest Rate: A Multi-Country Empirical Study', *Canadian Journal of Economics*, **17**, 283–311.

Mishkin, F.S. (1984b), 'Are Real Interest Rates Equal Across Countries? An Empirical Investigation of International Parity Conditions', *Journal of Finance*, **39**, 1345–57.

Modigliani, F. (1977), 'The Monetarist Controversy or, Should We Forsake Stabilization Policies?', *American Economic Review*, **69**, 1–19.

Modigliani, F. and T. Jappelli (1988), 'The Determinants of Interest Rates in the Italian Economy', *Review of Economic Conditions in Italy*, **88**, 9–34.

Monadjemi, M.S. and C. Kearney (1991), 'The Interest Rate Neutrality of Fiscal Deficits: Testing for Ricardian Equivalence and Capital Inflow', *Journal of International Money and Finance*, **10**, 541–51.

Mot, E.S., P.J. van den Noord, D.D. van der Schelt-Scheele, and M.A. Koning (1989), *HERMES–The Netherlands. Final Report on the Dutch Model*, Amsterdam: Foundation for Economic Research.

Mundell, R. (1963), 'Inflation and Real Interest', *Journal of Political Economy*, **71**, 280–83.

Nationale Bank van Belgie (1992), 'Weerslag van de Verlaging van het Tarief van de Roerende Voorheffing op de Financiële Markten en de Overheidsfinanciën', *Studienota's* 9, Bruxelles: Nationale Bank van Belgie, (in Dutch).

Nederlandsche Bank, De (1984), 'MORKMON Een Kwartaalmodel voor Macro-Economische Beleidsanalyse', in *Monetaire Monografieën* 2, Amsterdam: De Nederlandsche Bank NV/Deventer: Kluwer (in Dutch).

Neftçi, S.N. (1984), 'Are Economic Time Series Asymmetric over the Business Cycle?', *Journal of Political Economy*, **92**, 307–28.

Newey, W.K. and K.D. West (1987), 'A Simple, Positive Semi-Definite, Heteroscedasticity and Autocorrelation Consistent Covariance Matrix', *Econometrica*, **55**, 703–8.

Nijman, T. (1990), 'Estimation of Models Containing Unobserved Rational Expectations', in F. van der Ploeg (ed.), *Advanced Lectures in Quantitative Economics*, London: Academic Press.

Nunes-Correia, J. and L. Stemitsiotis (1993), 'Budget Deficit and Interest Rates: Is there a Link?', *Economic Papers* 105, Bruxelles: Commission of the European Communities.

Obstfeld, M. (1986), 'Rational and Self-Fulfilling Balance-of-Payments Crises', *American Economic Review*, **76**, 72–81.

OECD, *Economic Outlook*, various editions, Paris: OECD.

OECD, *Economic Surveys*, various countries, various editions, Paris: OECD.

Okker, V.R. (1994), 'Lagere Belastingen in de CPB-Modellen', *Economisch Statistische Berichten*, **79**, 462–65 (in Dutch).

Österreichische Nationalbank (1991), *Erneuerung durch Integration: 175 Jahre Österreichische Nationalbank*, Vienna: Österreichische Nationalbank (in German).

Ozkun, F.G. and A. Sutherland (1994), 'A Model of the ERM Crisis', *CEPR Discussion Paper* 879.

Patinkin, D. (1965), *Money, Interest, and Prices* (second edition), New York.

Perron, P. (1989), 'The Great Crash, the Oil Price Shock, and the Unit Root Hypothesis', *Econometrica*, **57**, 1361–401.

Persson, T. and L.E.O. Svensson (1989), 'Why a Stubborn Conservative Would Run a Deficit: Policy with Time-Inconsistent Preferences', *Quarterly Journal of Economics*, **104**, 324–45.

Plosser, C.I. (1982), 'Government Financing Decisions and Asset Returns', *Journal of Monetary Economics*, **9**, 325–52.

Plosser, C.I. (1987), 'Fiscal Policy and the Term-Structure', *Journal of Monetary Economics*, **20**, 343–67.

Quigley, M.R. and S. Porter-Hudak (1994), 'A New Approach in Analyzing the Effect of Deficit Announcements on Interest Rates', *Journal of Money, Credit, and Banking*, **26**, 894–902.

Ricardo, D. (1971), *On the Principles of Political Economy and Taxation*, (edited by R.M. Hartwell), Harmondsworth.

Rose, A.K. and L.E.O. Svensson (1991), 'Expected and Predicted Realignments: The FF/DM Exchange Rate During the EMS', *NBER Working Paper* 3695.

Rose, A.K. and L.E.O. Svensson (1994), 'European Exchange Rate Credibility before the Fall', *European Economic Review*, **38**, 1185–223.

Roubini, N. and J. Sachs (1989a), 'Political and Economic Determinants of Budget Deficits in the Industrial Democracies', *European Economic Review*, **33**, 903–38.

Roubini, N. and J. Sachs (1989b), 'Government Spending and Budget Deficits in the Industrial Countries', *Economic Policy*, **8**, 99–132.

Saunders, P. and F. Klau (1985), 'The Role of the Public Sector: Causes and Consequences of the Growth of Government', *OECD Economic Studies* 4.

Sargent, T.J. (1976), 'A Classical Macroeconomic Model for the United States', *Journal of Political Economy*, **84**, 207–38.

Sargent, T.J. (1983), 'Stopping Moderate Inflations: The Methods of Poincare and Thatcher', in R. Dornbusch and M.H. Simonsen (eds), *Inflation, Debt, and Indexation*, London.

Sargent, T.J. and N. Wallace (1976), 'Rational Expectations and the Theory of Economic Policy', *Journal of Monetary Economics*, **2**, 169–93.

Sargent, T.J. and N. Wallace (1981), 'Some Unpleasant Monetarist Arithmetic', *Federal Reserve Bank of Minneapolis Quarterly Review*, **5**, 1–17.

Schotman, P.C. (1989), *Empirical Studies on the Behaviour of Interest Rates and Exchange Rates*, Ph.D. dissertation, Erasmus University Rotterdam.

Seater, J.J. (1993), 'Ricardian Equivalence', *Journal of Economic Literature*, **31**, 142–90.

Siegel, J. (1979), 'Inflation-Induced Distortions in Government and Private Saving Statistics', *Review of Economics and Statistics*, **61**, 83–90.

Sims, C.A. (1980a), 'Macroeconomics and Reality', *Econometrica*, **48**, 1–48.

Sims, C.A, (1980b), 'Comparison of Interwar and Postwar Business Cycles: Monetarism Reconsidered', *American Economic Review, Papers and Proceedings*, **70**, 250–57.

Sims, C.A. (1982), 'Policy Analysis with Econometric Models', *Brookings Papers on Economic Activity*, 107–52.

Solano, P.L. (1983), 'Institutional Explanations of Public Expenditures among High Income Democracies', *Public Finance*, **38**, 440–58.

Sterken, E. (1990), *DUFIS An Econometric Model of the Dutch Financial System*, Ph.D. dissertation, University of Groningen.

Sterks, C.G.M (1982), *Begrotingsnormen*, Ph.D. dissertation, University of Groningen (in Dutch).

Stevenson, A., V. Muscatelli, and M. Gregory (1988), *Macroeconomic Theory and Stabilisation Policy*, Oxford: Philip Allan.

Sutherland, A. (1994), 'Target Zone Models with Price Inertia: Solutions and Testable Implications', *Economic Journal*, **104**, 96–112.

Svensson, L.E.O. (1991a), 'Target Zones and Interest Rate Variability', *Journal of International Economics*, **31**, 27–54.

Svensson, L.E.O. (1991b), 'The Term Structure of Interest Differentials in a Target Zone: Theory and Swedish Data', *Journal of Monetary Economics*, **28**, 87–116.

Svensson, L.E.O. (1991c), 'The Simplest Test of Target Zone Credibility', *IMF Staff Papers*, **38**, 655–65.

Svensson, L.E.O. (1992a), 'The Foreign Exchange Risk Premium in a Target Zone with Devaluation Risk', *Journal of International Economics*, **33**, 21–40.

Svensson, L.E.O. (1992b), 'An Interpretation of Recent Research on Exchange Rate Target Zones', *Journal of Economic Perspectives*, **6**, 119–44.

Svensson, L.E.O. (1993), 'Assessing Target Zone Credibility: Mean Reversion and Devaluation Expectations in the ERM, 1979–1992', *European Economic Review*, **37**, 763–802.

Svensson, L.E.O. (1994), 'Why Exchange Rate Bands? Monetary Independence in Spite of Fixed Exchange Rates', *Journal of Monetary Economics*, **33**, 157–99.

Tanzi, V., M. Blejer, and M.O. Teyeiro (1987), 'Inflation and the Measurement of Fiscal Deficits', *IMF Staff Papers*, **34**, 711–38.

Tanzi, V. and M.S. Lutz (1993), 'Interest Rates and Government Debt: Are the Linkages Global rather than National?', in H.A.A. Verbon and F.A.A.M. van Winden (eds), *The Political Economy of Government Debt*, Amsterdam: North-Holland, 233–54.

Thomas, A.H. (1994), 'Expected Devaluation and Economic Fundamentals', *IMF Staff Papers*, **41**, 262–85.

Thorbecke, W. (1993), 'Why Deficit News Affects Interest Rates', *Journal of Policy Modeling*, **15**, 1–11.

Thornton, D.L. and D.S. Batten (1985), 'Lag-Length Selection and Tests of Granger-Causality between Money and Income', *Journal of Money, Credit, and Banking*, **17**, 164–78.

Tran, D.T. and B.L. Sahwney (1988), 'Government Deficits, Capital Flows, and Interest Rates', *Applied Economics*, **20**, 753–65.

Tristani, O. (1994), 'Variable Probability of Realignment in a Target Zone', *Scandinavian Journal of Economics*, **96**, 1–14.

Tullio, G. (1987), 'Inflation Adjusted Government Budget Deficits and Their Impact on the Business Cycle: Empirical Evidence for 8 Industrial Countries', *Economic Papers* 62, Bruxelles: Commission of the European Communities.

Van Loo, P.D. (1984), 'De Hoogte van de Kapitaalmarktrente', *Maandschrift Economie*, **48**, 123–39 (in Dutch).

Verbruggen, J.P. (1992), *Van Macro naar Meso. Een Trendmatige Ontwikkeling in de Nederlandse Econometrische Modelbouw*, Groningen: Wolters–Noordhoff (in Dutch).

Von Hagen, J. (1991), 'A Note on the Empirical Effectivenss of Formal Fiscal Restraints', *Journal of Public Economics*, **44**, 99–110.

Von Hagen, J. (1992), 'Budgeting Procedures and Fiscal Performance in the European Communities', *Economic Papers* 96, Bruxelles: Commission of the European Communities.

Wachtel, P. and J. Young (1987), 'Deficit Announcements and Interest Rates', *American Economic Review*, **77**, 1007–12.

Wellink, A.H.E.M. (1989), 'Dutch Monetary Policy in an Integrating Europe', in M. Bub et al. (eds), *Geldwertsicherung und Wirtschaftsstabilität*, Frankfurt am Main: Deutsche Bundesbank, 391–410.

White, H. (1980), 'A Heteroskedasticity-Consistent Covariance Matrix and a Direct Test for Heteroskedasticity', *Econometrica*, **48**, 817–38.

Wilcox, J.A. (1983), 'Why Real Interest Rates Were So Low in the 1970s', *American Economic Review*, **73**, 44–53.

Williamson, J. (1991), 'FEERs and the ERM', *National Institute Economic Review*, **137**, 45–50.

Williamson, J. (1994), 'Estimates of FEERs', in J. Williamson (ed.), *Estimating Equilibrium Exchange Rates*, Washington: Institute for International Economics, 177–243.

Wolswijk, G.F.T. (1991), *The Structural Budget Deficit. Estimates for the Netherlands 1960–1987*, Groningen: Wolters–Noordhoff.

Zelhorst, D. and J. De Haan (1991), 'Federal Government Budget Deficits and Interest Rates: Comment', *Public Finance*, **46**, 324–30.

Zelhorst, D. and J. De Haan (1994), 'The Nonstationarity of Aggregate Output: Some Additional International Evidence', *Journal of Money, Credit, and Banking*, **26**, 23–33.

Author index

Abramowitz, M. 126
Alesina, A. 22
Allen, S.D. 1, 69, 71, 75
Andersen, T.M. 102
Arnold, I.J.M. 48
Artis, M.J. 48
Aschauer, D.A. 2, 21, 76
Atkinson, P. 71
Bakker, A.F.P. 100
Ball, C.A. 142
Barr, D. 48
Barro, R.J. 1, 2, 20, 21, 26, 29,
    30, 47, 48, 63, 68, 71, 75, 77,
    87, 89
Bartolini, L. 130, 159
Basmann, R.L. 11
Batten, D.S. 14
Bekx, P. 49
Bernheim, B.D. 29, 30, 31, 32
Bertola, G. 101, 106, 107, 109,
    130, 141
Beveridge, S. 10, 72
Bhandari, J.S. 1, 47, 75
Bischoff, C. 49
Bladen-Hovell, R.C. 48
Blanchard, O.J. 44, 47, 49, 69, 81
Bomhoff, E.J. 11
Boskin, M.J. 41-43
Box, G.E.P. 57, 63, 88
Brockwell, P.J. 115
Brunner, K. 20
Buiter, W.H. 38, 43, 44
Burdekin, R.C.K. 93
Cagan, P. 40
Caines, P.E. 15, 153
Cameron, D.R. 23, 25

Caramazza, F. 101, 123, 130, 151,
    153, 157, 158
Catsambras, T. 33
Central Planning Bureau, 11, 12
Chan-Lee, J.H. 11
Chen, Z. 101, 123, 130, 150, 151,
    157, 159
Chouraqui, J.C. 71
Claessens, S. 150
Clark, P. 149, 151
Clark, T.A. 91
Cooper, R.N. 100
Cornell, B. 91
Corsetti, G. 22
Cover, J.P. 80, 150
Cuddington, J.T. 10
Cukierman, A. 41, 93, 101
Cumby, R.E. 47, 53, 75, 78, 80,
    114
Darrat, A.F. 14, 33, 34
Datta, S. 87
Davis, R.A. 115
De Cecco, M. 100
De Grauwe, P. 100, 151, 155,
    156, 161, 162
De Haan, J. 1, 2, 18-21, 23-25,
    27, 30, 33-35, 38, 42, 47, 57,
    62, 64, 66, 76, 87, 89, 93, 116,
    140, 143, 152
De Kam, C.A. 20
De Nederlandsche Bank, 12, 111,
    163
Delgado, F. 108, 126, 142
Demopoulos, G.D. 93
Denslow, D. 2
Dhillon, U.S. 87

Subject index

accrual-basis 35
active stabilisation policies 19-20
amortisation 36-7
announcement effect methodology
    16, 87-98, 176
Austria 101
    credibility of exchange rate
        policy 132, 133, 162, 177
    devaluation expectations 143,
        144, 145, 146
    interest rate differentials and
        exchange rate 110, 111,
        115, 122, 123, 176
    public deficits and interest rates 3
automatic stabilisers 19, 20
balance-of-payments crises 150
    see also current account
Basle-Nyborg Agreement 1987 140
Belgium
    credibility of exchange rate
        policy 132, 134, 140
    devaluation expectations 143,
        144, 146, 155
    interest rate differentials and
        exchange rate 111, 116,
        122, 123, 176
    public deficits and interest rates 3
budget deficits
    causes 18-28, 44, 174
    effects 1, 18, 19, 28-34, 44-5,
        175
    fundamental determinants of
        interest rates 151-61 *passim*,
        177
    measurement 19, 34-44
    monetisation 89, 93-4

relationship to interest rates
    1-2, 47-8, 177-8
    announcement effect
        methodology 16, 87-98,
        176
    development ('double dip')
        7-9, 174
    Dutch macro-econometric
        models 11-13
    long-term interest rates
        50-68, 175
    short-term interest rates 75,
        81, 175-6
    trends 2-9
budgeting procedures 23, 25, 28
Bundesbank 93
    deficit news 90, 91-2, 93, 176
business cycle 7-9
capacity utilisation rate 49-50, 57,
    62, 66-8
capital markets 47-86, 175-6
    long-term interest rates 49-68
    short-term interest rates 68-81
capital mobility, international 2
    exchange controls abolished 100
    long-term interest rates 50, 51,
        52, 60-6, 67
    short-term interest rates 69-70, 75
capital stock 42-3
cash-basis 35
central banks
    independence 93
    intramarginal interventions
        107-8, 130, 140
    net worth 42
    see also Bundesbank